Applying Psychology to Forensic Practice

Forensic Practice

Series Editors: Dr Adrian Needs, University of Portsmouth, and Professor Graham Towl, HM Prison Service and the National Probation Service/University of Birmingham and University of Portsmouth

The books in this series take a research-based applied psychological approach to a wide range of topics in forensic psychology, and are aimed at a range of forensic practitioners working in a variety of settings. They will be of use to all those working within the criminal process, whether academics or practitioners.

Published

Applying Psychology to Forensic Practice
Edited by Adrian Needs and Graham Towl

Psychology in Prisons
Edited by Graham Towl

Lawrence Jones, 'Offence Parelleling Behaviour (OPB) as a Framework for Assessment and Interventions with Offenders', in *Applying Psychology to Forensic Practice* edited by Adrian Needs and Graham Towl

ISBN 0-4051-0542-9 paperback

Errata

On p. 36 the equation and first line of the key were printed without delta symbols. They are reproduced in full as follows:

$$\Delta R = (TE + GTI) - (TSR + TD + TIR) + (NTV)$$

ΔR = Post-treatment change in reconviction

On p. 38 the text starting 'Offence paralleling behaviour' and ending 'current offence-related issues' should have been replaced with the following:

Offence paralleling behaviour (OPB: Jones, 1997, 2000; Shine and Morris, 2000) is any form of offence-related behavioural (or fantasized behaviour) pattern that emerges at any point before or after an offence. It does not have to result in an offence; it simply needs to resemble, in some significant respect, the sequence of behaviours leading up to the offence. This construct was developed out of work done by McDougall and Clark (1991) and McDougall, Clark and Fisher (1994), in a risk-assessment context, as a strategy for working clinically on current offence-related (dynamic risk) issues.

The full reference for Shine and Morris is as follows:

Shine, J. & Morris, M. (2000) Addressing criminogenic needs in a prison therapeutic community. *Therapeutic Communities* 21(3), 197–218

Table 3.1 (p. 40) was incorrectly printed. It is reproduced in full as follows:

Behavioural Sequences	Parsed Behavioural Episodes							
	B_1	B_2	B_3	B_4	B_5	B_6	B_7	B_n
Childhood play behaviour	✓	✓	✓	✗	?	✓	✓	✓
Pre-offence offence related behaviour	✓	✓	?	✓	✗	?	✓	✓
Offence behaviour chain 1	✓	?	✓	?	✓	✓	?	✓
Offence behaviour chain $_n$	✓	✓	✗	✓	✗	?	✓	✓
Offence paralleling behaviour 1	?	✓	?	✓	✓	?	✗	✗
OPB $_n$	✓	✓	✓	?	✓	✓	?	✓
Current behaviour or fantasies	?	✓	?	✗	?	✓	?	✓

Figure 3.1 (p. 41) was printed incomplete. It is reproduced in full as follows:

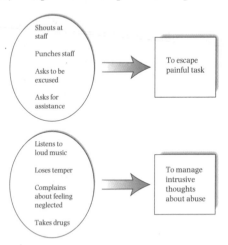

In Figure 3.3 (p. 49) all the labels on the periphery of the map (e.g. 'SAFE, ALONE, NOT VULNERABLE') should be in capitals, as described in the caption

In Table 3.3 (p. 53) closing parentheses were missing from the headings in column 1. These should read as follows: 'Sequence (Parsed behaviour) at onset of offending process'; 'Offence sequence (Parsed behaviour)'

Lawrence Jones, 'Offence Parelleling Behaviour (OPB) as a Framework for Assessment and Interventions with Offenders', in *Applying Psychology to Forensic Practice* edited by Adrian Needs and Graham Towl

ISBN 0-4051-0542-9 paperback

Errata

On p. 36 the equation and first line of the key were printed without delta symbols. They are reproduced in full as follows:

$$\Delta R = (TE + GTI) - (TSR + TD + TIR) + (NTV)$$

ΔR = Post-treatment change in reconviction

On p. 38 the text starting 'Offence paralleling behaviour' and ending 'current offence-related issues' should have been replaced with the following:

Offence paralleling behaviour (OPB: Jones, 1997, 2000; Shine and Morris, 2000) is any form of offence-related behavioural (or fantasized behaviour) pattern that emerges at any point before or after an offence. It does not have to result in an offence; it simply needs to resemble, in some significant respect, the sequence of behaviours leading up to the offence. This construct was developed out of work done by McDougall and Clark (1991) and McDougall, Clark and Fisher (1994), in a risk-assessment context, as a strategy for working clinically on current offence-related (dynamic risk) issues.

The full reference for Shine and Morris is as follows:

Shine, J. & Morris, M. (2000) Addressing criminogenic needs in a prison therapeutic community. *Therapeutic Communities* 21(3), 197–218

Table 3.1 (p. 40) was incorrectly printed. It is reproduced in full as follows:

Behavioural Sequences	Parsed Behavioural Episodes							
	B_1	B_2	B_3	B_4	B_5	B_6	B_7	B_n
Childhood play behaviour	✓	✓	✓	✗	?	✓	✓	✓
Pre-offence offence related behaviour	✓	✓	?	✓	✗	?	✓	✓
Offence behaviour chain 1	✓	?	✓	?	✓	✓	?	✓
Offence behaviour chain n	✓	✓	✗	✓	✗	?	✓	✓
Offence paralleling behaviour 1	?	✓	?	✓	✓	?	✗	✗
OPB n	✓	✓	✓	?	✓	✓	?	✓
Current behaviour or fantasies	?	✓	?	✗	?	✓	?	✓

Figure 3.1 (p. 41) was printed incomplete. It is reproduced in full as follows:

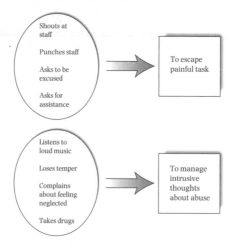

Shouts at staff

Punches staff

Asks to be excused

Asks for assistance

To escape painful task

Listens to loud music

Loses temper

Complains about feeling neglected

Takes drugs

To manage intrusive thoughts about abuse

In Figure 3.3 (p. 49) all the labels on the periphery of the map (e.g. 'SAFE, ALONE, NOT VULNERABLE') should be in capitals, as described in the caption

In Table 3.3 (p. 53) closing parentheses were missing from the headings in column 1. These should read as follows: 'Sequence (Parsed behaviour) at onset of offending process'; 'Offence sequence (Parsed behaviour)'

On p. 56 arrows were missing from the chains. They are reproduced in full as follows:

Simple behaviour chain OPB models

Simple behaviour chain OPB models are models that involve a repeat of the whole sequence of behaviours leading up to the offence, possibly including the offence itself. This is often suggestive of an overlearned process that has developed into a monopoly for the individual:

$$B_1 \rightarrow B_2 \rightarrow B_3 \rightarrow B_4 \rightarrow B_5$$

or similar behaviours in a varied order:

$$B_2 \rightarrow B_1 \rightarrow B_3 \rightarrow B_5 \rightarrow B_4$$

Stem and branch chain

$$B_a \rightarrow B_{a2} \rightarrow B_{a3}$$
$$\nearrow$$
$$B_1 \rightarrow B_2 \rightarrow B_3 \rightarrow B_b \rightarrow B_{b2} \rightarrow B_{b3}$$
$$\searrow$$
$$B_c \rightarrow B_{c2} \rightarrow B_{c3}$$

In this model, several different patterns can be identified in different offences, but they all appear to start with the same initiating sequence.

Branch and stem chain

$$B_a \rightarrow B_{a2} \rightarrow B_{a3}$$
$$\searrow$$
$$B_b \rightarrow B_{b2} \rightarrow B_{b3} \rightarrow B_4 \rightarrow B_5 \rightarrow B_6$$
$$\nearrow$$
$$B_c \rightarrow B_{c2} \rightarrow B_{c3}$$

In this model, a variety of different behavioural sequences lead up to a repeating sequence.

Response class chain

$$B_a \rightarrow B_{a2} \rightarrow B_{a3}$$
$$\nearrow \qquad \searrow$$
$$B_1 \rightarrow B_2 \rightarrow B_3 \rightarrow B_b \rightarrow B_{b2} \rightarrow B_{b3} \rightarrow B_7 \rightarrow B_8$$
$$\searrow \qquad \nearrow$$
$$B_c \rightarrow B_{c2} \rightarrow B_{c3}$$

In this model, whilst the initiating sequence and the ending sequence are repeated across contexts, there is some degree of variation at one, or more, points in the sequence. The behaviours that are interchangeable at these points are probably members of a response class and serve the same or similar function for the individual.

On p. 59 before 'Situational Variation', the following material was missing:

Schema contents and processes

Various 'schema' contents and processes (e.g. Young, 1994) can result in repeating ways of interpreting the world that result in repetitive behavioural outcomes.

Applying Psychology to Forensic Practice

Edited by

Adrian Needs and Graham Towl

BPS Blackwell

© 2004 by the British Psychological Society and Blackwell Publishing Ltd
except for editorial material and organization © 2004 by Adrian Needs and Graham Towl
A BPS Blackwell book

350 Main Street, Malden, MA 02148-5020, USA
108 Cowley Road, Oxford OX4 1JF, UK
550 Swanston Street, Carlton, Victoria 3053, Australia

First published 2004 by the British Psychological Society and Blackwell Publishing Ltd

Library of Congress Cataloging-in-Publication Data

Applying psychology to forensic practice / edited by Adrian Needs and Graham Towl.
     p. cm.
Includes bibliographical references and index.
    ISBN 1–4051–0542–9 (pbk)
  1. Forensic Psychology.   I. Needs, Adrian.   II. Towl, Graham J.

   RA1148 .A67 2004
   614 .1—dc21

                           2003004175

A catalogue record for this title is available from the British Library.

Set in 10 on 12.5 pt Photina
by Ace Filmsetting Ltd, Frome, Somerset
Printed and bound in the United Kingdom
by MPG Books Ltd, Bodmin, Cornwall

For further information on
Blackwell Publishing, visit our website:
http://www.blackwellpublishing.com

The views expressed are those of the authors and do not represent the views of their employing
organizations.

All proceeds from the book will be directly donated to 'Revolving Doors', a mental health charity
for offenders.

Contents

Contributors

Jo Barton – Department of Psychology, University of Portsmouth

Keith Baxter – JSAC Implementation Team, HM Prison Service

Jennifer Brown – Department of Psychology, University of Surrey

Ruby Bell – The Hutton Centre, St Luke's Hospital, Middlesbrough

David Boag – IMPACT Psychological Services, Bawtry, Doncaster

Jo Capelin – Kent, Surrey and Sussex Area Office, HM Prison Service

David Crighton – HM Prison Service, and the National Probation Service/ London Metropolitan University

Kirstin Davis – JSAC Implementation Team, HM Prison Service

Sue Evershed – Psychology Unit, Rampton Hospital

Eliot Franks – JSAC Implementation Team, HM Prison Service

Lawrence Jones – Psychology Unit, Rampton Hospital

Sonia Kitchen – JSAC Implementation Team, HM Prison Service

Jacqueline Law – Scottish Prison Service, Edinburgh

William R. Lindsay – State Hospital, Carstairs, Tayside Primary Care NHS Trust and University of Abertay, Dundee

Fiona MacLeod – Tayside Primary Care NHS Trust and University of Abertay, Dundee

Claire Nee – Department of Psychology, University of Portsmouth

Adrian Needs – Department of Psychology, University of Portsmouth

Pam Newlands – Department of Psychology, Glasgow Caledonian University

Graham Towl – HM Prison Service and the National Probation Service/ Universities of Birmingham and Portsmouth

Aldert Vrij – Department of Psychology, University of Portsmouth

Mark Wilson – Glasgow City Council, Glasgow

Series Editors' Preface

It is tempting to start this introduction with reference to the expansion in numbers of those who have the job title 'forensic psychologist'. This could be followed with a reminder of the stimulus provided by developments in professional training either within or under the auspices of the Division of Forensic Psychology of the British Psychological Society. Advances in relevant knowledge, skills and their applications could then be proclaimed with a final fanfare concerning forensic psychology's 'coming of age'. Certainly there would be some substance in such assertions.

The number of forensic psychologists employed in, for example, the Prison and Probation Services, in special hospitals and secure units, with the police and community mental health teams has increased impressively within the past decade, even within the last five years. Over a similar period the Division of Forensic Psychology has issued ethical guidelines, accreditation criteria for MSc courses and standards for supervised practice in the pre-chartership period. In addition, the adjectival title of forensic psychologist, mirrored by the change in name of the Division, now has widespread acceptance. Developments in research and practice have continued apace.

Many of the chapters are concerned with providing an introduction for students and practitioners alike to areas which have not received extensive coverage or integration within the more widely available literature. In several cases these are areas of considerable practical importance in meeting demands within settings of employment. Some chapters address areas of current development, which may be relatively unfamiliar to those whose primary interests and concerns lie outside these areas. A particular intention has been to provide examples of work which illustrate a view of forensic psychology as a branch of applied psychology.

The British Psychological Society's project on Occupational Standards in Applied Psychology during the 1990s identified substantial commonalities in patterns of work activity across the various specialist branches (including clinical, occupational, educational, health, counselling and forensic psychology). All branches recognized the relevance of certain major functions or 'key roles'. These include the problem solving cycle of investigation, formulation, action and evaluation; research; providing advice and support; and training other professionals.

The key roles vary according to how prominently they figure in the work of individual practitioners. Their manifestations certainly vary across the branches of applied psychology in the underpinning knowledge required and the contexts in which they are practised. Taken together, the roles reflect common demands on applied psychological services and areas where practitioners are often proactive in their contributions. The present volume gives examples of work within forensic psychology which are relevant to the exercise of the key roles. These examples are likely to be of interest to practitioners wishing to extend their contributions, particularly in contexts where multidisciplinary working is being given increased emphasis. Such examples may also be helpful to trainees who are facing the demands of the supervised practice component of eligibility for chartered status.

It is arguably the rather distinctive nature of the settings in which it is practised and the issues with which it is concerned which gives forensic psychology much of its discernible identity. This is not of course to claim that other practitioners of psychology never venture into contexts such as prisons, secure units, the police and the courts. Since the overriding aim of the book is simply to be useful to practitioners of psychology in such settings it is hoped that practitioners of a variety of professional affiliations will find it to be of some value. Indeed not all the chapters are by 'forensic' psychologists. (Perhaps concepts from cognitive and social psychology, such as those concerned with categorization, or group identity, should be applied to issues of professional definition!) Within this book the phrase 'illustrative rather than comprehensive' might also be applied to the coverage of settings. Nonetheless the examples of work presented here give a sense of practitioners and researchers not hemmed in by definitional boundaries, who are prepared to deploy what is relevant from within psychology in meeting demands and confronting issues in settings which are largely alien to most members of the public and to a sizeable number of other psychologists.

Awareness of work by others with whom one feels a degree of professional affinity can encourage new possibilities within one's own areas of concern to be glimpsed and elaborated. A creative synthesis of ideas from different areas can be a fruitful source of new insights. With appropriate development of skills it can also provide a basis for versatility, which is something that tends to be valued by employers. A parallel might be drawn with adaptive conceptual systems which combine differentiation with higher-order integration (e.g. Adams-Webber, 1979). Such systems provide a healthy basis for anticipating and responding to demands: their evolutionary prospects can be viewed with some confidence.

It is hoped that through presenting examples of applications of psychology to forensic practice this book, taken alongside existing texts, will make a worthwhile contribution to the evolution of the field and help stimulate new applications. In addition, the application of psychology to the testing-ground of complex and challenging issues encountered within forensic practice can be seen as having potential for valuable implications for psychology as a whole.

Adrian Needs and Graham Towl

Preface

There are two thematic sections of this book: Working with Offenders; Analysis and Intervention and Working with Criminal Justice Personnel

The first section begins with a focus on the offender's perspective. Claire Nee provides us with a salutary reminder of the need to consider offenders' perspectives when attempting to understand crime more fully. The acknowledgement of the offender as an 'expert' on their offending is the starting point of the chapter. Claire goes on to elaborate on this by describing research on residential burglary including her own impressive work in this area. One of the strengths of the chapter is in its practical advice for prospective researchers wishing to undertake specific work. This includes a discussion of some of the merits and demerits of particular methodologies for data collection. As Claire concludes (page 17), 'To undertake crime research without involving the offender's perspective should be seen as trying to write a play without characters.'

The next chapter, by Mark Wilson, proposes new directions in analysing and understanding offending. His focus is on the community, family and developmental context, in relation to crime by juveniles and young offenders. He draws upon public health and community psychology literature when addressing the issue of crime prevention in terms of primary, secondary and tertiary interventions. An ecological approach underpins the chapter.

Lawrence Jones calls into question the tradition within much forensic psychology of failing to consider the personal context and organization of offending behaviour in work on risk assessment and interventions to reduce the risk of reoffending. He applies the notion of 'offence paralleling behaviour' in describing how practitioners may formulate hypotheses in exploring individual offending patterns and their implications.

One major theme underpinning much of forensic psychological practice is that of risk assessment and management. David Crighton reviews the language, logic and psychology of risk assessment. He outlines the 'Cambridge model of risk assessment' and its application to forensic practice. Finally he addresses the challenging issue of risk communication. This is an important but frequently neglected area.

Ruby Bell and Sue Evershed address the demanding area of working with 'difficult' clients. They draw from clinical experience, therapeutic approaches and empirical research in giving guidance to practitioners. They begin by exploring the question of who, exactly, falls under such a heading. They go on to examine 'what works?' with difficult clients, beginning with an emphasis on the importance of establishing an effective therapeutic alliance. They bring their chapter to a close with a discussion of some key environmental issues to consider when working with difficult clients.

Bill Lindsay, Jacqueline Law and Fiona Macleod examine linkages between intellectual disabilities and crime. They begin with a concise historical account going on to review more up-to-date literature. Case examples in the chapter richly illustrate some of the challenges in this area. The authors conclude with a focus on the nature and outcomes of treatment interventions.

In the second section, Aldert Vrij and Jo Barton outline a model of decision-making to use lethal force by police marksmen. They describe some studies carried out utilizing a Fire Arms Training System (FATS, an American shooting simulator) drawing conclusions in terms of factors which impact upon decision-making in critical situations.

Psychologists have contributed much in the area of eyewitness testimony. Pam Newlands examines developments in this important area in a detailed chapter. She outlines contributions to facilitating both recall and identification during an investigation. The chapter concludes with a number of reflections on future directions.

Jennifer Brown gives a stimulating account of occupational stress, concentrating upon uniformed criminal justice workers. She examines some of the common sources of stress in their organizational contexts. A review of the evidence on occupational stress interventions follows, finishing with some key conclusions from the territory covered in the chapter.

Job Simulation Assessment Centres (JSACs) have been used extensively in HM Prison Service in recent years in the assessment (and development) of staff. Keith Baxter, Kirsten Davis, Eliot Franks and Sonia Kitchen cover this area of inovation in their chapter, which is informed by both research and practice. They describe the development of the JSAC and its application particularly in relation to the HM Prison Service staff including prison officers, senior officers and operational managers.

David Boag begins his chapter by sharing some personal examples from his extensive experience of staff training within criminal justice settings. In a lively (one might even say a trainer's) style he cautions that it should never be assumed that training is the only, or even a relevant, solution to every performance-related problem. Following on from this he gives a detailed description of what is involved in a systematic and comprehensive approach to the development of training.

The work of many forensic psychologists now involves multidisciplinary teams, and the facilitation and oversight of teams responsible for the delivery of offending behaviour programmes is a conspicuous example of this. To date, however, the field has been dominated by a concern with the tasks for which the teams exist, rather than the teams themselves. The chapter by Adrian Needs and Jo Capelin aims to stimulate awareness of issues relevant to understanding and working with teams, encouraging examination of practice in relation to programmes and ultimately to other contexts.

In the final chapter Graham Towl gives an account of the context and work of applied psychologists in HM Prison Service and the National Probation Service. He highlights some of the recent professional history of the growth of forensic psychology in prisons in particular, and also comments on the recent development of a national infrastructure for psychologists working in probation services.

Dr Adrian Needs and Professor Graham Towl

Section One

Working with Offenders; Analysis and Intervention

Chapter One

The Offender's Perspective on Crime: Methods and Principles in Data Collection

Claire Nee

This chapter outlines the importance of including the offender's perspective on his or her own behaviour in any analysis of criminal activity. In particular, it argues that research on specific types of crime, patterns of crime and interventions into offending behaviour must benefit from including this perspective. The first part of the chapter focuses on work done on residential burglary to show how fruitful this 'grounded' approach to research can be. It then goes on to discuss how reliant we are on self-report methodologies in this type of research and describes some general principles and recent developments that have improved the validity and reliability of crime data collected in the field.

Why Interview the Offender?

In the latter half of the last century the eminent criminologist David Matza (1970) cautioned the research world that it was becoming very distant from the key 'actors' of our subject matter: offenders. In fact, in our quest to understand criminality, offending behaviour and criminal careers, it would seem sensible and obvious to go to the 'experts' in the field. Yet, half a century later, aside from a thin but tenacious strand of empirical research (some of which is reviewed below), we rarely pay heed to offenders' view of things, and relatively little investment is made into looking at their perspective. While criminal justice practitioners spend a large amount of their time interviewing offenders, as researchers we often focus on the analysis of large data-sets and statistical modelling without much reference to the 'raw material' of our subject.

If we can show that we can research offenders' understandings of their own behaviour reliably – and this chapter describes many such examples of this – then surely a grounded approach to research, using the offender as expert, is a method we ignore at our peril.

Using the Offender as Expert

Using a grounded approach to data collection, it is very important that the offender is actively involved in the formulation of the basic research questions, and each further stage of methodological refinement until a stage of theoretical elaboration is reached (Glaser & Strauss, 1967). This ensures that the enquiry begins and remains as relevant, valid and reliable as possible. A first stage in this is to fully involve offenders in pilot work so that research questions are judged as pertinent by them as by the research team. An important part of the pilot stage is to ensure that correct and appropriate terms of reference and language are incorporated into subsequent research instruments. Once exploratory research questions are formulated, the researcher embarks on preliminary data collection with a sample of the 'experts' in their enquiry. In an ideal world this should be done in a loosely structured way at this point of the investigation, to allow the offender (rather than the researcher) to focus the enquiry more sharply. Appropriate methods here might include semi-structured interviews and focus groups.

The next stage will be to test out offenders' verbal reports about their criminal experience in a more empirical way, in other words getting closer to their actual observed behaviour. This has been done in a variety of ways including simulations (Bennett & Wright, 1984; Nee & Taylor, 2000) and quasi-participant observation (Carroll & Weaver, 1986; Cromwell, Olsen & Avary, 1991; Wright & Decker, 1994).

Each enquiry will throw up new information, the validity of which can be tested by triangulating research methods (Brewer & Hunter, 1989) and getting as close as resources and ethics will allow to observing the actual behaviour of the offender at work. Relying on offenders in this way to tell us and show us how they operate will get us closer to the 'truth' of what we want to know and, of course, to theoretical elaboration.

Again, in an ideal world, these stages should be adhered to within each piece of proposed research. In reality, though, it is more often the case that separately commissioned pieces of work build on and extend previous pieces of work in the same vein. A compelling example for this is the work on residential burglary at the end of the last millennium, to which I contributed, and the next part of the chapter gives an overview of this work to exemplify how productive a grounded approach can be.

Research on Residential Burglary: an Example of the Grounded Approach

Empirical work on residential burglary first came to prominence in the United States in the 1970s with the largely descriptive studies of Scarr (1973), Shover (1973), Reppetto (1974) and Waller and Okihiro (1978). In the 1980s there followed an outbreak of activity in this type of work, on both sides of the Atlantic, which addressed offending behaviour and decision-making at the scene of the crime. This increase in offender-based work had been fuelled by a gentle shift in emphasis over the preceding decades from individual to environmental explanations of crime, including the idea that the physical opportunity to commit crime may be as important as individual factors in explaining the criminal event (see for example Mayhew et al., 1976). The theoretical underpinning of this new 'situational' perspective on crime was adapted from an econometric model of human behaviour known as rational choice theory. Cornish and Clarke's (1986) work entitled *The Reasoning Criminal* is seen as the definitive text in this development.

It was no coincidence that much of the British research on burglary was either government-based or government-funded at this time. Policy-makers encouraged the shift, since changing the focus of research to the environment in which crime occurred had popular policy spin-offs. In particular, situational crime prevention rose to the fore as an alternative and very promising way to address the problem of crime. Target hardening, or reducing the physical opportunities for crime, allowed for a cost-efficient, more immediately rewarding approach to crime reduction (for both the public and politicians). Crime-reduction policy relied heavily on this approach in the 1980s and early 1990s, in tandem with renewed emphasis on punishment and deterrence. In recent years we have seen a more balanced approach emerge in the UK, which acknowledges the need to address individual and societal factors that cause criminality (secondary and tertiary crime prevention) alongside reducing opportunity (primary crime prevention) and deterrence.

The exploratory American work with burglars in the 1970s alluded to earlier is an example of the very early stages in a grounded approach to understanding this type of offending behaviour. As well as describing burglars' lifestyles and motivations, it provided the first suggestions that a specialized type of learning and discrimination might be taking place at the scene of the crime. This sparked interest and generated the research that followed in Britain and Ireland.

In 1982, Maguire and Bennett published the first major work on residential burglary in Britain. By examining police data and interviewing victims and incarcerated offenders regarding burglaries in the Greater London area, they provided us with a wealth of data on patterns of offending and target selection in burglars. They identified middle-range' burglars as most typical, those characterized by skill and discrimination at the scene of the crime but lack of organization away from it. They provided evidence that environmental cues influenced target selection in a systematic way, simultaneously weakening the assumption that burglary was an impulsive, indiscriminate act.

Based on these findings Bennett and Wright (1984) developed a series of more focused empirical studies, challenging the assumptions made by situational crime prevention experts about the way burglars think. Involving several hundred imprisoned burglars, their research involved a variety of methods, including structured and semi-structured interviews; videos; and photographic methods. Their findings strongly supported the degree of skill or 'bounded rationality' (Cornish & Clarke, 1986) described by Maguire and Bennett with respect to target selection and importantly, looked closely at the staged decision making typical of most burglars. This was manifested as noting potentially lucrative residential areas and burglary targets during routine daily activities (Felson, 1993) and returning to those areas later in order to burgle. Once in these areas, burglars would choose targets according to the range of environmental cues presenting themselves at that time: e.g. to do with occupancy, surveillability, accessibility and security levels in the property.

One can already trace an exemplary pattern in these pieces of work. Each new project builds on and extends the findings of its predecessors, always returning to the offender to verify and lead new researchers in their future enquiries. As a next stage Max Taylor and I undertook a series of projects in the late 1980s that used these two British studies as their foundation. Working in the Republic of Ireland, we had three broad aims:

> to verify the ground-breaking British findings on burglars, in another country;
> to tease out systematically,in an empirical setting, the nature and importance of varying types of environmental cues in burglars' target selection;
> to compare burglars' assumed 'expert' decision making with non-burglars.

We began by interviewing imprisoned burglars selected on current conviction and from recommendations by other burglars (see Nee and Taylor, 1988 and Taylor and Nee, 1988 for fuller details of sample selection). We found that recommendation by other burglars was more fruitful than using index offence. Many of those serving a sentence for burglary did not consider it the focus of their criminal activity and many more 'expert' burglars were serving sentences for other crimes. An added advantage of not using only those convicted of burglary was that it countered to some extent any bias in relying solely on 'failed' burglars, i.e. those who had been caught. We covered criminal career, lifestyle and target selection in interviews with fifty burglars. The end of the interview was used to rate the relative importance of a variety of environmental cues, identified by our respondents and British burglars as useful in selecting properties to burgle.

The results of the interviews with Irish burglars produced overwhelming support for the kind of behaviour and decision-making processes discovered earlier in the British context. The results were strongest in relation to the sequence of decision making, the level of skill and organization (good and poor respectively) and the use of cues in target selection. The two key areas of divergence lay in the Irish burglars' preparedness to travel a considerable distance to find a target (this may have been to do with the more rural nature of the geography in Ireland) and that they were less concerned that the target be unoccupied. Like British burglars, they considered the size and nature of the target and its position on the street as most important at the scene of the crime, at least according to their verbal reports.

We had replicated the British studies in terms of verbal response, but as is well known in social-psychological literature, people's actual behaviour does not always reflect their reported behaviour (LaPiere, 1934). It was important to take the investigation a stage further and try to validate empirically what burglars said they did in a more realistic observational setting. It was not possible to accompany active burglars during their criminal activities for ethical reasons, so we created a simulated residential environment using maps, slides and a random access slide carousel. The earlier British research in the area had examined the importance of different types of cues sequentially and it now seemed preferable to look at the whole range of identified cues together, as they would appear in reality.

In the first simulation (Taylor & Nee, 1988), cues were deliberately manipulated on five 'adjacent' houses, in line with what burglars had reported as attractive or not in a target. For example, one house was detached, had good cover, easy access and was unoccupied. The remaining properties were a terrace of four town houses made to look adjacent on the simulated map, with a variety of positive and negative cues. We were attempting a basic empirical validation of what burglars had said in a variety of interview studies, including our own. We also compared burglars' responses to those of householders for the first time. Burglars and their householder comparison group were asked to 'wander' around the simulated environment by calling up random slides and 'thinking out loud' as to what they found attractive or unattractive in terms of target selection.

Burglars, and indeed non-burglars, all said they were most likely to burgle the 'attractive' detached house. However, householders overestimated the importance of many cues, while completely missing a whole range of other cues used by the burglars when discriminating between all five houses. For instance, householders had no awareness of the increased vulnerability of the corner properties on the terrace, or that one house looked more 'lived-in' and therefore more lucrative. Householders were also significantly more random in their slide choice and took significantly longer to reach a decision (for a fuller description see Taylor and Nee, 1988).

It was clear that cues were being used in target choice and it was also clear that burglars had a certain expertise in comparison to their householder counterparts. But the 'burglars as experts' had raised a further set of issues. It appeared that they were not using a single hierarchy of cues in relation to target selection. A more complex picture emerged, in which the effects of cues seemed to be interacting with and mediating each other. We therefore decided to explore this in a more realistic, less manipulated setting.

This second experiment (Nee & Taylor, 2000) constituted a more sophisticated simulation using five houses roughly equal in terms of size, market value and potential lucrativity. This time we did not manipulate natural cues in line with previous burglars' preferences. This produced a more realistic environment with greater ecological validity. We used a new set of incarcerated middle-range burglars and a random sample of homeowners selected from a housing area similar to that in the simulation.

Not surprisingly, a richer and more enlightening picture emerged from the burglars' responses. While there were clear trends in preference for particular houses, it became apparent that these could change depending on aspects such as the time of day; the time of year; changes in the neighbourhood in terms of population movement, transport and architecture. No single set of cues seemed central to decision making. It was the combination of cues at any one time, in any one scenario that burglars were appraising and changes in these cues at another point in time might lead to a different decision. For instance, an extremely attractive house in terms of potential lucrativity, cover (from vegetation or other buildings), access and lack of occupancy was considered less popular than a house with a dog and less cover because of the comprehensive target hardening on the former house (i.e. solid windows, doors, deadbolts and alarm). Householders were even more indiscriminate than they had been in the first experiment. Burglars demonstrated a practised, experienced decision-making process that was flexible in the face of varying contingencies, and this was something situational crime prevention planners had not bargained for.

The next logical stage of enquiry in this research was to observe and interview offenders in their natural operational context, i.e. on the streets – the most ecologically valid setting possible. Two excellent studies, based on an ethnographic approach, were published in the 1990s in America that did precisely this (Cromwell, Olsen & Avary, 1991; Wright & Decker, 1994). Going to great lengths to involve active burglars in their samples, they interviewed participants at the scene of a recent burglary and each others' burglaries, asking them to reconstruct their decision-making process and behaviour (this avoided the ethical problems of observing an actual burglary). Despite the dramatic cultural differences between the American and British samples (the former had a far greater ethnic mix and were heavily drug dependent) both research teams found overwhelming support for the earlier, prison-based work particularly in terms of: motivation (money for an expensive lifestyle); a sequenced decision-making process (beginning away from the scene of the crime); degree of planning (mostly falling into the 'searcher' category identified in Bennett and Wright's [1984] work); and the use of cues at the scene of the crime to select a target. Both teams in the US also used samples of non-offending students to evidence the burglars' expertise. These two early-90s studies extended our knowledge by giving us insight into burglars' patterns of decision making once inside the target (Wright and Decker's 'cognitive scripts' [1994]) and with their excellent discussion of enhanced target selection under the influence of drugs (Cromwell, Olson & Avary, 1991).

Pulling all of these studies together at the end of the last millennium has taken us some considerable way along the road to theoretical elaboration in the field of burglary research.

The key elements of what we have learned can be summarized as follows:

the lifestyle, motivation, career trajectory and general characteristics of burglars from different cultural backgrounds;

the greater level of expertise typical of most burglars compared to non-offenders and the bounded rationality within which they operate (Cornish & Clarke, 1986);

the complex nature of target selection, together with the 'nuts and bolts' of entering and operating within the property and how this applies to situational crime prevention;

the burglars' sequential use of thumb based on earlier successful learning and flexible response to contingencies (cues) once at the scene of the crime, in accordance with the use of rules and contingencies in operant conditioning (Taylor & Nee, 1988; Parrott, 1987);

the performance-enhancing effect of drugs on target selection, reducing anxiety and differentiating central cues in relation to peripheral cues (Cromwell, Olson & Avary, 1991).

Naturally, research should not stop here. We are now aware of the impact that an ever-changing environment has on target selection, and should remain alive to the importance of changing local, national and international cultural developments over time (for example in the use of drugs, or changes in crime prevention policy). It is now nearly twenty years since some of this work was done and it is important theoretically as well as for crime-prevention policy that we continue to learn about changing motivations, attitudes and behaviours regarding residential burglary (and of course for every type of criminal activity). Burglary rates, while still high in Britain, continue to reduce year on year and we should ask offenders why. Have householders, for instance, become more vigilant? Has technology improved? Are there easier ways of making illicit money? Are there changes in the characteristics or demographics of the typical burglar?

As already noted, emphasizing a grounded approach to the findings from several different studies, allows for the extension and continuation of work over time and encourages the triangulation of methods. There is no reason, for instance, why researches could not investigate the salient findings from the more recent American studies (namely those of target selection under the influence of drugs and decision making within the target) on this side of the Atlantic. This would be important in order to replicate these findings but also to unearth important local variations of value to policy-makers and service-planners.

It is worth pointing out, before going on to discuss more general principles in offender-based research, that although the focus above has been on burglary, many other types of crime and criminal behaviour have been studied from the offender's perspective. A sample includes: shoplifting (Carroll & Weaver, 1986), car theft (Light, Nee & Ingham, 1992), armed robbery (Wright & Decker, 1997), interpersonal violence (Felson & Steadman, 1983) sex offending (Murray, 2001) and the use of lethal weapons in violent crime (Wells & Horney, in press). There are also studies on variations in the patterns of criminal activity for a wide range of offenders (Horney, Osgood & Marshall, 1995; Mande & English, 1988; Chaiken & Chaiken, 1982).

Increasing Accuracy in Offenders' Accounts

The next part of this chapter offers a summary of useful guidelines that I have adopted as a researcher in this field and suggests ways in which we can enhance the quality of information we glean from our time spent with the offender.

Observing offenders carrying out a crime is unethical, illegal and potentially dangerous, so researchers are usually constrained to interviewing offenders either in groups or on a one-to-one basis (albeit sometimes at the scene of a recent crime). For this reason, this part of the chapter concentrates on issues around interviewing offenders.

Interviewing offenders about their lives clearly relies on their own verbal accounts of what has occurred or what is commonly known as 'self-report' methodology. Can we be sure that what the offender is telling us is reliable? There are obvious reasons why offenders' accounts might not be the whole truth: self-protection; overconfidence; and inaccuracies of memory to name just a few. However, many of these problems can be minimized by taking care to organize and carry out data collection with reference to the many methodological developments made over the last two decades in this type of research (see Junger-Tas and Marshall, 1999 for an extensive review). When carried out competently, self-report methods provide us with an infinitely richer picture of offenders' experiences. They fill in substantial gaps in our knowledge about criminal activity such as motivation, decision making, circumstances and methods used that are simply not held on official criminal justice records (Horney, in press). As well as obtaining information about offences from which no convictions have resulted, Horney (in press) points out that self-report methods can shed light on potential offences that were avoided for some reason – perhaps because the offender changed their mind or was interrupted. This area of offender decision making is of great potential interest to the criminologist and policy-maker, but is not captured by official records at all.

Important methodological factors to consider when planning offender-based research include: the inclusion of offender-focused pilot work (usually done in groups, to identify, for example, the appropriate type of language to use); sampling; the location of the data-collection exercise; the methods used in data collection including the use of memory-enhancing techniques.

Groups or Individual Interviews?

I would suggest that, whenever possible, it is preferable to use a one-to-one format when working with offenders. Groups can be useful at a preliminary stage in order to identify salient issues, tighten research questions and clarify terminology to be used. In my experience, however, the dynamics in a group can negatively affect the validity of data collected and should be avoided if possible once research becomes more focused. Further, the problems that can arise in groups of offenders, such as limited literacy and verbal skills, shyness, overconfidence or hostility towards other group members, are considerably more pronounced with younger age groups (teens and below). All of these difficulties can be significantly reduced by an experienced interviewer who takes care to build up a rapport with the offender in a one-to-one situation. Interviewed competently, younger age groups have been found to be particularly forthcoming about their illegal activities, as they have yet to develop the more prosocial attitudes of older offenders and are less ashamed of what they have done (Junger-Tas & Marshall, 1999).

Sample Parameters and Locality of Data Collection

Some research projects which have attempted to estimate the general incidence of offending in society have used random samples of the general population, such as Graham and Bowling's (1995a, 1995b) *Young People and Crime*. Offender-focused work, however, often singles out a particular offence as a basic parameter and consequently samples are purposive or convenience based.

Recent forensic ethnographers such as Cromwell, Olson and Avary (1991), Wright and Decker (1994) and Shover (1996) have cautioned us about the fuzzy recall and lack of context-specific cues offenders from these samples experience if they are interviewed in, for instance, a prison setting. They also suggest that prison-based samples involve too many 'failed' criminals. Wright and Decker (1994) have contended that the only valid way to explore the thought processes and decision making of the offender is to interview him or her within their crime-specific context, meaning at the scene of a recent or potential crime. On the face of it, this does seem the ideal scenario – to interview in the most meaningful, ecologically sound environment. There are though, drawbacks with this type of interviewing and there are several good reasons why a sample drawn from an incarcerated population can be used just as effectively.

Ethnographic samples are often achieved using a snowballing technique in which one contact in a local neighbourhood will recommend other potential interviewees with a similar degree of knowledge and experience of a particular subject, who will then recommend others and so on. While the accounts of offenders sampled in this way are certainly worthwhile in their own right, they will be skewed by a very specialized and localized view of events. For instance, in the research on burglary reviewed in the first part of this chapter, Wright and Decker's (1994) sample was taken from the chronically poor 'rust-belt' of St Louis. Most participants were African-American in origin, and most were heavy users of 'crack' cocaine. A positive aspect of this type of sample is that it may well yield very valuable information for local service-planners and policy-makers. However, in terms of methodological rigour, this sample will be less representative of burglars in general than prison-based samples, which will include a greater geographical and behavioural mix.

The notion that offenders in custody comprise only 'failed' criminals is also easily challenged. It is well documented that the majority of offenders engage in a mix of high-rate property crime (Tarling, 1993) and are likely to serve time in prison at some time in their criminal careers, thus increasing the representativeness of any given prison sample. Further, prison samples can be drawn, not just using index offences – a method sometimes less than fruitful because it may not reflect the offender's most common offences – but through recommendations from other offenders and prison staff (which can subsequently be validated against official criminal records). In this way, one can have reasonable confidence that one is selecting those really experienced in the field in question.

For particular types of less common crime, such as those involving sex and violence or those involving female offenders, Horney (in press) points out mportantly that the only practical method of data collection is with convicted, incarcerated offenders, as it is simply too difficult to achieve a large enough sample from the general population. Junger-Tas and Marshall (1999) have also noted that young offenders are under-represented in general population surveys, probably because of the transient, more chaotic nature of their lifestyles in comparison to their non-offending peers.

Finally, it could be argued that using the real-world context within which to interview offenders has markedly greater face value than interviewing in a prison setting. However, the simulations used in prisons that Richard Wright himself carried out with Trevor Bennett for research on burglary (Bennett & Wright, 1984) and later those by Max Taylor and myself (e.g. Taylor & Nee, 1988) suggest that this setting can be used very effectively if the right cues for recall are utilized. The fact that later ethnographic interviewing by Wright and his colleagues fully supported the findings of the earlier experimental work indicates that prison-based samples are a valid source of data collection, to say nothing of the ethical issues which arise when taking active offenders back to scenes of recent crimes, and those of their colleagues. My recent involvement through the Home Office Policing and Crime Reduction Unit in using virtual reality as means of carrying out offender-based research convinces me there is still further and exciting potential in exploring simulated situations with incarcerated offenders.

Assisting Recall in Data Collection

As well as complex simulations and risky ethnographic encounters, many researchers continue to yield valuable qualitative and quantitative information using traditional face-to-face interviews with offenders. As researchers, then, and in the broader criminal justice arenas of police investigations and the court process, we are very reliant on the recall of events. Any process which can improve the accuracy of memory for criminal events will benefit all of us working in these fields. We can, therefore, learn many lessons from cognitive psychologists working in this area.

In their excellent review of research evidence on the effects of memory in remembering autobiographical sequences, Bradburn, Rips and Shevell (1987) make three points particularly relevant to the current discussion. Firstly, when asked a question about the incidence of a particular event or behaviour over a protracted period of time, people do not utilize a clear, quantitative strategy of recall to answer the question. They rely on fragmented memories about the past and make inferences and approximations based on this. Secondly, some types of information are remembered far more readily than others. For instance, memories about the critical details of daily events can be accessed more easily than street names in a familiar area (and there is good evidence that memories of sequences of offending can be retrieved quite well, as the discussion of life history calendars below indicates). Thirdly, there is greater room for overestimation when numerous very similar incidents are recalled – and this may well affect persistent offenders' recall. Multiple occurrences of an event are more likely to be remembered erroneously. They may be 'telescoped' by memory into greater numbers of events and telescoped forwards in time to have happened nearer the present time.

Experience in the world of survey research (e.g. Sudman, Bradburn & Schwarz, 1996; Schwarz & Sudman, 1994), cautions those constructing questionnaires that wording should try to involve retrieval cues compatible with memory. A preferable way to achieve this, if we have the luxury of choice, may include any research setting which involves appropriate visual stimuli, such as the simulations and ethnographic interviews already described above and the calendar methods to be described below. These methods more freely represent the images, contexts and emotions that draw out memories. Although these methods can be difficult to incorporate due to time and resource constraints, we should try to include them whenever possible, and encourage those working with us to do so. They result in a clear pay-off in terms of the quality of the data we can yield and, therefore, what we learn from the offender.

Experiments show that people recall more accurately if they begin with the most recent events and work backwards (Loftus & Marburger, 1983; Fisher & Geiselman 1992). Over 70 per cent of a whole range of life's details can be remembered accurately up to two years into the past (Bradburn, Rips & Shevell, 1987). After this, accuracy recedes quickly, if no appropriate cues and prompts are given to improve and assist it.

Later, in work on survey methodology with Schwarz and Sudman (Sudman, Bradburn & Shwarz, 1996; Schwarz and Sudman, 1994), Bradburn recommends using the shortest time period feasible in self-report research and not to expect absolute accuracy. These authors also found evidence that proxy reporting (e.g. by a parent for a child, or a significant other for an offender) can be highly correlated with self-reporting if carried out competently and with an awareness of the boundaries of memory (Mingay et al., 1994).

Other important lessons can be learned about recall from the field of witness testimony, in particular 'cognitive' interviewing (Fisher & Geiselman, 1992), in our quest for more valid data collection. These authors emphasize once again the importance of attempting to recreate the context when reconstructing an incident in terms of physical environment, smells, emotions, others present. They value the recall of isolated pieces of information and emphasize the importance of working backwards and forwards from well-remembered sequences, enabling the individual to piece together the jigsaw of memory.

Developed in the 1980s as a technique for collecting retrospective data (Freedman et al., 1988), the life events calendar has been developed for use in criminological, psychiatric and socio-economic research in the last decade (see, for example, Caspi et al., 1996, for work in psychiatry; Horney, Osgood and Marshall, 1995, for work in criminal careers and Belli, Shay and Stafford, 2000, for work in the socio-economic field). All of these studies have shown it to be a robust and effective tool for collecting detailed data about events and sequences of events and superior in collecting accurate information than simple questioning.

It too includes many of the memory-enhancing 'mnemonics' referred to above which increase accuracy in our potentially faulty recall. These include visual cues (a card or computerized calendar); relevant retrieval cues (significant events in one's life); and a clear time-frame moving from the most recent memories backwards, all of which help to match and retrieve representations in memory such as particular works, images and emotions (Wagenaar, 1986). Further, research evidence shows that we group memories of events into autobiographic sequences in which individual events (e.g. criminal activities) are remembered within more encompassing sequences (such as summer holidays, periods of unemployment: Bradburn, Rips and Shevell, 1987; Loftus and Marburger, 1983). The life events calendar provides an unrivalled method of identifying the reference points and anchors of these encompassing sequences within which to locate episodes of criminal activity.

The life events calendar method involves using a hard copy or computerized calendar that incorporates months presented chronologically backwards from the last time the offender was at liberty, and going back in some cases as far as three years (see Horney, in press). At first, the basic contextual features of a person's life are recorded on the calendar: when they were out of prison; such as who they were living with; where; birth dates of children or significant others; employment; training. During an important preliminary pilot phase (see the grounded approach in the first part of this chapter), areas of significance to particular offending groups will have been unearthed.

For example, football fixtures were very important reference points and mnemonics to a recent group of very young offenders. These would therefore be incorporated as the next step in the calendar exercise. Once general life events have been plotted, offenders then find it far easier to temporally locate periods of, for example, criminal activity, alcohol and drug use or problems with relationships, in a much more accurate, highly structured way.

The calendar method clearly encompasses many of the key features that might assist us in recall. Secondly, offenders and researchers using it have described it as enormously helpful in remembering more accurately (Horney, in press; Lewis & Mhlanga, 2001). In discussions with Julie Horney, she and I have come to the view that when using the calendar or other demanding cognitive tasks such as responding to the simulations in our burglary research, there is evidence that the actual intellectual engagement in the task increases the validity of the response and decreases deliberate deception. Offenders become completely absorbed in the task with the researcher and often correct or refine reports of particular incidents or decisions they have made as their appreciation of the task in hand and memory of the period becomes more focused. Findings from the first study of its kind to compare the calendar method with free recall of events in the field of crime research (Lewis & Mhlanga, 2001) tend to support this view. This Home Office-funded study attempted to estimate the incidence of offending among nearly 2,000 incarcerated property offenders over their previous eighteen months at liberty. Offenders were asked to freely recall their criminal activities in the first part of the interview and then repeat the exercise using the calendar. They significantly down-weighted the number of offences reported when using the calendar method, suggesting that it considerably reduced the forward telescoping and overestimation that Bradburn and his colleagues described (Bradburn, Rips & Shevell, 1987) when recalling numerous similar events over a bounded period of time.

As well as giving us important data about the incidence of offending (for instance, persistent offenders are not persistent all the time) the calendar method has enriched our understanding of links between crime and continuity and change within the offender. In other words, it simultaneously allows us to look at factors affecting the criminal career of a person and the impact that the immediate situation and circumstances have on criminal decision making (Horney, in press). This perspective has certainly been neglected in the past and has been facilitated greatly by the development of the calendar method.

Recommendations in Undertaking Offender-based Research

To summarize the main thrust of this chapter, the main rules of thumb I would use when embarking on work with offenders are as follows:

use the offender as expert throughout the study;

undertake preliminary groundwork using focus groups to ensure research questions are relevant and language used for future stages is appropriate;

after groundwork, choose one-to-one interviews with offenders over group interviews wherever possible, and especially with younger offenders;

use memory-enhancing retrieval cues such as visual aids (simulations) and meaningful daily experiences (life events calendars) wherever possible;

begin with recent events and work backwards, wherever possible and appropriate;

when asking offenders to recall events, use the shortest time period feasible.

This chapter began with a cautionary note from Matza (1970) about distancing ourselves from a most important source of information – the offender. Hopefully, the chapter has provided convincing evidence for the reader of the value of making the offender central to our investigations. To undertake crime research without involving the offender's perspective should be seen as trying to write a play without characters.

Chapter Two

The Community and Family Context in Understanding Juvenile Crime

Mark Wilson

For ten years I worked as a community psychologist in a housing scheme on the periphery of a large Scottish city. The question 'Why do our children grow up violent and badly behaved?' was posed to me one day by Cathy McCormack, a mother, writer and community activist. The scenario she described was from the previous evening, where she had witnessed a fight between a group of boys from her own street, against a large group from the community across the main road. Such battles had been a constant feature of the summer nights for all the years she could remember. She described the gang-related behaviour of stone-throwing and stick wielding as 'stone age'. As our society has progressed, she asked, why is it that our teenage boys end up behaving like men from the stone age? She articulated her own fear of living in the midst of violence, coupled with an awareness that her own sons possess risk factors for future offending, simply because of where they live.

In this chapter, I hope to build upon the focus taken by forensic psychology, in drawing upon theories which can inform professional practice. I also hope to build upon McCormack's passionate desire for all citizens to participate in building better communities for our young people (McCormack, 1995). Rather than focusing largely on products of risk and failure (such as 'stone age behaviour') this chapter hopes to address forces which might prevent such failure. The majority of Scottish fourteen–fifteen-year-old pupils admit to offending (Jamieson, McIvor & Murray, 1999), so adolescence itself will be viewed as a hazard. In parallel with theories of adolescence, this chapter will attempt to build a focus on forces which are fluid, dynamic and changing, nevertheless. The psychologist who seeks to work with forces impacting upon human development will often face immediate challenges of responding to the cognitions and behaviour of people, in order to find solutions. At times, this will contrast with the approach from academic psychology, where there is the intellectual challenge of reviewing, interpreting and balancing results from psychological theory and research, in search of general descriptive principles.

In this chapter, theory from developmental psychology and community psychology will receive attention, alongside clinical concepts that have established themselves with adult forensic populations. In particular I will refer to experiences in Scotland where there has been a 'welfare' approach to dealing with offenders aged under sixteen for most of the last thirty years. This approach to identifying 'needs' has rarely resulted in a diagnosis and treatment approach, but rather in a range of empirical interventions aimed at finding what variables might make a difference. The Scottish approach to working with young people who offend is subject to review at present, and questions are certainly being asked about whether it can learn from the research into effectiveness of treatment programmes (Smith, 2000). Equally, I will seek to question whether models of prevention, as developed in Scotland, might be an important feature in future research and interventions within forensic psychology.

Review

Risk, and opportunity: perspectives from developmental and community psychology

Ecological theory of human development (Bronfenbrenner, 1979) provides an academic framework for examining whether the community and family context is of crucial importance to a young offender, and to their risks of future reoffending. The framework has now been modified to form a statutory tool for assessment of 'Children in Need' in England and Wales (Horwarth, 2001). In this section, some evidence for the usefulness of this perspective will be discussed.

In young offenders, crime-related factors exist in tandem with needs associated with the biological and social changes of adolescence. Whyte (1998) suggests that the 'most important single fact about crime is that it is committed mainly by teenagers and young adults'. He goes on to suggest:

> many young people, whatever their background, offend at some time, though not frequently;
> youth crime is not rising out of control;
> the range of crimes up to the age of seventeen tends not to be very serious;

most young people who offend do not come to the attention of the authorities;

most young people who offend stop without formal intervention.

The prevalence of offending increases to a peak in the teenage years and then
decreases in the twenties (Farrington, 1986). The Cambridge Study in Delinquent Development found that 55 per cent of those convicted between the ages
of ten and sixteen were conviction free between ages twenty-five and thirty-
two. This compares with 92 per cent of those not convicted as juveniles. Graham
and Bowling (1995a) found that although offending is widespread amongst
the eleven-to-sixteen age group, about 3 per cent of offenders accounted for
approximately a quarter of all offences reported. Thus, risks of offending and
reoffending are high amongst teenagers, but risks of serious persistent
reoffending apply only to a small minority.

What are the forces that lead some children to become offenders, and then
severe/persistent adult offenders? Antisocial behaviour associated with early-
onset hyperactivity has a strong genetic component, according to Rutter (1997),
though he also clarifies that the genetic contributions are to the various risk factors rather than to a discrete categorical disorder. Antisocial behaviour carries
different consequences over time, of course. Children aged under eight in Scotland (and under ten in England and Wales) are below the age of criminal responsibility. Antisocial behaviour may often be seen as mischief in children, but as a
crime in adolescents; the same antisocial tendency may sometimes be underlying, but the adolescent lawbreaker reflects greater individual maturity and new
risks and opportunities in his environment. Their interactions with new peer
groups, new ideas, emotions, roles and identities lead to a second question, of
much greater interest to many: might it be possible to identify the processes in
adolescence which prevent the offending child from becoming the serious/per-
sistent adult offender?

In order to answer such a question, context requires to be an integral part of
our research design. This is an integral feature of Urie Bronfenbrenner's ecological model, which involves

the scientific study of the progressive, mutual accommodation between an active,
growing human being and the changing properties of the immediate settings in
which the developing person lives, as this process is affected by relations between
these settings, and by the larger contexts in which the settings are embedded.
(Bronfenbrenner, 1979, p. 21)

Such a model contrasts, firstly, with much of developmental psychology, which
can be seen as 'the science of the strange behaviour of children in strange

situations with strange adults' (Bronfenbrenner, 1979, p. 2), and secondly, with much of forensic psychology, where the focus has often been on 'risk' factors which change little with time.

The ecological model affirms multi-linear patterns of causation, so it easily accommodates the recent advances in biological models; much is undoubtedly still to be learned about how biological variables function and interact with time and development. A number of age-related issues can be identified. For example, psychosis is very seldom a factor in adolescents with high-risk behaviour (Sheldrick, 1999). Another predictor of criminal behaviour in adults, Factor 2 of the Psychopathy Checklist (PCL-R), shows risks declining with age (Harpur & Hare, 1994). Fahlberg (1994) has influenced thinking and practice in adoption and fostering, with her research about how the young child's brains can be affected by trauma, leading to future behavioural difficulties. As medical care for highly vulnerable babies has improved, it is suggested that increased numbers of children are living with neurological difficulties (Garbarino, 1999). This may manifest itself as behavioural difficulties, and 1 per cent of children may have characteristics of Attention Deficit Hyperactivity Disorder (National Institute for Clinical Excellence, 2000).

It is open for academic discussion whether biological models (possibly involving diagnosis) can complement the development of useful psychological models, based upon assessment of context and human development (Pilgrim, 2000). In talking about individual development, we have to be clear about two concepts, *change* and *time*. Time is not the same as development, but development always has a temporal dimension. If a person's distinctive pattern of characteristics remains unchanged across time, no development has occurred. Consequently, processes that go on in an unchanged manner, within existing structures, do not constitute development (Moen, Elder & Luscher, 1995). Biological models and approaches to identifying 'traits' in individual characteristics tend to emphasize variables which change little over time, so they are of critical importance in the prediction of offending behaviour. Social contexts, by contrast, are rather poor predictors when taken in isolation. Models from psychology and information on social contexts are critical for the prevention of offending, nevertheless. The ability to predict may be important if we are to be able to evaluate our prevention efforts.

Writing about interactions of biological and environmental forces, Michael Rutter emphasizes that the alleviation of environmental adversities is most crucial for individuals at genetic risk because they appear to be the people most vulnerable to those adversities (Rutter, 1997). An example comes from Mednick and Kandel (1998), who studied children with signs of minor neurological damage. They found that 70 per cent of these children were arrested for a violent crime by the age of twenty-one, if they had been brought up in unstable and

troubled families. This compared with 20 per cent of physically normal children reared in similar families. Children with signs of neurological damage were
found to be at no greater risk for violent crimes than physically normal children, however, if they grow up in well-functioning, stable families (the arrest
rate by age twenty-one was about 15 per cent for both groups). In another study,
Losel, Bender and Bliesener (1998) studied the role of child temperament in
teenage bullies and victims, starting with the general finding that a low resting
heart rate in children is associated with antisocial behaviour. They found that
this difference in heart rate was significant in low-risk families (i.e. those with a
low levels of stressful events and trauma and a high level of effective family functioning). There were no differences in the heart rates of bullies, victims and other
young people in high-risk families, however.

There is recognition of a continuing and interlinking importance of family,
parenting, poverty and education in the development of antisocial behaviour
throughout a child's school years (Loughran, 1998). Longitudinal studies have
identified clusters of factors which significantly differentiate between groups
who go on to be convicted as juveniles, and those who do not (Kolvin et al.,
1988). The predictors noted can be easily identifiable to parents and teachers:
children who were troublesome and dishonest in their primary schools, generally from poorer or larger-sized families, living in poor accommodation, supported by social agencies, and suffering physical neglect from parents, are more
likely to get into trouble with the law (Loughran, 1998). Boys who become delinquent are more likely to show low intelligence and poor attainment, and to
be rated as 'daring' by parents and peers. Teachers are likely to say they are
hyperactive, and have poor concentration. The boys are likely to have below-
average height and weight (West & Farrington, 1973).

Low intelligence has correlated with delinquency, even after controlling for
other variables such as social class and race (Lynam, Moffitt & Stouthamer-Loeber,
1993). Wilson (1980a) concluded that the most important correlate of convictions, cautions and self-reported delinquency was lax parental supervision at age
ten. West and Farrington (1973) found that the differences between juvenile delinquents and non-delinquents at age fourteen were similar in many respects to
the differences identified at age eight–ten. Importantly, the convicted delinquents
still tended to have cruel, passive or neglectful parents who were in conflict with
each other – their development had continued on a high-risk trajectory, because
there had been no significant change in their family environment.

The chapter on Risk Assessment by David Crighton in this volume emphasizes the importance of specifying exactly which risks are being identified. This
general point is particularly pertinent when considering the validity of risk assessment for young people. Risk assessment will undoubtedly have greater predictive validity when applied to adults, than when done with children and young

people. Adults have had time to rehearse particular patterns to their offending, whereas children and young people tend to be more impulsive, and much more likely to offend with peers. The features held in common by 'persistent' young offenders have less to do with offending patterns, and more to do with their adverse personal and social circumstances (Hagell & Newburn, 1994). Fundamentally, the development of delinquent behaviours in a child is clearly correlated with other life experiences from an early age, and any strategy that reduces delinquency and offending will inevitably have positive spin-offs in other areas also. In the words of David Farrington: 'Any measure which reduces crime will probably also reduce alcohol abuse, drink driving, drug abuse, sexual promiscuity, family violence, truancy, school failure, unemployment, marital disharmony and divorce' (Farrington, 1994, p. 221).

Treatment

Perhaps the 'treatment' approach to young people who offend was put 'on trial' in the Scottish Children's Hearing system. Scotland's unique approach to juvenile offending has existed since 1971, aiming to ensure that the needs of the child are always taken into account in making decisions about offenders. It is an example of the 'welfare' model of juvenile justice, where disposal is based upon a professional's assessment of the needs of a child, rather than in proportion to the severity of the offence. The Children's Hearing system considers the welfare of children who require protection from abuse and truants, as well as offenders. It is a system that encourages diversion away from official agencies, but also provides for the formal supervision of juvenile offenders in the community or in residential settings. In nearly all cases, decisions about what should happen to a child are made by the Children's Panel, not a court (see Lockyer & Stone, 1998).

An assessment of the child's 'needs' is therefore the cornerstone of decision making. The original expectation was that assessment would identify the following themes (May, 1971):

1   The explanation for delinquency would be found in the characteristics and the motivational systems of delinquent youths.
2   Delinquents would be identifiably different from non-offenders.
3   The delinquent would not be held fully responsible for his or her actions because of the psychological constraints or family influences, or both, that he or she suffered from.
4   Delinquent behaviour as such would not be seen as the problem, but as merely a symptom of a more intractable 'disease'.

In practice, in most areas of Scotland, residential centres were established allowing an 'in-depth' assessment of a child's functioning to be prepared in a three-week intensive residential period. Clayton (1979), observing parallel developments in England, suggested that the philosophy behind such residential assessment centres was rooted in the idea that human behaviour is constant, and that the child's behaviour would be relatively consistent over time and across situations, and that these personality factors would be measurable and predictable. It was assumed that the child (usually a boy) removed from his usual environment and admitted to an assessment centre would take his problem with him to be assessed. This assumption corresponded well with the 'medical model' underlying much of the new Children's Hearing system.

Linear models of psychology were popular in the earlier days of the Children's Hearing System, where staff focused on 'treatment' of an identified underlying variable. This focus of assessments and interventions on the 'need rather than the deed' (Lockyer & Stone, 1998) led to a tendency to categorize children with terms like 'List D material' (meaning residential school), 'Maladjusted' or 'Deserves another chance/saveable'. One memorable residential assessment centre report referred to a child suffering from 'Al Capone Syndrome' (Wilson, 1980b). There was a kind of belief that if staff could describe the 'root of the problem' and find out 'what makes the child tick' then they could allocate the child to a resource which would fit them best. Later research suggested, however, that assessment centres found it difficult to conceptualize community solutions, and led to children being inappropriately recommended for residential placements (Mapstone & Buist, 1980). The practice also often became frustrating for social work staff, because other professionals such as psychiatrists and psychologists often refused to become involved where there was a 'social problem' (Wilson, 1985; 1994a).

Now practice is much more firmly rooted in a multi-linear approach to psychology, focusing on points of interaction between child and the environment. Instead of trying to match a child's difficulties to an individual treatment, practice is more like an 'empirical model', where a number of variables might be altered, and the effects noted. Nowadays, in approaches to Children's Panel supervision, families, social workers, teachers, psychologists and others are much more likely to be involved in multi-agency plans, where assessment and intervention are seen as two interrelated pieces of work, and where it is recognized that the child is constantly growing and changing. In terms of psychological theory, the assessment involves an evaluation of the child's response to interventions in different settings. Although traditional assessments, focusing on the child's characteristics, were high in reliability, assessments where interventions are evaluated as part of an ongoing process, done in naturalistic settings, should maximize validity (Wilson, 1991; McPhee, 1992).

Recent studies utilizing techniques of meta-analysis have clarified effective treatment approaches with young offenders (Lipsey, 1992). Features of effective programmes are summarized by McGuire (1995) and Martin (1998). Research does not identify any one approach as suitable for all young offenders, but broadly, the more effective programmes are targeted at high- and medium-risk offenders, challenge ways of thinking as well as ways of behaving, and adhere to agreed objectives and structures. In Scotland, formal 'treatment' programmes have been developed in community as well as residential settings, within the childcare settings as well as within the Young Offender Institutions. Initial results in Scotland appear impressive (e.g. Cadbury, 1998; Scottish Prison Service, 2000) and have led to a government initiative to ensure high standards of effective practice (Galbraith, 2000).

Reliance on 'treatment' programmes alone is inadequate, however. 'Treatment' programmes are most effective when there is some stability in the child's residence, and some motivation to participate. Both of these requirements are frequently lacking amongst children in trouble, or in the young offender population. For example, in Polmont Young Offender Institution, over half of the sixteen- to twenty-one-year-olds admitted in any year will be released within three months, and will therefore not be there long enough to do any of the programmes on offer (Wilson, 1998a). Some young people are not suitable for treatment programmes. It seems important to offer interventions aimed at motivation for change (Buchanan, 1999), and resources designed to ensure that the young people do not drift into a 'no-man's land' between children's services and those designed for adults (Winchester, 2000). Work to develop effective practice following a 'prevention' paradigm will be discussed in the next section.

Prevention

We may believe that 'a stitch in time saves nine' and 'prevention is better than cure', but Orford (1992) contended that past practice in applied psychology has 'undoubtedly been an overconcentration upon existing disorder, to the virtual exclusion of attempts to prevent disorder ever happening in the first place' (p. 154). Adolescence, moreover, has received little attention in the prevention literature (Mrazek & Haggerty, 1994; Wolfe, 1994).

In the previous section, I have discussed the important place for treatment, but also highlighted some of the limitations of this paradigm. Adult conditions such as 'psychopathy' have restricted utility in practice with children or young people, but there may, nevertheless, be a desire to reduce risks, or promote an individual's 'resilience' (Rutter, Giller & Hagell, 1998). Social problems cannot be 'cured' by psychological answers, yet there is a desire to respond to the many young people at risk of becoming serious or persistent offenders (Galbraith, 2000;

Barnardo's Matrix, 2000). Even in an institutional setting, paradigms of prevention can provide a paradigm for effectively preventing today's young offender becoming tomorrow's hardened criminal (Gunn & Wilson, 1999). The paradigm of 'prevention' has been developed within the field of community psychology during the last thirty years, and appears to hold particular relevance to issues of youth crime at this time (Wilson, 1998b; 1998c).

Ken Pease points out that 'crime' covers such a wide range of different behaviours, that it would be inappropriate to look for a single technique of prevention: 'The behaviour itself must be understood, to determine where change could best be brought about' (Pease, 1997, p. 964). A useful distinction between different forms of crime prevention was made by Brantingham and Faust (1976). Drawing on terms in public health and community psychology literature (see Orford, 1992), they make a distinction between 'primary prevention', which seeks to reduce the opportunities for crime with no reference to criminals themselves; 'secondary prevention', which seeks to prevent those who may be tempted into a criminal career from doing so; and 'tertiary prevention', which aims to prevent known criminals from committing further crime.

Primary prevention

Ainsworth (2000) talks of successes in situational and environmental approaches to crime prevention, of relevance to all ages of (potential) offenders. Settings where there are high densities of young people provide opportunities for effective work utilizing this model. Resources are targeted at a situation (rather than individuals) to prevent the onset of a problem, thereby reducing incidence. For example, assessing aggregate needs may lead to anti-bullying work in a Young Offenders Institution, based upon models of primary prevention (Power, Dyson & Wozniak, 1997). In Glenthorne Youth Treatment Centre, the high concentration of young people has enabled work aimed at mitigating effects of violent TV and computer-game images upon cognitions (Browne, 1999). In a community setting, changes in opportunities available to children in the evenings are reported to lead to a reduction in offending (McGallagly, 1998). Primary prevention approaches also offer the prospect of influencing the 85 per cent of children who commit serious, violent offences as juveniles, but who do not get caught (Dunford & Elliot, 1984).

The recently reported gun violence at schools in the United States seems to have led to widespread public discussion about prevention strategies (Garbarino, 2000). Violence, which has long existed in ghetto areas, seems now to have been spreading into more prosperous areas. Children recently responsible for school shootings have often come from prosperous backgrounds, but they are going out into a world where they feel their parents can't protect them any more (Garbarino, 1999). Scotland has some of the worst youth homicide statistics in the Western world, with a murder rate about four times higher that England, Ireland or France (Garbarino, 2000). Children growing up in some of our impoverished peripheral housing schemes may prepare their cognitions and behaviour to face situations which they perceive to be risky, and often this will mitigate against their personal needs being met (Garbarino, Kostelny & Dubrow, 1991; Wilson, 1994b).

Although we have much to learn about how to work with young people's perceptions of dangers and inequalities in their communities and world, the 'ethos' of the school has been identified as crucial in assisting children to build a resilience against violence in their communities and homes (Morley, 1998; Rutter, Giller & Hagell, 1998; Munn, 2000). Battistich and Hom (1997) examined relationships between students' sense of the school as a community and their involvement in problem behaviours. It was found that school context may moderate relationships between individual risk factors, protective factors and developmental outcomes, and that schools that are experienced as communities may enhance students' resilience.

Meta-analysis of effectiveness in primary prevention programmes by Durlak and Wells (1997) affirmed that interventions targeting change in environments can be beneficial in reducing a variety of risks facing children. They concluded that two other approaches have also demonstrated their effectiveness: 'transition programmes', where resources are focused on easing the passage of children through potentially traumatic events, and 'person-centred strategies', where programmes employing behavioural or cognitive behavioural forms of intervention were found to be particularly effective.

Secondary prevention

Whereas the approach of primary prevention is to prevent crime, 'secondary prevention' focuses on the prevention of criminality (Farrington, 1996). Secondary prevention might also be referred to as 'early treatment' (Mrazek & Haggerty, 1994). This approach to prevention characterizes the approach of the Children's Hearing System, as planned by Lord Kilbrandon (1964). The plan had been that children might be identified young. Arrangements would be made for them and their families to receive individual programmes of treatment or re-education. Lord Kilbrandon had predicted that the new Children's Hearing System would probably lead to an increase in numbers of children being received into residential educational settings, and this is indeed what happened. The approach was not cost-effective; there were not enough personnel available in community settings to meet the needs which could be identified, and although residential settings sometimes met individual needs, the cost (of disrupted family relationships, as well as finance) was too high.

Now we are more aware of risk factors associated with children who become persistent offenders, and simplistic expectations of 'nipping things in the bud' have lessened. Rather than focusing simply on an individual's personality characteristics, it is likely that useful knowledge will result from studying their cognitions, and how these are mediated to growing children and young people. What type of interactive construing is likely to produce agreement or non-agreement amongst young people, and the adults around them? There would seem to be circumstances where the young person will set high score on being independent of others, forming their own opinions, and being nonconformist, or disobedient (Fromm, 1981). There will be other circumstances where the young person will wish to sum up each particular situation on its merits, or see it as extremely important to get along with the other people present. Don Bannister suggested that 'trait theories' may not be particularly helpful with adolescents; they are 'tautological in two senses – they inhibit the development of concepts of process and change and they produce unelaboratable concepts of original cause' (Bannister, 1970, p. 412). 'State' may sometimes be an appropriate focus of treatment interventions, in order to reduce the risks of a particular 'trait' developing.

Garbarino writes of how children develop a sense of personal self and morality in response to traumatic events in their life (Garbarino, Kostelny & Dubrow, 1991). Cairns and Cairns (1994) talk of the cognitive changes of adolescence, which develop from their interpretations of experiences. The cognitive growth of the adolescent is intertwined with their construing of a sense of self, and perceiving themselves as part of a world in which they have a chance of a reasonable future. Kelly (1992) emphasizes the need of the adolescent for experiences which lead to helpful constructive answers to four questions:

1   Who am I?
2   What kind of person am I?
3   How will people react to me?
4   Am I OK?

Few other behaviours so poignantly call into question our membership of mainstream society as being officially labelled an offender. For most children and young people, criminals immediately are excluded from our concept of 'people like us'. We know that many young offenders will commit offences with co-offenders, and we face a challenge of preventing the individual from developing criminal potential and characteristics (e.g. self-concepts and cognitions associated with roles, social opportunities and behaviour: Kelly, 1992; Farrington, 1996).

Approaches to secondary prevention, therefore, now tend to focus on the dangers that any interventions might increase the risks of future offending. They target young people at risk of exclusion and/or custody, to enhance their opportunities for remaining in mainstream roles in society. Successes of such 'diversion' policies are discussed by Asquith and Samuel (1994).

Tertiary prevention

'Tertiary prevention' is work aimed at preventing the reoccurrence of a problem. Whereas conventional treatment approaches may be appropriate irrespective of age, tertiary prevention approaches seek to make the most of the opportunity to intervene before patterns are fully consolidated. Whereas 'treatment' programmes are necessary and beneficial for young offenders serving long-term sentences, other approaches are necessary to make an impact on those persistent offenders who serve repeated short sentences (Scottish Prison Service, 2000). This also applies to those at a 'pre-contemplation' stage of change (Prochaska, Norcross & Di Clemente, 1994).

It seems clear that a substantial proportion of the young offender age group constitute a high risk in terms of reconviction, but it is also during these years that many young offenders will engage in personal growth, change their patterns of social networks and will start the process of disengaging from offending. On a Scottish population, Cooke and Michie (1998) found that about half of young offenders would be back in custody within two years of release. Within Scotland's largest young offenders Institution (HM YOI Polmont), this means 1,300 young offenders finishing their sentences each year, and 650 coming back within twenty-four months. Cooke and Michie's research feeds some optimism, because of the half who have not reappeared within two years, few have returned to prison within four years.

One example of tertiary prevention might be to target work with cognitions at key points when the young offender is at risk of forming attachments to criminal patterns of identity (e.g. work with young people experiencing remand or custodial sentence for the first time). This approach can be found within the childcare system; the first three months of residential placement are often a time of particularly intensive intervention, which addresses maintaining family relationships, focusing the child's thinking, the circumstances and variables behind the decision to provide accommodation, and seeking means of changing variables.

In 1994 the US Institute of Medicine reported to Congress, reviewing evidence for the effectiveness of prevention approaches (Mrazek & Haggerty, 1994). They concluded that it would be helpful to classify prevention work in a way that separated it clearly from treatment work. The three means of targeting prevention work which they suggested were: 'universal' approaches, aimed at the total population; 'selected' approaches, targeted at groups of individuals show signs of being at risk; and 'indicated' approaches with individuals.

Following these principles, as well those from Durlak and Wells (1997), Guerra, Tolan, and Hammond (1994), and Asquith (1996), pilot strategies at HM YOI Polmont have included 'universal' efforts to promote helping, 'soften the culture' and create a more constructive ethos. 'Selected' approaches have included 'Early Intervention Programmes', targeted at young offenders serving their first custodial sentence, and have also focused on the opportunities of the induction period for assessment of change in repeat offenders. For individuals, it has been considered important to maintain contacts with people outside the institution, such as partners or family and outside agencies, to discourage the process of identity-formation based upon the institution. Whereas long-term and adult prisoners require sentence planning, the young offender requires assistance with 'life-planning' (Gunn & Wilson, 1999).

Practice

Psychologists working with children who pose a risk to others also work in a context which mandates them to protect those same children against dangers. As a result of the UN Convention on the Rights of the Child, children up to age eighteen are entitled to services which promote their well-being. A child has a right to a service because of their situation/context, and a service does not require to be justified because of a particular pathology or diagnosis.

The best people to help a 'troubled' child may be those who know the child best (Buchanan, 1999). There are roles to be developed by psychologists in working with others to address factors that enhance the child's abilities and reduce the risks facing the developing child. Strathclyde Regional Council defined a priority for their psychologists in education and social work settings as 'to prevent unfavourable conditions in the home, school or community from hindering the appropriate psychological, educational and social development of children and young people' (Strathclyde Regional Council, 1988). As we have seen in the section on secondary prevention, work to ensure effectiveness of practice is particularly important in the sphere of young offending, because professionals face a responsibility to ensure that interventions done with good intentions are not actually serving to increase risks of adult offending. Risks require to be managed, and reduced, by action concerning environmental as well as individual variables. Assessment may not aim to attribute blame to any particular individuals or situations, but certainly does work towards a sharing of responsibility for sustainable developments.

Policy makers have recognized that 'ecological' models of psychology (Bronfenbrenner, 1979) are essential for broadening the range of interventions beyond that of clinical treatment. (Strathclyde Regional Council, 1988; Department of Health, 2000). Implications for practice include the following (adapted from Garbarino and Stocking, 1980):

1 Behavioural problems in adolescents relate to characteristics of the environment as well as characteristics of the individual; stresses, opportunities, and supports are relevant factors.
2 Efforts to bring positive changes to the lives of young people in trouble require understanding of children, families and their environments.
3 Efforts to involve personal, peer and social networks in responses to troubled or troublesome behaviour require a shift in professional role and perspective – from 'caregiver' and 'policy maker' to 'participant in caregiving and policymaking'.
4 Approaches to social interventions need to be tested and evaluated, so we base our practice on knowledge of what is working, what does not, and why.

In line with the above, assessments cannot be deficit-led. Although many prevention initiatives are focused on risk reduction, efforts to promote wellness and resilience are seen as invaluable (Rutter, Giller & Hagell, 1998). In order to be effective, prevention initiatives need to be integrated within a comprehensive continuum of interventions (Adelson & Taylor, 2000)

To focus treatment efforts on the child alone, without also involving significant others in the child's life, makes it unlikely that the benefits will be sustained (Bamberger-Schorr, 1991). Multi Systemic Therapy (Henggler et al., 1996) is an example of how environmental forces can be harnessed to maintain benefits of a multi-modal programme, in community settings. In Scotland, Barnardo's Matrix Project is a government-funded initiative to pilot interventions with children aged eight to eleven who are at risk of becoming persistent offenders; importantly, their approach focuses considerably on the adults who influence the children and who mediate the cognitions which they are developing (Sharron, 1997; Barnardo's Matrix, 2000). In schools, thinking skills are developed through the mainstream curriculum (Times Educational Supplement, 2000), though Feuerstein's 'Instrumental Enrichment' curriculum is also developed in some schools for children with social, emotional and behavioural difficulties (Head & O'Neil, 1999).

When we try to understand how to respond to the psychological issues of young offenders, we can see that adolescents coming to our attention are often facing developmental paths that are normal, but hazardous nevertheless. We know that young offenders will take risks, believing they are invincible, perhaps as a test of their masculinity. Community-based interventions are not always going to be successful; many individuals will fail and find themselves in custody. Coming to a penal establishment is not neutral; the change of context can have developmental significance (Bronfenbrenner, 1979). When they reach a Young Offenders Institution, it is important to ensure that traumas associated with the move are minimized, and that opportunities for cognitive development are maximized. Garbarino (1999) writes of the need to ensure safety in care or custody, so that young people continue to make use of the higher parts of the brain (cortex), where they can think clearly, rather than the limbic and mid-brain regions, which are directed towards survival. If the ethos is constructive and purposeful, there will be opportunities for young people to learn that the issues they face are less about their toughness and ability to survive, and much more about their thoughts and the decisions they are making.

In custodial settings, I believe the psychologist can assist staff to face the challenge of softening the culture, and creating a positive ethos of constructive learning. Links with community are important to maintain. In all settings, teamwork is important. There are many opportunities to work with parents, families and other professionals to promote individual resilience. The empirical psychological model is useful to all, in clarifying goals, appraising processes of change and evaluating achievements. The psychologist can be a welcome ally in efforts to ensure that practice is theory-driven and designed for effectiveness.

Future Directions

In this chapter I have attempted to clarify examples of how new developments in forensic psychology might come from psychological rather than clinical models. With child and young adult offenders, there are opportunities to focus a bit less on the individual's psychopathology, and more on the normal forces surrounding adolescence.

Key issues for future development include the following:

In postgraduate training courses in forensic psychology, there may be a need to construct a new focus on developmental psychology and the specific issues in work with children and young people.

In risk assessment, there may be a need to focus more upon longitudinal studies, in order to identify variables that can make a difference. Retrospective and correlational studies may have value in clarifying issues that do not change much with time, but it is important to acknowledge that all children have rights to interventions which enhance their well-being.

In practice and research, there may be a need to move out of the 'treatment' paradigm, and examine issues of effective 'prevention' practice. Our focus, moreover, has to be not only on 'what works' but also on what makes it sustainable.

A variety of local authorities and voluntary childcare organizations are participating in strategies concerned with offending by young people. There may be a locus for employment of numerous forensic psychologists in the future. Strategies developed for institutional settings will often be unsuitable for community settings, however, and will require to be changed to take account of options which might enhance the individual's freedom to shape his own environment.

Chapter Three

Offence Paralleling Behaviour (OPB) as a Framework for Assessment and Interventions with Offenders

Lawrence Jones

'present concepts of behaviour appear to be inadequate, especially with respect to long temporal sequences and interactions between behaviours . . . behaviour should be studied as meaningful sequences (acts, practices etc.)'

(Hallam (1987, p. 326))

Forensic psychologists, perhaps more than any other group of applied psychologists, need to work with various types of historical narrative, often describing the same set of events. Unfortunately, most methods for analysing behaviour in the psychological literature (e.g. functional analysis) focus on discrete episodes. With the notable exception, perhaps, of Gresswell and Hollin's (1992) 'multiple sequential functional analysis' paradigm, there is a general paucity of literature that attempts to grapple with the complexity of behaviour as a diachronic process. This problem comes, I believe, out of the more fundamental methodological problem of finding ways of modelling and operationalizing hypotheses about offences as processes as opposed to events. The concept of an 'offence' is not defined scientifically, it is a particular, socially defined value-driven way of describing certain types of behaviour. This chapter attempts to open up some of the questions about why and how, as forensic psychologists, we need to look at behaviour as a sequential development. In addition, it explores the ways in which viewing behaviour in this way enables practitioners to work with a broader range of psychological and behavioural processes that are helpful to the tasks of risk assessment and addressing offending behaviour.

Traditionally, forensic psychologists have focused on past, discrete episodes of offending behaviour in their work on both risk assessment and in interventions addressing offending behaviour. Jones (1997, 2000) argued that this strategy has some significant problems associated with it, and that focusing on offence paralleling behaviour (OPB) is one way of, at least partly, addressing some of these shortcomings. Firstly, he argued, when assessing risk using actuarial assessment instruments such as the HCR-20 (Webster et al., 1997a, 1997b) it is important to ask what exactly is being predicted. Crime surveys suggest that the majority of offending behaviour goes undetected. The 'dark figure' in the 1998 British crime survey, for instance, was estimated at 76 per cent (though it is different for different crimes). Myhill and Allen (2002) estimate that 80 per cent of rape offences are not reported to the police. Attrition rates for rape allegations actually reaching a conviction are high, Harris and Grace (1999) found that 'only 6% of the cases originally recorded by police as rape resulted in convictions for rape'; out of 483 cases of allegations of rape being brought to the police, in 64 per cent of cases a suspect was identified, 31 per cent were charged, in 23 per cent a decision was made by the criminal prosecution service to prosecute, 21 per cent led to court proceedings, there was a conviction for any offence in 13 per cent of cases and a rape conviction in only 6 per cent. By multiplying the percentage reported by the percentage of reported offences reaching conviction it is possible to get an estimate of the proportion of all offences resulting in a conviction. In the case of rape this is 20 x 6 = 1.2 per cent (see also Friendship & Thornton, 2001). This implies that an estimated 98.8 per cent of all rapes committed do not result in a conviction. Lloyd, Mair and Hough (1994) estimate that only 3 per cent of all offences, of any kind, result in a conviction. It must be the case, then, that all that any actuarial measure, based on reconviction, is capable of predicting is the unusual event of *being reported, getting caught and being convicted* for a particular crime. Rather than arguing that past offending is the best predictor of future offending, it is more accurate to be arguing that past arrest or past conviction or conviction-related behaviour predict future arrest or future conviction. The relative absence of detection/prosecution-evasion skills and/or the inability to implement these skills must play a significant part in the process of getting caught for further offending. As most actuarial measures are reliant on reconviction as an outcome measure, they must systematically underestimate the rate of reoffending.

If we then take into account the degree of inaccuracy in the instrument the proportion of offending predicted is even less. The PCL-R, for instance, which is thought to be one of the better predictors of general recidivism, has been found by Hemphill, Hare and Wong (1998), pooling data across seven predictive studies (N = 1,374), to have a correlation (r) of 0.27 with general recidivism. This gives an estimated percentage of variance accounted for (r^2 x 100) of 7.29 per cent. If we multiply this by the 3 per cent (suggested by Lloyd, Mair and Hough,1994, see above) estimate of crime for which convictions are obtained we get an estimate of the proportion of crime that the PCL-R predicts as 0.2187 per cent. Clearly, these estimates will be different for different subgroups; however, this serves to illustrate the problem.

The impact of this distortion on treatment outcome studies, if too much reliance is made on actuarial measures or reconviction-based measures, is potentially serious. It is possible to have interventions resulting in an apparent reduction in offending behaviour (with the treated group being reconvicted far less compared to either what was expected from the actuarially assessed probability of being reconvicted or to the untreated group), but which in reality have not changed offending behaviour at all. An example might be a thinking skills intervention. If the treated individual became more adept at thinking about creative detection-evasion strategies or effective prosecution-evasion strategies and developed the self-restraint not to offend in an impulsive way, the reconviction rates might plummet, whereas the actual offending could remain unchanged or even increase. Alternatively, an intervention could have the effect of increasing reconviction rates, this being a desirable outcome if the treatment graduates go on to hand themselves in to the police more readily, perhaps as a self-regulatory relapse-prevention strategy to prevent an escalation in offending. Or perhaps the intervention fosters honesty and a genuine concern about being lawful, which leads to disclosure to police of offences that the individual previously would not have disclosed. Finally, it is also possible for interventions to make people worse (cf. Jones, 2002a) and increase the rate of reconvictions – a fact that is often obfuscated by using aggregated data without looking at the individual cases within the sample.

Captured as a single equation this can be expressed as:

$$R = (TE + GTI) - (TSR + TD + TIR) + (NTV)$$

R = Post-treatment change in reconviction
TE = Treatment impact on increasing reconviction evasion (= Treatment impact on evading being reported + Treatment impact on evading getting caught + Treatment impact on evading conviction)
GTI = Genuine treatment impact on reducing reconviction
TSR = Treatment impact on increasing self-regulatory offending (offending to avoid more serious offending)
TD = Treatment impact on increasing disclosure of offences
TIR = Treatment impact on increasing offending which also results in reconviction
NTV = Other treatment and non-treatment sources of variance

Unfortunately the 'what works' literature and third-generation actuarial assessment strategies (for reviews see McGuire, 1995; Gendreau, 1996; Andrews & Bonta, 1998) have been seriously compromised by their heavy use of reconviction as an outcome. This *does not* mean that we should stop using this kind of approach; it does, however, mean that we need to think carefully about interpreting results based on them. Until we have better instrumentation we need to think very carefully about the 90 per cent (or more) of offending that is not predicted, particularly for people who have evidenced change in treatment and for people who have low scores on actuarial measures.

Secondly, Jones (2000) argued, actuarial assessment has the effect of moving the focus of assessment and intervention away from the present 'flow of behaviour'. Many interventions with offenders use a model that involves systematic exploration of the offence using various analytic procedures aimed at generating insight into the offence process. Whilst this may have some use in developing conceptual frameworks for the individual to think about their offending behaviour, it can fail to address aspects of the individual's offence-related thinking, feeling and behaviour that are likely to be emerging in the current treatment setting. Various models of learning processes emphasize the importance of bringing the learning experience as close as possible to the problem that is being learned about. It is a simple behavioural truism that the closer the consequences are to the behaviour (e.g. Lee-Evans, 1994) the more likely they are to have an impact on the behaviour.

For many people engaged in interventions addressing their offending behaviour the offence is something that has happened months if not years prior to the intervention. Furthermore, offenders have often had to go over the offence repeatedly in a variety of judicial and therapeutic contexts, consequently the account may have lost the ability to have any emotional impact on the individual. In recent years clinicians, from a variety of backgrounds, have been increasingly emphasizing the importance of working with issues as they present in the individual's *current* functioning. Kohlenberg and Tsai (1994) have developed an intervention strategy called Functional Analytic Psychotherapy (FAP). For example, in this they advocate working with various forms of 'Clinically Relevant Behaviour' (CRBs), behaviours that reflect the presenting problem, but which emerge in the session, whether it is the problem behaviour itself or some form of changed behaviour emerging in the session. This kind of formulation is also at the heart of Linehan's (1993) Dialectical Behaviour Therapy.

Similarly Young (1994) has developed an approach to intervention that involves actively working with schemas in the session, using gestalt techniques to activate the 'schema' in the session, rather than talking at one step removed about schema that the individual might have. Safran and Muran (1996) also emphasize the importance of working on relationship problems, described as 'ruptures', as they emerge in the therapeutic relationship; not just as a way of maintaining the therapeutic alliance but also as a critical opportunity to address the repeating pattern of relationship disturbances that have been affecting the individual's life.

When applied to offending behaviour this approach indicates that it is important to address offending behaviour or offence-related behaviour as it emerges in the current treatment setting. It also suggests that any behaviour that represents a shift away from an offence-related lifestyle and towards a positive lifestyle (Wanigaratne et al., 1990; Ward 2002) needs to be identified and reinforced, validated and encouraged.

Thirdly, reconviction-based measures do not allow for focus on distressing non-criminal aspects of interpersonal functioning that might also be a significant target for intervention aimed at the goal of maximum reduction in distress caused to self and others. Much behaviour is distressing to self and others but does not qualify as 'a crime'. Behaviours like interpersonal hostility and exploitation, for example, are also legitimate treatment targets for offenders but are sometimes neglected.

In the face of these various challenges to the validity of interventions and assessments focused primarily on historical data a framework for working with current functioning is clearly called for. Jones (2000) proposed that we need to look at *process variables* (e.g. Thornton, 1987) and the *model of change* underlying the intervention in order to validate the assertion that *offence-relevant* change has taken place. OPB is one way of doing this.

Offence paralleling behaviour (OPB: Jones, 1997, 2000) is any form of offence-related behavioural (or fantasized behaviour) pattern that emerges at any point before or after an offence. It does not have to result in an offence; it simply needs to resemble, in some significant respect, the sequence of behaviours leading up to the offence. Ideally, it can be monitored in the current treatment setting. This construct was developed out of work done by McDougall and Clark (1991) and McDougall, Clark and Fisher (1994), in a risk-assessment context, as a strategy for working clinically on current offence-related issues. Towl and Crighton (1995) criticized the McDougall et al. model as an assessment strategy on the grounds that it was dependent on file information and that much of this originates from an adversarial context and is therefore likely to be biased. They also challenged its predictive validity as there is, as yet, no evidence that 'risk factors' identified using this technique are actually linked with offending. Finally, they felt that, as an assessment strategy, it was too open to cognitive bias in the assessor along the lines identified by Kahneman, Slovic and Tversky (1982).

Unlike the model developed by McDougall and Clark (1991) and McDougall, Clark and Fisher(1994) Jones emphasizes the fact that offending behaviour and consequently OPB is not just a single event but a culmination of a process or chain of events. Consequently, it is possible to have OPBs that are not obviously similar to the offence, in terms of the eventual action taken, but which have many similarities in terms of the *pattern of behaviours, thoughts and emotions leading up to* the offence. As such, it has much in common with the idea of an offence cycle and with thinking in the literature on personality disorder, which highlights the way in which some people find themselves repeating the same self- or other-harming behaviour over time. Recent thinking on behavioural regulation (Carver and Scheier, 1998) describes this sort of pattern, using models drawn from chaos theory, as a 'behavioural attractor'. No matter what starting point, the pattern of behaviour gets drawn towards a particular repeating configuration. In offender-profiling literature, this is similar to the construct of a Modus Operandi. This concept also has something in common with Birchwood's (1994) construct of relapse signatures, 'prodromal' experiences, disturbances in cognitive functioning such as attention and memory and behaviours that are not always obviously relevant to the outcome (psychosis) but which are reasonably reliable predictors of relapse in psychotic patients. In Kelly's (e.g.1955) personal construct theory terms this may be seen as a repeating behavioural experiment where, for various reasons, the results do not answer the question posed by the behaviour.

Jones (2001) suggests various strategies for developing a formulation of an individual's offence paralleling behaviour. Initially a cognitive, affective and behavioural protocol is systematically developed. What follows is simply a guide to one possible approach to this task.

Serial Analysis of Offending

Essentially this involves identifying sets of behaviours that may have a similar function or developmental structure for an individual (see table 3.1). In doing this it is important not to just look at single events but to try and capture the antecedents to the behaviour and to describe these as a sequence of discrete behavioural/cognitive/affective/situational (in the interests of brevity I shall refer to all of these as behavioural from here on) episodes. There is no objective way of parsing a behavioural flow into discrete behavioural events as what we define as a behaviour is fundamentally socially constructed. However, it is possible to use a criterion of episodes being socially and psychologically meaningful to the investigator. Clarke and Crossland (1985, p. 103) also suggest 'judging where the greatest discontinuities of form or function lie' as a strategy for parsing behaviour (see also below).

Behavioural Sequences	Parsed Behavioural Episodes							
	B_1	B_2	B_3	B_4	B_5	B_6	B_7	B_8
Childhood play behaviour					?			
Pre-offence offence related behaviour			?			?		
Offence behaviour chain 1		?		?			?	
Offence behaviour chain $_n$						?		
Offence paralleling behaviour 1	?		?			?		
OPB $_n$					?		?	
Current behaviour fantasies	?		?		?		?	

Table 3.1 Offence behaviour chain 1 is in bold as it has been used as the initial model of the set of behaviours being investigated. Ticks indicate that the behavioural episode, or a functional equivalent, was present; crosses indicate that they were absent; and question marks indicate areas to investigate suggested by other parallel behavioural processes. The 'n' symbol in the left-hand column indicates that the row is the 'nth' one paired with Offence behaviour chain 1/Offence paralleling behaviour 1, highlighting the need to look at all behaviour chains in order to identify themes.

Behaviours that can be usefully included are previous offences, both prosecuted and those disclosed by the individual and various behaviours observed or reported during the course of intervening. It is also useful to get information from the offender and from significant others about any form of offence-related behaviour prior to the offence. This might include behavioural 'try outs', fantasies about offending, crisis behaviours that had not culminated in offending, offending behaviour where the individual had managed to inhibit the act of offending by using, for example, various substitute behaviours. Sometimes it can be useful to look at offence paralleling playground behaviours and the repertoire of 'games' the individual had as a child (e.g. sexual play with sex offenders and bullying and fighting for violent offenders). Once the sets of behaviours have been identified, it is useful to contrast different behavioural sequences, generating hypotheses about why a particular behaviour was present in one but absent in another. This might include, for example, testing the hypothesis that parts of the behaviour chain manifested in the current context (e.g. 'crisis' behaviour) were also present in the context of the offence and vice versa. This might be done by further questioning of the individual, seeking collateral information or a re-examination of file information. It may also be that a particular antecedent was present but was not recorded or reported by the individual, or that some other behaviour served the *same or a similar function* in that particular behavioural sequence.

Testing hypotheses linking current and offence behaviours with proximal and distal antecedents can also be useful. Offending behaviour can often be a replay of childhood abuse or of abusive behaviour witnessed by the individual. Similarly it can be linked with recent salient experiences. If the practitioner wants to test the hypothesis that, in this case, the offence was a re-enactment (see below) of a witnessed or experienced offence (or other traumatic experience) then the sequence of behaviours leading up to the witnessed/experienced event can be included as a row in the matrix and the same kind of testing out of component behaviours can be undertaken. If the sequences of behaviour are fundamentally different then the hypothesis can be refuted.

Behaviours can be clustered together as members of response classes (cf. Sprague & Horner, 1999), or as having some morphological similarity.

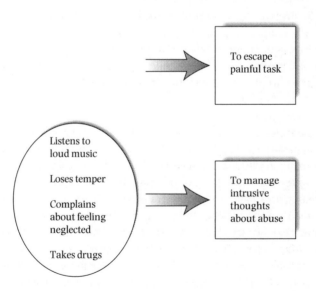

Figure 3.1 Two examples of response classes (based on Sprague and Horner, 1999)

Response classes (see figure 3.1) are sets of behaviours that serve the same kind of function. Morphological similarity is similarity of form. It should be noted, however, that similar behaviours do not necessarily have the same function. Consequently, morphological similarity is only really of interest if it is sequential, because sequences of similar behaviour are more likely to be serving a similar function than discrete behavioural episodes that are similar.

A useful approach in this context is to use the Kellian strategy of triadic elicitation. This procedure involves presenting the individual with triads of behavioural sequences and asking in what way are two of these similar and different from the third. One might, for instance, present an individual who has robbed a bank with:

1 approaching the bank (during the index offence);
2 approaching a fellow patient with money (on the ward as part of a sequence of intimidatory behaviour);
3 approaching a drug dealer in order to get drugs;

and they might reply: 'approaching the bank and approaching the fellow patient are similar in that I felt a buzz of anticipation, they are different from number three in that when I got drugs I didn't feel anxious but I still had a buzz of anticipation'. This then enables the practitioner to identify hypotheses about the function of the behaviour in the moment, and thereby establish the degree to which a particular behaviour is a parallel process to the offence. Needs (1988) suggests simply contrasting pairs of behavioural episodes in order to make the task less cognitively challenging. If the person being assessed does not want to engage in the assessment process then the practitioner can undertake a similar exercise and use other sources of information, such as accounts of the offence previously given, to identify the states the individual moved through during the lead-up to the offence.

In generating hypotheses about the function of behaviour hermeneutic strategies (see Valentine, 1992, for a review of hermeneutic methodology from a psychological perspective) can be useful. Originally developed as a strategy for analysing narrative, this approach can be useful in analysing behaviour also. When attempting, for example, to understand the meaning of a word in a sentence, a common strategy is to look at its context within the sentence in order to establish its meaning. An iterative process of moving from the part to the whole and back to the part in order to establish the meaning and function of a specific behaviour is an equivalent process with behaviour. In addition it is useful to use a general framework for understanding offending such as the CLASP framework (Context, Life history, Agenda, Sequence, Personal meaning: Needs & Towl, 1997) in order to generate and test hypotheses about what was going on in a particular behavioural sequence.

Organization of the Offence Process

Ressler et al. (1992) discuss a typology of crime scenes which involves looking at the extent to which the offence 'reflects a methodical, well-organized subject who did not leave a single print or piece of physical evidence behind' as opposed to more disorganized offences which are 'spontaneous and disarrayed with a great deal of evidence at the scene' (p. 9). They describe this as a continuum of crime scenes going from organized to disorganized. This structural characteristic of offending needs to be examined in offence paralleling behaviour on, for example, a ward. Highly 'organized' OPBs will be less easy to detect but will contain various components of the individual's offence-detection and -evasion repertoire. This information can be useful in ascertaining whether apparent treatment-induced changes in behaviour are actually due to an increase in the individual's capacity to 'organize' their offending processes.

Using Mapping to Generate and Test Hypotheses about OPB

One way of generating and testing hypotheses about OPBs is to map the OPBs in the same space as the offence. Whilst similar in some respects to the behavioural mapping methodology used by Canter (e.g. Canter & Fritzon, 1998; Canter & Hodge, 1998; Canter, Hughes & Kirby, 1998) this approach is essentially idiographic and has been developed out of work by Kelly and Taylor (1981) on analysis of behavioural sequences. The procedure is as follows.

1   Identify key points in offence(s) and OPB(s). Clarke and Crossland (1985, p. 103) describe this as 'parsing', 'unitizing' or 'segmenting' the 'behaviour stream'. They indicate that the best method for doing this involves 'judging where the greatest discontinuities of form or function lie within the behavioural stream, sometimes by combining the views of a number of judges'. In the clinical context this can be done collaboratively with the client. Other clinicians can also be used.

It is useful to include both antecedent and subsequent or consequent behaviours in the behavioural frame being investigated.

Then generate a list of affective and cognitive states, associated with offending behaviour to rate each parsed behaviour against. An affective/cognitive 'state' is a complete state of mind, not just a specific cognitive content. So it might include, for instance, a process such as dissociation, confusion, a kind of attention (e.g. focused as in 'tunnel vision' or unfocused), racing thoughts; a content, such as thoughts of escaping, thoughts of offending; and an affective state, such as frightened, sad, angry etc. It can also include interpersonal processes e.g. conflict, affection, love, hate. A useful strategy for generating 'states' is to use the standard triadic elicitation procedure, contrasting pairs or triads of parsed behaviours (see above). Another dimension to explore is the individual's experienced agency; the extent to which they felt like the author of their own actions as opposed to passively experiencing behaviour as if it were something done to them by some external agency. For a similar conceptualization of 'states' see the Golynkina and Ryle (1999) development of the multiple self states model.

If a standard set of supplied affective states is needed (e.g. in order to contrast affective processes between subjects) then it might be useful to use Gerald, Jones, and Chamberlain's (1990) UWIST mood adjective checklist or the standardized affective headings from Hermans' (1995) valuation theoretical approach.

2   Generate a behaviour by state matrix for each of the offence and offence paralleling behaviours being examined. Data are derived by either rating presence or absence using a binary variable, or by using ratings (table 3.2 below).

		Emotional and cognitive states					
		E_1	E_2	E_3			E_n
	B_1	1	0	1			
	B_2	1	1	0			
	B_3	0	1	1			
	B_n						

(Behavioural sequence)

Table 3.2 Behaviour by state matrix, indicating associations between behavioural sequences and emotional and cognitive states relevant to offending

3   Then use multidimensional scaling/Repgrid methodology to map both (all) behaviours in the same space using packages designed for multidimensional scaling like PERMAP (Heady, 2002), or to map each of the behaviours separately and to compare them using GRIDSCAL (Bell, 1999).

4   Chronology is then represented, within each plot, by joining behaviours sequentially on the plot (Kelly & Taylor, 1981). This is equivalent to a phase diagram in the chaos theory literature (Carver & Scheier, 1998).

5   Cognitive/affective 'state' can then be used as a clue to the function of behaviour; behaviour is seen as a way of travelling in cognitive/affective state space.

6   Each state can be seen as consequence of 'arriving' behaviours and antecedent of 'departing' behaviours.

For more complex ways of modelling sequential behaviour, including Markov chains and developing 'behavioural grammars', sets of rules that describe the behavioural flow, see Clarke and Crossland (1985).

Evaluation of OPB Formulation

In order to evaluate the OPB formulation it is important to predict specific OPBs, using the OPB formulation as a model (see also McDougall & Clark, 1991; McDougall, Clark & Fisher, 1994). Predictions are more robust if they specify both a context and a time-frame for the predicted behaviour. Obviously, it is also important to design pre-emptive interventions if and when the predicted behaviours begin to emerge. OPBs and possible offending behaviour should be anticipated. They can then be seen as 'Therapy Interfering Behaviours' (Linehan, 1993; Jones, 1997) or as possible crisis behaviours (covert and overt) that require intervention.

It is unethical not to intervene pre-emptively and, as such, one is constantly trying to prevent one's own predictions from coming true. This makes for an unusual kind of scientist practitioner approach. Unfortunately, even with pre-emptive interventions, predictions based on a clear formulation often materialize.

If the observed behaviour is different from the OPB model it can be revised so that a model is cumulatively built up in a manner akin to the 'serial deviant case analysis' approach of Kelly and Taylor (1981) (see also Needs, 1988). Essentially this methodology involves repeatedly revising the model in the face of cases that do not fit, until the model describes all new presentations.

Vignette: A Case Illustration

The John vignette, described below, was developed in order to illustrate the development of an OPB model. It is based on real cases which have been changed in various significant ways in order to maintain confidentiality.

John

Offence history:

1. At school he got into trouble for grabbing breasts of girls in class
2. Has a history of stalking women and of previous sexual assaults (preceded by stalking behaviour).

Offence:

1. Drinking and using glue in room
2. Fantasizing about offending
3. Has row with dad
4. Leaves house
5. Follows woman
6. Catches up with her
7. Grabs her breasts
8. Pushes her to the floor
9. Assaults her
10. She stands and fights back
11. Punches her
12. Passer-by shouts
13. He runs away
14. Masturbates in room thinking about her.

On ward:

1. Intimidated by peer (gives him tobacco without wanting to)
2. In his room he fantasizes about assaulting member of staff
3. He goes to the day room
4. Watches TV
5. Is called in to side-room alone with staff member, to look at property in property box
6. Staff member leans over box
7. John looks down her top
8. He feels an urge to grab her breasts
9. Manages not to act
10. Returns to room and masturbates
11. Has cigarette.

The behaviours were parsed by checking with John what he felt were 'steps' in the process, and by identifying significant changes in location or in mental state. The offence paralleling episode, on the ward, is interesting in several respects. It was an episode described by John as an example of his frequent need to *inhibit* offence-related urges. In many respects, the behaviour resembles the sequence of behaviours leading up to and during the index offence. Prior to the index offence, he reported that there had been numerous attempts to stalk and assault other women. He had not disclosed other attempts reaching the same stage as the index offence but this is a real possibility. He described the sequence as a repeating pattern and recognized it as such himself.

Both sequences involve: fantasy, some form of intimidation or 'row', gaining proximity to object of fantasy, offending or offending covertly, being inhibited by presence of others, returning to room and masturbating thinking about the episode. In this example the sequence isn't exactly the same in each episode. In one the fantasies preceded the intimidation, in the other the fantasies came after feeling intimidated. This may be an artefact of describing things in a linear sequential way. It may be that he was fantasizing all the time and that it was the intimidation or the row that was the trigger for offending behaviour. Comparisons between episodes can help to generate hypotheses about both the underlying psychological process and possible omissions from accounts.

Contrasting behaviours (see above for account of triadic elicitation) generated the following set of 'state' constructs:

1   Safe
2   Alone
3   Not vulnerable
4   Sexually active
5   Sexually aroused
6   Self-conscious about looks
7   Powerful
8   Adrenalin rushing
9   Angry
10   Disliked
11   Vulnerable
12   Stoned
13   On edge
14   Hearing voices

In this example constructs are not the Kellian (Kelly, 1955) bipolar variety, though this would be an equally feasible approach. It is possible to infer the absence of an attribute at the opposite side of the diagram; for example, in the diagram 'safe' is situated at the top and 'unsafe' at the bottom.

A behaviour by state matrix, for both the offence and the ward behaviour (OPB), was completed by asking John to rate whether or not each state was present during each behaviour (0=absent, 1=present). This was then analysed, as one matrix including both offending and offence paralleling behaviours, using PERMAP (Heady, 2002). The state map (figure 3.2) shows a spatial representation of the relationship between different states identified for John.

Using Differences Between the Two Mappings to Generate Hypotheses

On the basis of the joint mapping it is possible to generate hypotheses about ways in which the current environment inhibits offence paralleling behaviour.

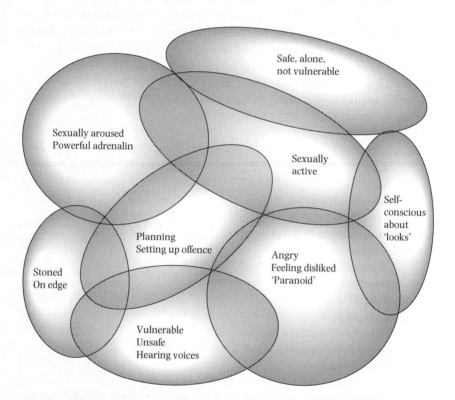

Figure 3.2   The oval areas represent the region in the behavioural mapping where different 'states' were most in evidence. In following diagrams, the labels are pushed to the edges of the behavioural map in order to facilitate analysis of changes in state accompanying different behavioural episodes.

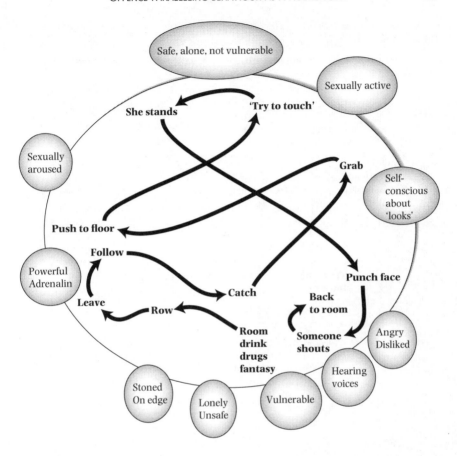

Figure 3.3   In this mapping of John's index offence the sequence of behaviours is illustrated using arrows linking each episode. States associated with different parts of the map are described, in capitals, on the periphery of the map.

If we look, for example, at the areas on the joint mapping where there is little overlap it is possible to identify behaviours like 'leaving' and 'following' that do not appear to have any obvious equivalents in the ward setting. This is probably because it is not easy to leave or follow anybody in the ward setting. However, when this issue was raised in the clinical team staff began to specifically focus on his following behaviour. Behaviours like staring at and tracking female staff and walking behind female staff were then observed. These can be seen as vestigial behaviours. Even when the context inhibits the emergence of behaviour, it is often possible to identify this kind of vestigial version of the behaviour.

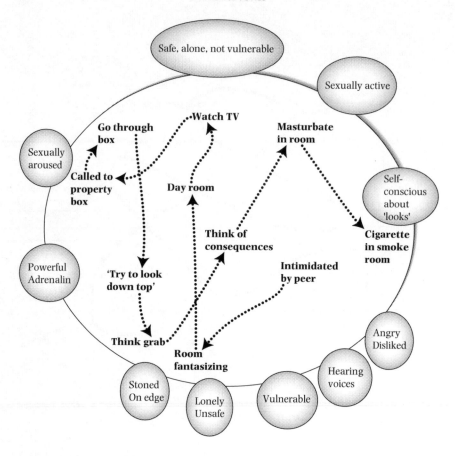

Figure 3.4 The sequence of on-ward, offence paralleling behaviours is mapped using the same strategy as the mapping for the offence behaviour.

A similar process of inference can be used by looking at the ward offence paralleling behaviour and testing hypotheses, based on these observations, about possible antecedents to the offence.

Similarly, the actual acts of violence in the index offence do not overlap with any equivalent behaviours in the ward episode. Again this is possibly because the fact that the individual knows that they are being watched and monitored and consequently does not act on offending impulses; offending stays in the realm of fantasy that is being played out without culminating in offending.

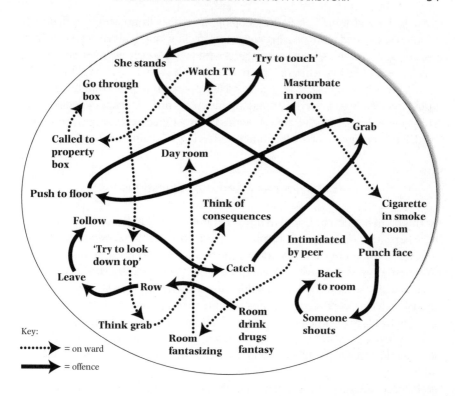

Figure 3.5   In this mapping the two sequences of behaviours are overlaid illustrating the extent to which the offence paralleling behaviour involves the same states as the offence. State descriptions have been omitted so as not to clutter the diagram too much.

Using 'State' as a Key to the Function of the Behaviour

One of the advantages of this form of mapping is that it highlights the complexity of offending behaviour. Rather than being something that can be easily captured by conducting a functional analysis looking at the headings of long-term antecedents, proximal antecedents, behaviour and consequences, the offence process needs to be analysed as a complex interplay of sequentially organized stages. It hints at the unparsed nature of raw behaviour.

Each moment of behaviour is both a consequence of the antecedent moments and an antecedent to the following moment. Each transition represents a moving away from one state and into another. Analysis of the preceding and subsequent states helps to clarify what the function of the behaviour at that stage is.

So, looking at John's on-ward mapping: he moves from 'being intimidated', which is associated with 'hearing voices' and feeling 'angry and disliked', to 'fantasizing in his room', which is associated with being 'lonely' and 'stoned and on edge'. It might be hypothesized, then, that John was in a psychotic state at the time, he was hearing voices and he was feeling persecuted. Also that he uses fantasies specifically as a way of managing his voices and his sense of persecution. The general thrust of the vector is towards feeling stoned, on edge and more powerful. It doesn't get rid of the loneliness and feeling of alienation, however.

Behaviour as a Series of Questions

At this point it might be useful to think about the way that John's behaviour has been parsed into a series of problems and a series of potential solutions that he has selected. Early on in such a sequence the failure of an effort to manage can be tolerated. However, if a series of solutions are attempted unsuccessfully then an accumulative sense of increasing failure, frustration and anger is likely to accrue. In Kellian terms, each step of behaviour is an attempt to get an answer to a question; each failure to anticipate is a piece of refutation and can challenge core construing. As a consequence the individual may need to try and force the data to fit their world. Offence paralleling behaviour and offending processes often take the form of an escalating sequence of unsuccessful attempts to solve interpersonal problems resulting in more and more extreme attempts to force the data to fit the theory. It is in such terms that Kelly (1955) defines anger and hostility.

The Interpersonal Nature of the Offence Process

Each step in the sequence represents a particular form of interaction between the victim and the perpetrator. It is possible to generate a model of the individual's construal of the perpetrator–victim relationship configuration at each step. This enables us to analyse the offence as a form of interpersonal behaviour (Table 3.3).

The victim's and the perpetrator's changing relationship can be seen as a movement, of both protagonists, in the interpersonal circumplex described by Blackburn (1990). Most repertory grids will give an idiographic version of structures identified in more nomothetic studies of interpersonal perception. They usually have, when analysed, dimensions that are similar to (sometimes with the help of a little rotation) the Dominant/ Submissive, Hostile/Friendly dimensions identified in the interpersonal circumplex literature. Emotions associated with being dominant/submitted to, being submissive/dominated, being hostile

Table 3.3 Interpersonal dynamics of offence

	Relationship Configuration	
Sequence (Parsed behaviour at onset of offending process	John	Father (as construed by John)
In room alone	Alone, lonely	In the background, possibly seen as neglecting him
Row with father	Feels intimidated, defeated and punished (victim stance)	Aggressive, punitive and Victimizing
Leaves house	Angry, vengeful	Left behind possibly worrying about him
Offence sequence (Parsed behaviour	John	Victim (as construed by John)
Follows woman	Following, anticipating offending, victim feelings subsiding	Innocent to intentions or feeling followed
Catches up with victim	Feels anticipation affects, prepares for action	Feels intimidated and scared
Grabs her breasts	Sexually aroused feeling very dominant	Terrified, violated
Pushes her to the floor	Aggressive, aroused, dominant	Terrified, subjugated
Assaults victim	Aggressive, aroused, dominant	Terrified, subjugated
She stands and fights back	Frightened, defied, intimidated	Defiant, anticipating escape
Punches her	Aggressive, aroused, dominant	Terrified, subjugated
Passer-by shouts	Frightened	Rescued
He runs away	Frightened, triumph of running away	Rescued
Masturbates in room	Dominant, vengeful, aroused, aggressive	Victim (as fantasy now) subjugated and punished

or being affectionate define the space. Cognition and affect are usefully conceived as being socially embedded.

John's grid has a clear 'powerful' v. 'self-conscious about looks' dimension which is an interesting affective rendition of John's experience of being dominant or being submissive in this context. It also has a 'vulnerable', 'hear-ing voices', 'unsafe' v. 'safe', 'sexually aroused' dimension which is a rendition of his experience of being hostile or being 'friendly' in this context. Each state is the inside view of an interpersonal behaviour. Each behaviour is aimed at achiev-ing a particular interpersonal goal as part of an interpersonal project from this perspective: 'it is useful to see people as being interested in specific *interpersonal projects* – coherent goal oriented behaviours – linked with each of these [inter-personal] dimensions. Offenders are often preoccupied with managing the dis-turbances they experience in relationships' (Jones, 2002b, p.37).

Relationship 'projects' are exemplified by 'seeking a relationship, forming a relationship, going through a honeymoon period, maintaining a long term re-lationship, becoming estranged in a relationship, grieving a lost relationship, or avoiding relationships altogether' (ibid, pp.37–8). They can also be exempli-fied by being actively hostile towards a particular person, e.g. wanting revenge, or hating somebody with whom they have a grievance. Status 'projects', on the other hand, are exemplified by 'seeking status, defending newly acquired sta-tus, bullying, reorienting to lost status or being bullied, maintaining status, form-ing strategic alliances, reacting to authority or deferring to authority' (ibid, p.37).

Looking at the mapping for John's offence, when he grabs the victim he becomes more 'self-conscious' about his 'looks', clearly concerned about being rejected or seen as undesirable. The next action in the sequence is to push the victim to the floor, it is this act that dispels the feeling of being subject to rejec-tion and installs a sense of being 'powerful'. Even at this fine-grained level of analysis there are quite clear status and relationship projects driving behaviour at each step. For this individual there were some concerns relating to having been adopted and being subject to racism that made the issue of acceptance and rejection central to his construing of interpersonal situations.

From this kind of analysis, it is possible to develop models for exploring offence paralleling interpersonal behaviour patterns. In the example above this might mean exploring ways in which John felt he was relating to the member of staff at different stages of the sequence on the ward. Jones (1997) looked at the ways in which interpersonal behaviour in therapeutic groups mirrored aspects of interpersonal behaviour at the time of the offence. For example he found that a measure of dominance of offender group members, as rated by group facilitators, correlated with nominal victim status: dominant offenders (e.g. armed robbers) tending to offend against groups of people, medium-status offenders against individuals, and low-status individuals offending against older people or children. A similar basic measure of hostility in the group setting also correlated with the extent to which violence had been used in the offence.

Another useful framework, not inconsistent with the interpersonal paradigm outlined above, is to explore the possibility that the offender is evidencing rapid shifts between the kinds of incompatible representations of the self and others described by Liotti (1999) within an attachment theory framework (see also Golynkina and Ryle's (1999) multiple self states model). Liotti (1999) presents evidence to suggest that individuals with 'disorganized attachment' patterns have 'multiple, incompatible, and thereby unintegrated (i.e. reciprocally dissociated) representations of self-with-others' (p. 300). Moreover he argues that the 'general pattern of these segregated . . . representational processes . . . suggests the simultaneous presence of the three poles of the 'drama triangle' (Karpman, 1968)' (p. 301). Essentially this involves seeing the self or others as being either *victims, rescuers* or *persecutors* at any moment. It also involves switching between roles and seeing others as switching roles, sometimes quite rapidly over time. The Karpman triangle can be seen as a special case of the kinds of typology of roles described by narratologists – derived from the analysis of large numbers of folk stories and plays – e.g. Greimas (1966, 1970), Propp (1968) and Souriau (1950). Typically these typologies involve the following roles: protagonist, opponent and helper and an end or goal that is being aimed for (for a review see Elam, 1988). Offence accounts can usefully be analysed in these terms. Bush (1995) has developed a formulation linking offending to taking a 'victim stance' but there is little in the literature that describes the complexity of the changes in role and perception of others that can take place in the course of an offence chain, and is frequently paralleled in interpersonal interactions in other contexts including the current treatment context as part of OPB.

If the function of the offending behaviour is to meet specific, if complex and changing, interpersonal needs, then these same interpersonal needs can be used to organize observations in the custodial setting, in order to identify, and make sense of, offence-paralleling behaviour. This approach is also central to any risk management strategy.

Offence Paralleling Behaviour Models Can Take Various Different Forms

Typically practitioners identify a characteristic linear pattern in behaviours that culminate in an offence. Most accounts of offending that use the concept of some form of offence cycle use this kind of model. However, it is possible for behaviour to have a structure that is not necessarily of a linear nature. Sequential analysis needs to recognize this possibility.

Simple behaviour chain OPB models

Simple behaviour chain OPB models are models that involve a repeat of the whole sequence of behaviours leading up to the offence, possibly including the offence itself. This is often suggestive of an overlearned process that has developed into a monopoly for the individual:

$$B_1 \quad B_2 \quad B_3 \quad B_4 \quad B_5$$

or similar behaviours in a varied order:

$$B_2 \quad B_1 \quad B_3 \quad B_5 \quad B_4$$

Stem and branch chain

$$ B_a \quad B_{a2} \quad B_{a3}$$
$$B_1 \quad B_2 \quad B_3 \quad B_b \quad B_{b2} \quad B_{b3}$$
$$ B_c \quad B_{c2} \quad B_{c3}$$

In this model, several different patterns can be identified in different offences, but they all appear to start with the same initiating sequence.

Branch and stem chain

$$B_a \quad B_{a2} \quad B_{a3}$$
$$B_b \quad B_{b2} \quad B_{b3} \quad B_4 \quad B_5 \quad B_6$$
$$B_c \quad B_{c2} \quad B_{c3}$$

In this model, a variety of different behavioural sequences lead up to a repeating sequence.

Response class chain

$$ B_a \quad B_{a2} \quad B_{a3}$$
$$B_1 \quad B_2 \quad B_3 \quad B_b \quad B_{b2} \quad B_{b3} \quad B_7 \quad B_8$$
$$ B_c \quad B_{c2} \quad B_{c3}$$

In this model, whilst the initiating sequence and the ending sequence are repeated across contexts, there is some degree of variation at one, or more, points in the sequence. The behaviours that are interchangeable at these points are probably members of a response class and serve the same or similar function for the individual.

Developmental Analysis of OPBs

Behaviour rarely emerges from nowhere, it usually develops over time. Developmental analysis of the way in which a non-offending behavioural sequence develops into an antecedent offence paralleling behaviour and eventually into offending behaviour and then into post-offence offence paralleling behaviour can be very useful.

For John this was: chasing girls in primary school, initially just chasing them; then chasing them into the girl's toilets; then chasing them and pulling up their skirts; then, in secondary school, grabbing girls' breasts in the school corridors. After many of these behaviours he had been told off by teachers. However, there had also been numerous occasions when the behaviour had gone unobserved and unreported to adults.

The Origins of Repeated Offending and Repetitious Offence Paralleling Behaviour

As we have seen not all offending and offence paralleling behaviour is repetitive. However, when it is there is a strong likelihood that there is a narrower response class and that certain components of an individual's behavioural repertoire have come to monopolize their behaviour in certain settings. The process of developing repeating patterns of behaviour is complex and cannot be understood by using a single model. Some possible developmental processes are outlined below.

Repeated reinforcement and the automation of behaviour

Essentially this is a classical notion of behaviour being shaped by the consequences for the individual. Repeatedly reinforced behaviour results in more extinction-resistant, experienced as more automatic, behavioural habits. Reinforcement schedules where the reinforcement is intermittent are considered to be most resistant to change. General models of offending such as Andrews and

Bonta (1998) follow this kind of model. Addiction to crime (e.g. Hodge, 1997) models are a version of this kind of formulation, but also emphasize the process of escalation, withdrawal and tolerance in crime series. With this kind of model the behaviour develops gradually over time.

Trauma-induced learning

Less often explored in the literature are the kinds of learning associated with traumatic experience. Horowitz (1986) and Van Der Kolk (e.g. 1989) discuss various ways in which people can have intrusive experiences following a traumatic experience. Of particular note in the context of offence paralleling behaviour is the concept of post-traumatic re-enactment of all or parts of the traumatic experience. Kruppa, Hickey and Hubbard (1995) present evidence for offenders being traumatized by their own offending. Hodge (1997) suggests the possibility that offence-related Post-Traumatic Stress Disorder (PTSD) can lead to further episodes of violence. Van der Kolk (1989) proposes various models for the way in which trauma can lead to repeated re-enactment of aspects of the traumatic experience. He notes that there are two common forms of re-enactment: re-enactments of the victim role (e.g. victims of sexual abuse going on to become heavily involved in prostitution), apparently more common amongst women victims; and re-enactments of the perpetrator role (e.g. victims of sexual abuse going on to perpetrate sexual abuse on other people), apparently more common amongst male victims of abuse. The learning process leading to this form of re-enactment is thought to take two forms. Firstly, the perpetrator who offended against the would-be re-enactor acts as a model and is imitated in the resulting re-enactment of the abuse. Secondly, behavioural re-enactment is construed as a form of intrusive memory of unprocessed traumatic material. This is seen as no different from other forms of intrusive memories of abuse such as auditory, visual or emotional flashbacks in which discrete aspects of the abuse are relived in an involuntary fashion.

This kind of model would suggest a rapid learning process.

Sexual trauma

Theorists such as Money (1986), in developing accounts for the development of paraphilias, another behaviour pattern that is repeated and difficult to change, give some evidence for a process whereby early sexual experiences can have a significant impact on later sexual development often defining the kinds of experiences the individual seeks out in later life in a way which is difficult to change.

The more intense the experience of sexual arousal, or trauma – associated with the early experience – the more likely the individual is to be affected by it. The kinds of learning associated with sexual experiences – traumatic and non-traumatic – may have many of the same characteristics as are observed in PTSD, i.e. intrusive thoughts, affects and behaviours and various forms of dissociative states contingent on high levels of arousal.

Stress and strong emotion linked with fragmentation of the capacity to monitor and manage intentions

Williams (1996), drawing on Frith's (1993) work on the neuropsychology of psychotic experiences, presents a model suggesting that individuals with schizotypal and borderline personality disorder diagnoses may be more vulnerable to losing the capacity to monitor intentions when under stress. This then has a cascade of effects including disruption of the pursuit of goals and reduced capacity to inhibit impulsive behaviours. This process is thought to be accompanied by experiences of loss of agency and dissociative states. The behaviour is experienced as 'just happening' rather than as something that the individual is actively engaged in. With a diminished sense of agency the individual is less likely to feel able to actively change the behavioural process as it is ongoing. Williams argues that this kind of phenomenon is not just associated with personality disorder and that people who have experienced extreme and or prolonged trauma (e.g. war traumas) can also experience this. Personality serves only to render the individual more vulnerable. The constructs of disorganized crime scenes (Ressler et al., 1992) are possibly linked with offending of this kind. Other factors that can have a similar effect are substance/alcohol abuse.

Situational Variation

It is a mistake to assume that an individual will always exhibit the same behavioural patterns in the same situation. Theorists like Mischel (1999) and Shoda (1999) have attempted to respond to the challenge that situational variance presents to any attempt to identify consistency in individual behaviour. They highlight the importance of the interaction between the person and the situation and advocate a model in which the individual's unique construal of the situations they encounter is emphasized. For Shoda, a behavioural signature is a characteristic profile of the extent to which a particular individual will behave in a particular way when they are in a specified situation. Shoda challenges the orthodox notion that cross-situational aggregation of behavioural observations alone is useful in predicting behaviour. What is interesting, he argues, is the way that an individual can be inconsistent across situations but often is consistent in the ways that their characteristic behaviour emerges out of a self-organizing interaction between mutually influencing social-cognitive variables. Using a social-cognitive model (e.g. Gollwitzer & Bargh, 1996) focusing on goals, expectancies, and values to select the features of situations that are relevant and interact with the characteristics of the person is an essential feature of developing hypotheses about potential offence paralleling behaviours. The question is: what features of which situations encountered in which states will invoke which OPBs?

Of particular importance in the analysis of situational factors contributing to offence paralleling behaviour is the analysis of the different ways in which custodial settings can suppress or inhibit offence paralleling behaviour. The absence of significant cues for offending behaviour, opportunities to offend and detection-evasion opportunities can have the effect of inhibiting OPBs. In order to allow this kind of behaviour to surface, it is important to allow as much situational variety within the custodial setting in the hope that the behaviour can be identified prior to the individual being released. Unlike the proverb 'give them enough rope and they will hang themselves', the aim of this must be to catch and intervene with offending processes before they have developed or had the opportunity to evolve into offences.

Using Offence Paralleling Behaviour as a Focus for Intervention

The psychodynamic literature explores the way in which patterns of relating are generalized from earlier attachment experiences into current interpersonal functioning. Typically this is seen as playing itself out in the relationship between the therapist and the patient. However, it is seen as a protocol for all relationships that the individual engages in.

The kinds of interpersonal behaviour evident in the development of the OPB often constitute a pattern of behaviour like this. The individual can often play out in the offence aspects of interpersonal functioning that derive from learned attachment styles (see above). As such, the kinds of interpersonal projects that were around at the time of the offence are likely to be evident in the current setting, in relation to the therapist, other staff and other patients.

An example might be somebody whose offence involved sadistic sexual assault on a stranger and whose current girlfriend is reported to have returned from a recent visit with significant bruising, who, on questioning, reported that it was caused by her partner punching her covertly when they met. Analysis of the behaviour indicated that he had been getting hostile with staff on the ward prior to these episodes. In sessions with the therapist he had become verbally abusive and threatening and appeared to enjoy watching the therapist's distress. He had previously disclosed that he had been bullied by his mother and, later in life, he had been bullied at school. The trigger for the relapse into sadistic behaviour was a combination of factors including an episode in which he had been bullied by one of his peers.

In this example there is an apparent link between the earlier attachment and interpersonal experiences and the current behaviour. However, interestingly, the roles have been reversed. The trigger is also linked with the theme of bullying. Intervention with this kind of behaviour requires a regime that is attuned to the individual's characteristic pattern of interacting and particularly to the links between this and their offending. This then allows people to ensure that the interpersonal project is explored and alternative behaviours introduced. It is also important that appropriate, non-OPB behaviour is recognized and validated (Linehan, 1993; Kohlenberg & Tsai, 1994). This kind of attunement to the clinical relevance of behaviour can only be developed through building a milieu culture *where all behaviour*, on and off groups and individual interventions, is seen as relevant to the change initiative.

Using Offence Paralleling Behaviour as Part of a Risk-management Strategy

Developing models of offence paralleling behaviour can facilitate much more effective risk-management strategies. It enables supervisors to develop a clear understanding of some of the patterns of behaving that might be indicative of an imminent lapse or relapse. Working collaboratively it is possible to catch this kind of issue early in its development. Of particular importance here is modelling previous breaches of confidence with supervisors and identifying the underlying motives for this. An example might be the following.

Peter, prior to reoffending, had formed a relationship with one of the auxiliary staff in the hostel where he was living. This had the effect of cutting him off from the staff team, who were clear with him about the boundaries, informing him that they did not feel that this relationship was appropriate. On the ward, he had become increasingly isolated from the clinical team and had formed an intense therapeutic relationship with one of his named nurses. He had withdrawn from other people and would not talk to any other member of staff.

For people who have repeatedly reoffended there is a process where they have either duped their supervisors or where their relationship with their supervisors has gone through a period of estrangement. This has meant that they have not been able to turn to them for support and assistance. Peter's characteristic 'splitting' behaviour was an indication that he was engaged in an offence paralleling process. Often any boundary violation is an indication that something is amiss and that some form of parallel process is underway. Working with this information decisively is critical to effective risk management. Clinicians and case managers must always expect that the past will repeat itself, and not be surprised by it when it does. The onus on the patient is to prove them wrong, and not to react adversely to the sense of being labelled inherent in any risk monitoring that is underway.

Of particular importance in developing a formulation of an individual's risk is a systematic understanding of their various detection evasion skills. As noted in the introduction this is a critical factor in understanding the individual's risk of offending and not getting caught. Through historical analysis of evasion-detection skills and the various ways in which these are manifested in the current setting, the practitioner can develop a more detailed understanding of the individual's real risk, or at least the probability of detection should the individual offend again.

Other Forms of Paralleling Behaviour

Jones (2002a) describes various ways in which a similar form of behavioural analysis can be used to identify possible ways in which an individual can drop out of treatment. This involves analysing previous treatment drop-out processes, and any other form of relationship that the individual has 'dropped out of', for example jobs, education or intimate relationships. From this analysis, an attempt is made to identify and predict future treatment drop-out. Often treatment drop-out behaviours and therapy-interfering behaviours (Linehan, 1993; Jones, 1997) are also components of offence paralleling behaviours. Similar analyses can be done to look at crisis behaviours, self-harm and suicidal behaviour. It is also possible to explore the ways in which newly developed behaviours, post-treatment, are being generalized into non-treatment settings.

Conclusion

In this chapter, I have identified several ways of understanding, describing and analysing behaviour as a sequential process. A critique of some of the shortcomings inherent in using actuarial assessment and in focusing interventions on past behaviour, rather than any current manifestation of the behavioural underpinning for that behaviour, has been elaborated. A model of the way in which an individual's unique learning history inevitably presents itself in the current setting and, when this history has involved a significant amount of offending behaviour, the way in which the behavioural processes involved in that offending are likely to surface as offence paralleling behaviour, has been described. Possible models for the development of frequently repeating offending and offence paralleling processes have been outlined. Finally some of the implications of this kind of behaviour analysis for assessing, managing and intervening with offence-related issues have been proposed.

Whilst it has not been the purpose of this chapter to dismiss the use of actuarially derived measures of risk and treatment outcome, it has been the aim to open up debate and provoke ways of thinking about the ways we as practitioners can work with offending behaviour and offence paralleling behaviour as historically embedded processes.

NOTE

Thanks to Sean Hammond for suggesting using GRIDSCAL for comparing mappings, to Jason Davies for general discussion and checking the stats at the beginning of the chapter, and to Ron Tulloch for provoking thought about the interpersonal aspects of offence processes.

Chapter	Four

Risk Assessment

David Crighton

Introduction

Many of the areas of forensic practice discussed in this text are, directly or indirectly, concerned with issues of risk. Such risks are often towards others but can also be self-directed. For example, assessment and intervention work with substance abusers will often be concerned with the risks to the communities in which they live, but also to the risks of physical harm to the individual client.[1] Similarly areas such as 'sentence management' and 'throughcare'[2] are often concerned with the ways in which future risks can be minimized.

As such it can be argued that risk assessment and risk management are fundamental aspects of forensic work. In undertaking assessments and interventions, either at an individual or an organizational level, forensic practitioners need to have a clear awareness of the issues of risk. Equally, they need to have a clear technical understanding of the ways in which such risks may be assessed and, in turn, managed. In addition they need to have a grasp of the ethical values which underpin practice in this complex area.

Given the importance of issues of risk and risk management it is perhaps somewhat surprising that the research base has developed slowly. However, in recent years there has been a marked growth in pure and applied research. There has also been a great deal of discussion, debate and confusion about what risk assessment involves (Monahan, 1981, 1997; Steadman et al., 1993; Prins, 1996; Towl & Crighton, 1996, 1997).

In order to discuss risk assessment it is therefore helpful to begin by scrutinizing a number of fundamental issues. Firstly, the use of language in relation to risk has often been confused and terms have been inadequately defined. For the purposes of this chapter it is important to look at three commonly used terms which are key to effective practice: 'dangerousness', 'prediction' and 'risk assessment'.

Following on from this a number of significant contributions to the area of risk assessment have been made in cognitive and social psychology. Such research has concerned the processes and biases associated with perception, memory and decision making in a social context. Related to this, research has also been undertaken looking at the ways in which information in general, and about risk in particular, is communicated and received. Each of these areas is briefly discussed in the review section below. The implications for practice of such research are then outlined with the intention of suggesting ethical decision-making approaches in relation to risk assessments, judgements about risk assessments and also the effective communication of risk assessments.

Review

The language of risk assessments

As noted above there are three key terms that are often used when discussing risk: 'dangerousness', 'prediction' and 'risk assessment'. Each of these is considered in turn.

Dangerousness

One dictionary definition of 'dangerous' is: 'involving or causing danger' (*Concise Oxford Dictionary*, 1995), whilst 'danger' is defined as: '1. liability or exposure to harm; an unwelcome possibility. 2. a thing that causes or is likely to cause harm. 3. Brit. the status of a railway signal directing a halt or caution' (*Concise Oxford Dictionary*, 1995).

In the literature, and forensic practice, this broad term is used in a number of different ways. It is sometimes used to refer to a particular hazard or to indicate that there is a significant probability of a hazardous event occurring. It has been noted, some time ago, that such differing uses of the term may result in confusion (Scott, 1977; Monahan, 1981). Thus some have used the term dangerous to mean violence to others (e.g. Bowden, 1996), others use it to mean violence to others or oneself (e.g. Gunn, 1996). Some (e.g. Monahan, 1981) simply prefer the term 'violent behaviour' to notions of dangerousness because of its semantic clarity. A number of commentators have also sought to distinguish between violence and dangerousness (see Monahan, 1997). Prins (1996) made a helpful distinction between danger as the degree of harm arising from an event and risk as the likelihood of the event. The broad usage of the term 'dangerousness' in the literature reflects, to some extent, the breadth of its usage in practice (Towl & Crighton, 1996). Indeed, the notion of dangerousness has long been a pervasive theme in many areas of criminal law.

Recent highly publicized cases of mentally disordered offenders returning from inpatient care to the community and committing serious offences have served to both stimulate and stifle discussion and debate on 'dangerousness' (see Blom-Cooper, Hally & Murphy, 1995; Blom-Cooper et al., 1996; Prins, 2001). Similarly, recent developments in relation to 'Dangerous Severe Personality Disorder' have served to further muddy the waters by confounding issues of 'dangerousness' and 'personality disorder'. However, both areas and the resultant media attention have served a useful function in highlighting some of the difficulties associated with the appropriate management of mentally disordered offenders.

Prins (1996) suggests that there are a number of difficulties arising out of such enquires. From the Christopher Clunis case he highlights the evident importance of seeking corroboration of accounts given by clients, rather than uncritically accepting such accounts. Discussion and debate are also sometimes stifled in that one organizational and professional response to such media attention is simply to become averse to taking any risks, and develop defensive professional practices.

The term 'dangerous' is enshrined in a range of legislative frameworks addressing the management of offenders both in the UK, e.g. the Mental Health Act (1983), Criminal Justice Act (1991), and elsewhere: an international example would be the New Zealand Criminal Justice Act (1985). Such legislation has, it can be argued, contributed to the erroneous dichotomous classification of individuals as either 'dangerous' or 'not dangerous'. This process has been referred to as bifurcation (Bottoms, 1977). Research into the utility of such dichotomies have suggested them to be both an inaccurate and often an unjust means of assessing risk (see Towl & Crighton, 1996; Towl & Forbes, 2000).

What is evident from this brief review of the usage and abuses of the term 'dangerous' is that it is still used by numerous researchers and practitioners. It is also enshrined in some of the legislation that is highly relevant in forensic practice.

The term needs, however, to be treated with a considerable degree of scepticism and circumspection. It is important that forensic practitioners are aware of the usage of the term in legislation. This does not mean that it is necessarily helpful to use such ill-defined terms in professional practice. The term is, at best, vague. Perhaps more importantly, it is clear that it is used with a range of different unspecified meanings, leading to spurious dichotomies and conceptual confusion (Towl & Crighton, 1997).

Prediction

A dictionary definition of 'prediction' is: '1. the art of predicting or the process of being predicted. 2. a thing predicted; a forecast' (*Concise Oxford Dictionary*, 1995).

Thus from variable 'x' we may predict outcome 'y'. Criminological studies on prediction have traditionally been characterized by the identification of a predictor variable such as age (e.g. Monahan, 1981) or the offence type (e.g. Copas, 1982). These are then tested to assess their predictive power for a given criterion variable (e.g. reconviction for violence within two years of the prediction). Well-defined predictor and criterion variables are key elements in the methodology of prediction studies in criminology (see Farrington & Tarling, 1985). Such studies aim for the accurate prediction of specified events (i.e. criterion variables) within a given time-frame.

In terms of the complexities of any human social behaviour it is logically implausible to maintain that such predictors will ever be 100 per cent accurate in terms of predictor variable 'x' *always* predicting criterion variable 'y'. Complete accuracy, in this context, would be an unreasonable expectation and a practical impossibility. Thus to judge the utility of prediction studies on the basis of whether or not the predictor variable always predicts the criterion variable would be absurd. A more useful test of prediction studies is to check the degree of accuracy of the estimated probability of the relationship between the predictor and criterion variables. Thus, for example, if a specified predictor variable was shown to predict a specified criterion variable 70 per cent of the time, data could be examined to test and retest this estimate of the statistical relationship.

One logical consequence of such a conceptualization of prediction studies is that if the presence of the predictor variable does not result in an individual case in the manifestation of the criterion variable, then this does not 'disprove' the prediction. A direct parallel of this can be seen in forensic decision making. Towl and Crighton (2000) provide a further and fuller discussion of this within the context of suicide, where, for example, the identification of risk may lead to the mobilization of resources to support that individual. Where this is successful the individual may not complete suicide. However, in such a case, this does not negate the validity of the initial assessment of risk.

Linked to this is the thorny issue of decision rules in terms of the acceptability or otherwise of what is a reasonable level of risk to take (Monahan, 1981; Towl & Crighton, 1996). The findings from prediction studies have provided us with a range of useful data to help inform our decision making in forensic practice. Perhaps some of the most notable and influential of such studies on practice have been on the development of prediction scales for parole (e.g. Copas, 1982). Another series of influential studies has been the research into 'criminal careers'. These prospective studies on the development of delinquency and criminality provide us with a huge data set on factors contributing to the development and manifestation of criminal activity (see Farrington & Wilkström, 1994; Maughan & Rutter, 2000). Clearly, prediction studies offer significant potential for helping to inform decisions about risk assessment as discussed below.

Basic concepts in risk assessment

Three basic concepts lie at the root of good practice in risk assessment. Firstly, *predictor variables* (PV) and *criterion variables* (CV). These are central to the language of prediction (Monahan, 1981, 1997). Predictor variables are those variables that may be used to predict an event (or criterion variable) at a specified level of probability. For example, a conviction for a violent offence within two years might constitute a criterion variable, whilst age, level of alcohol consumption and previous convictions for violence may constitute predictor variables.

Secondly, it is important to have an understanding of *base rates*. The base rate is the relative frequency with which a specified event occurs (Plous, 1993). The base rate for public order offences, for example, is high. The base rate for homicide, in the UK, is relatively low. Low base rates result in particular problems of prediction with infrequently occurring events being particularly difficult to predict (Needs & Towl, 1997).

Thirdly, there is the notion of the acceptability of a specified level of risk of a criterion variable occurring. This is an important and conceptually distinct issue. Attempts to set guidelines for such areas of practice are sometimes referred to as decision rules. Thus the problem is in how judgements about the cut-off point where levels of risk are deemed acceptable are made.

Decision making

As noted previously (e.g. Towl & Crighton, 1996), a number of aspects of decision making about risk are 'trans-scientific', relating as they do to notions such as 'justice'. This is not, however, to suggest that psychological research cannot contribute significantly to elucidating and indeed improving such decision-making processes.

Research into decision making can, it has been suggested, be divided into two major approaches: (i) decision analysis and (ii) judgement analysis. The former approach involves a priori decomposition of the process by which decisions are reached. Judgement analysis in contrast involves a posteriori decomposition of decisions (Connolly, Arkes & Hammond, 2000).

Decision analysis

A priori approaches involve separating a decision into its likely component parts before it is made. This is generally done by looking at the probabilities of a range of likely outcomes, while also attempting to estimate the utility of these outcomes. For example, decisions about whether to utilize particular medical treatments can and have been broken down in this way.

Taking the example of medical interventions, the probability of the treatment being successful can be input into a decision tree. Figure 4.1 is a simplified summary of such a decision tree, using the example of surgery.

The term utility is used in this process, in preference to the term value, since value is something which will be judged differently by different people (Connolly, Arkes & Hammond, 2000). Utility is generally scored on a scale from 0 to 1.0 and can be seen, in essence, as the degree to which the outcome is positive. Thus a utility approaching 0 would suggest an outcome with a very low level of desirability. A utility approaching 1.0 would suggest a very desirable outcome.

Studies using this methodology generally involve multiplying the probability of an outcome by its estimated utility. It can be argued that this approach has value in that it makes explicit decision processes that people undertake. It has also been argued that such decision analyses may provide a useful aid to making decisions (Connolly, Arkes & Hammond, 2000). The approach, though, suffers from a number of weaknesses. These would include the fact that the probability of an event is often difficult to assess. Studies to date have often focused on decisions such as whether to apply particular medical treatments. This area is quite untypical in that good data often exist on the probabilities of the full range of specific outcomes. The concept of utility is, if anything, even more challenging, yet the value of any decision tree is completely dependent upon the accuracy of the estimates of probability and utility.

One way around this has been to look at the sensitivity of decision trees to

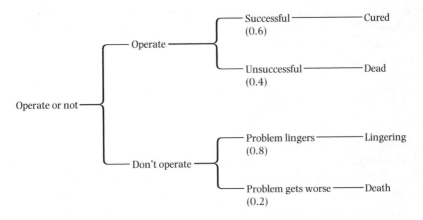

Figure 4.1 A simplified decision tree diagram for a decision whether or not to undertake a surgical operation (reproduced from Connolly, Arkes and Hammond (2000). With permission of Cambridge University Press)

changes in the probability and utility estimates. Where similar results follow from reasonable changes in probabilities and utilities, then, it can be argued, the decision tree is more robust and can be treated with greater confidence.

Judgement analysis

In many respects this approach is the obverse of decision analysis. Here decisions are analysed, after they have been made, using a process of working backwards, to explicate the basis upon which those decisions were made: 'judgements are made from *tangible* data, which serve as *cues* to *intangible* events and circumstances' (Connolly, Arkes & Hammond, 2000, p. 7).

One possible example of such studies is the area of weather forecasting. Here tangible data such as temperature, barometric pressure and so on are combined to produce a prediction about future weather. However, it is clear that such data are used in a complex way, in which different cues are given differing weights. Thus cues where a strong relationship with specific patterns of weather can be shown to occur will be of more use in making judgements that those with weak associations. To further complicate this situation, it is also clear that specific cues may have different types of relationship with future weather patterns. So, for example, a cue may have a positive linear relationship (e.g. increased cloud cover and increased rainfall). Relationships may also be negatively linear or non-linear. Judgements involving curvilinear types of relationship tend to be even more difficult to make than for linear relationships.

Cue data can also be combined in various ways from simply summing data through to using such data in complex patterns. Interestingly most experts report using such complex patterning to produce analyses. Empirical studies however suggest that many such judgements can, in fact, be accounted for using relatively simple patterns of summing and averaging (see Plous, 1993; Connolly, Arkes & Hammond, 2000).

Enhancing decisions

As noted above, studies of diagnostic decision making have provided a particularly good paradigm for studies of applied decision making. This is because diagnostic situations often involve making repeated choices between competing alternatives. In turn most, if not all, of the competing alternatives are often known and can generally be identified with a high degree of reliability.

It is also worth noting that all diagnostic decisions involve the use of probabilistic information. For example, no diagnostic test is 100 per cent accurate. Because of this such decisions will inevitably include false positive decisions, for example, where cancer is incorrectly diagnosed on the basis of information from diagnostic tests (e.g. mammograms). The inverse of this will also occur, where false negative decisions are made and genuine cases of cancer are either not identified or are identified as non-cancerous.

One logical consequence of this is that to get more true positive diagnostic decisions we need to accept an increase in the number of false positives. Conversely, if we wish to have fewer false positives then we will miss more true positives. Where the threshold is set for such decisions will, to a large extent, depend on the consequences resulting from false positives and negatives. So, for example, in the identification of cancers a low threshold would generally be seen as appropriate, due to the grave consequences where a cancer was missed. The costs associated with false positive diagnoses (i.e. anxiety, distress and expense) may be seen, at least by practitioners, as undesirable but acceptable.

Base rates, costs and benefits

Base rates will also have an impact on where we choose to set our threshold in any risk assessment in addition to the relative costs and benefits of decisions. Together these provide the strongest means for deciding on a logical decision threshold (Swets, 2000). Typically, however, other factors are involved such as the capacity to undertake tests, financial costs, availability of resources and so on. This perhaps goes some way to explaining the fact that in the USA 3 out of 10 breast cancer biopsies are positive, whereas in the UK this is closer to 5 in 10, suggesting a higher threshold for the deployment of testing in the UK (Swets, 2000).

Swets notes that any decision-making system has its own inherent level of inaccuracy. The accuracy of such decisions, though, may be increased by improving the accuracy of the evidence being used to help make the decisions. It is evidently difficult, if not impossible, to make accurate assessments on the basis of inaccurate information.

In turn it is also possible to focus on the key aspects of evidence that can be shown to be associated with more accurate decisions. Using again the example of breast cancer, a number of aspects of mammograms (i.e. x-ray pictures of the breast) have been shown to be predictive of the presence of cancer (e.g. the clustering of microcalcifications). These indicators can be combined into a checklist and such information has also been computerized, as an aid to radiologists undertaking such assessments. By giving a probability of malignancy based on use of those indicators which are the most reliable and valid indicators the accuracy of decisions is increased. This approach has been shown to increase levels of accuracy from medium to high, with a gain of 0.15 in true positive probability and a parallel decrease in false positive probability (Getty et al., 1988; Swets et al., 1991). It is important to note that such approaches have been based on empirical studies of effective practice. They are also used as an aid to decision making, not as a replacement.

Swets (2000) also reports a similar approach in a contrasting area of risk assessment, with a study looking at the ability of US Air Force technicians to detect cracks in aircraft wings. The study showed what the authors worryingly described as a 'complete range' of decision thresholds, over a sample of 125 technicians, varying from pure chance to good levels of accuracy. Decision thresholds used by individuals ranged from very strict to very lax. Interestingly, the accuracy levels at a particular base tended to be similar. Thus at a poorly performing base all technicians tended to be similarly poor and vice versa. As with radiologists it was possible to identify the specific cues used to make effective decisions and the way these were used. In turn it was possible to codify these for use by poorly performing technicians, bringing the performance of these individuals into line with the best technicians.

Practice

There are many areas where risk assessments may appear less immediately accessible to the methods outlined above. Studies from cognitive psychology have, to date, had limited impact on forensic practice. A number of possible explanations exist for this. For forensic practitioners the situation faced is complicated by a number of factors. These would include often very poor levels of understanding about what the likely outcomes of risk assessments may be. Previous studies of complex constructs such as 'dangerousness', it has also been argued, have done much to retard the development of much-needed research into specific outcomes. Taking up his earlier distinction (Prins 1996) between danger as harm from an event and risk as the likelihood of such an event, Prins (2002) notes that concepts of risk and dangerousness are often confused.

The definitional and conceptual confusion inherent in concepts such as 'dangerousness' not only makes it difficult to make sensible and valid decisions about risk but may also serve to impede effective study and research.

In addition, the situation faced by forensic practitioners is often more akin to that faced by atmospheric physicists trying to predict weather patterns (Monahan, 1997). Human behaviour takes place in a complex, and poorly understood, social environment. In this environment apparently small changes may have strong and unforeseen effects. In much the same way small changes in weather systems may go on to have strong and unforeseen effects on the weather. Because of this it has been suggested that the mathematical approaches developed by chaos theorists may have greater utility than traditional linear models (Monahan & Steadman, 1996; Crighton, 1997).

Overall it seems clear that there remains a great deal of fundamental research that needs to be undertaken in relation to risk assessment and decision making in forensic contexts. Priorities in this area would include the need for adequate studies of outcomes in relation to risk assessments. There is also a clear need for methodologically adequate research into the effects of a range of interventions on subsequent outcomes. It could also be suggested that there is a need for a better understanding of the ways in which judicial and quasi-judicial bodies make judgements about risk. The current state of knowledge in these key areas is, at best, rudimentary and developments have often been based on studies with serious methodological weaknesses (West, in press). That said, forensic practitioners are faced with the reality of needing to improve the quality of risk assessments now.

Outlined in figure 4.2 is the 'Cambridge model of risk assessment' (Towl & Crighton, 1996, 1999, 2000). This conceptual model serves two main purposes. Firstly, it provides a systematic way in which practitioners might structure their approach to assessing risk. In turn this, to a significant extent, makes explicit the basis for the decision-making process involved. Secondly, it has the potential to provide a basis for the systematic gathering of a much-needed knowledge base. By moving away from multi-faceted concepts such as 'dangerousness' the model requires the identification of specific areas of risk. It also requires the specification of the evidence that is thought to suggest increased and decreased risk. This limited level of precision simply brings forensic risk assessments into line with other, further-developed, areas of risk assessment. In doing this it also allows for testing of the empirical relationships between the specified variables.

The Cambridge framework for risk assessment

Figure 4.2 outlines a framework for undertaking risk assessments. It is derived directly from earlier work (see Towl & Crighton, 1996, 1999, 2000). It also draws on the work of others in the area of forensic risk assessment (e.g. Monahan & Steadman, 1994; Prins, 1996).

Stage one of this framework refers to the specification of the relevant criterion variables as the first step in the risk assessment. There may be more than one criterion variable for each client, for example a client may have a history of arson attacks and assaults. Hence two criterion variables may be reconviction for each criminal activity within a twelve-month period. This is crucial since it

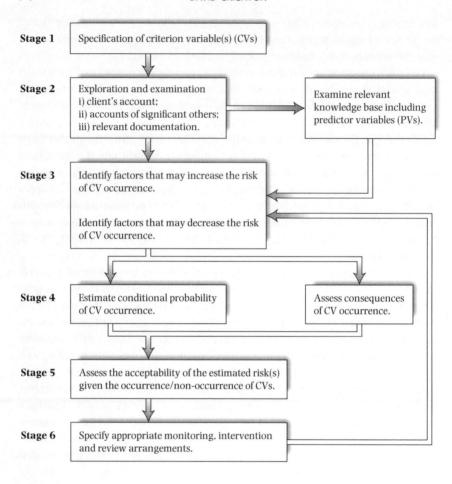

Figure 4.2   The Cambridge Framework for Risk Assessment

enables practitioners to structure risk assessments so that distinctions may be made between the likelihood of the occurrence of distinct offences. This distinction of ostensibly different risks is important partly because of the unfortunate tendency for some practitioners simply to write in terms of the risk of reoffending as a global and homogeneous term. It is also important to place a time limit on any assessment, since it seems highly unlikely that an individual's level of risk will remain the same indefinitely.

Stage two essentially consists of the information-gathering process. It is important that practitioners have a well-developed and developing knowledge base in areas where they are conducting risk assessments. To take the risk of suicide as an example, there is a substantial and developing body of knowledge about the factors that are correlated with suicide in the community (Charlton et al., 1992; Hawton, 1994) and in specific settings such a prisons (Crighton, 2000). There are also psychometric tests that can be used as effective aids to assessing risk (Beck, Kovacs & Weissman, 1979; Beck & Steer,1989; Plutchik, 1997; Plutchik & Van Praag, 1990; Palmer 2001).

It is only by accessing such a knowledge base that practitioners may best be enabled to fully explore and examine individual cases. The client's account of events will be of paramount importance in the assessment process since, as Prins (2001, 2002) notes, the hazards that an individual may present as a risk are the product of certain 'vulnerabilities' in certain situations. It is therefore important to have the best possible understanding of what these individual vulnerabilities are and the contexts in which they may occur. An example of this might be someone who expresses ideas that others are prone to persecute and conspire against them. An understanding of the client's construing of their environment is often therefore key to understanding the nature and extent of the risks involved. It is also clearly distinct from simply accepting the client's account in an uncritical manner (Needs & Towl, 1997).

Linked to this, the observations and views of significant others will also provide important information. For example, the accounts given by friends and the individual's family may serve to confirm or contradict the client's account. Also, it may be that the assessment is taking place in an institution, for example, a prison or secure hospital. In such cases it would be particularly prudent to solicit the observations of a wide range of staff such as mental health nurses, probation officers, social workers, occupational therapists, prison officers and police officers. The importance of good and effective communication between professionals is absolutely imperative to help inform accurate risk assessments. Prins (1996, 2002) stresses the central role of effective communication in making valid assessments. Prins perceptively observes that 'Denial is by no means the sole prerogative of offenders' (1996, p. 49). Related to this, he stresses the need to effectively listen to the views of others.

Stage three involves the identification of factors that may serve to either increase or decrease the level of risk. The nature of these factors will depend on the nature of the risk or risks identified in stage one and the information gathered during stage two. In addition forensic practitioners will be able to draw on the developing knowledge base within forensic practice to inform their assessments.

Stage four of the model involves the attempt to integrate two distinct areas of the risk assessment: (i) the probability of a criterion event happening; and (ii) the likely effects should it occur. Stage five is, in turn, closely linked, involving the practitioner in outlining their assessment of the acceptability of the estimated risk. In many areas of forensic practice the individual practitioner will not make such decisions alone. Rather, decisions will be made as part of a process by judicial or quasi-judicial bodies, for example Mental Health Tribunals, Discretionary Lifer Panels and so. In turn these statutory bodies will draw on input from forensic practitioners.

The final suggested stage is the specification of monitoring and review arrangements. Historically, risk assessments have often failed to include this. Such an approach is, though, seriously flawed, since an individual's level of risk is unlikely to be static over an indefinite period of time. It also seems to be a missed opportunity in terms of structuring intervention work to reduce levels of risk over time.

Having made such a detailed assessment of risk, practitioners will then need effectively to communicate their findings and opinions to others.

Risk perception and communication

In undertaking risk assessments practitioners need to have an understanding of risk perception. It is also important that they are able adequately to communicate risk assessments.

In making effective risk assessment decisions there is a need to understand the risks and benefits associated with alternative courses of action. There is also a need for a clear understanding of the limits of 'expert' advice in relation to risk assessment and management. Specifically it has been demonstrated that 'experts' often do not differ from 'non-experts' when making unstructured assessments about risk (see Monahan & Steadman, 1994). Both types of assessor under such conditions tend to use simple algorithms to make their assessments and tend to be subject to systematic cognitive biases. A number of research studies exist which illuminate this area for practitioners.

Lichtenstein et al. (1978) suggest that estimates of risk are subject to the following systematic cognitive biases:

1   Internal consistency – individuals seemed to have a moderately well-articulated internal risk scale, which they could express even in unfamiliar response modes. However, such scales do appear to differ significantly between individuals.
2   Anchoring bias – direct estimates appeared to be influenced by the 'anchor' given. For example, individuals told that 50,000 people died from car accidents estimated a higher number of deaths from other causes than those told that 1,000 people died from electrocution.

3 Compression – individuals' estimates showed less dispersion than statistical estimates of risk.

4 Availability bias – at any level of statistical frequency, some causes of death received consistently higher estimates than others. These proved to be causes that were disproportionately visible (e.g. received high levels of TV coverage). This in turn seemed to be associated with frequency and ease of recall or imagining. Interestingly, people showed very little insight into the fallibility of this as an index of risk.

5 Miscalibration of confidence judgements – here people tended to be insensitive about the limits of their judgements, tending to be markedly overconfident about their accuracy.

6 Response mode problem – people tended to use quantifiers differently from others and also for different types of risk. Thus the term 'very likely' to kill again referred to a much lower probability than 'very likely' to rain.

7 Perceived invulnerability – most people, in most circumstances, see themselves as facing less risk than the average for others, even though this cannot logically be true for more than half the population.

Scientific estimates of risk require detailed data on conditions. For example, risk assessments for coronary heart disease would depend on accurate estimates of blood pressure, blood cholesterol levels, weight and so on. Missing or inaccurate data will inevitably lead to less accurate risk assessments. This imposes marked limits on the accuracy of current risk assessments in forensic practice, for the simple reason that there are substantial amounts of missing data.

In the absence of explicit data people appear to fill in the gaps for themselves in a more sophisticated way than has been assumed in many early psychological studies. Individuals do, however, vary markedly in the assumptions they make to fill in such missing data (Fischoff, Bostrom & Quadrel, 1993). Most people, when faced with such decisions, are concerned with data that are related to the risks being assessed. This is not true for everyone, though, and some people show an interest in data that are irrelevant to the risk being assessed. People also appear to show 'blind spots'. For example, teenagers asked to assess various risks saw the amount of alcohol consumed as relevant to a drink-driving scenario; in contrast the number of incidents of sexual intercourse was not be seen as relevant in an HIV scenario (Quadrel, 1990).

In fact this finding appears to be a specific example of a more common problem, whereby people are insensitive to cumulative risk. Thus people tend to produce estimates of risk but fail to increase the level of risk as a result of multiple exposures. Thus people tend to maintain, quite incorrectly, a constant estimation of risk from death in a car accident whether they drive 5,000 or 50,000 miles per annum. This is clearly at odds with the statistical level of risk as evidenced by, for example, insurance premiums.

Communicating risk assessments

Fischoff, Bostrom and Quadrel (1993) argue that the first step in designing communications relating to risk assessments is selecting the information that should be contained. They suggest that often communications about risk are predicated on the basis of what the recipient ought to know rather than a realistic appraisal of what they do know. For example, in communicating levels of risk, 'experts' often make assumptions about the level of prior knowledge amongst recipients. To illustrate this they report the findings of a survey of the US public following a series of health promotion initiatives. This survey found that 41 per cent knew that a virus caused HIV. The value of this information was compromised by the fact that the survey did not say what respondents understood a virus to be. In fact the researchers found very considerable variation in the understanding of what a virus is.

They go on to suggest three systematic approaches to the structuring of risk communications:

1   *Mental models analysis.* Here communications are designed to convey a comprehensive picture of the process of formulating and controlling a risk, therefore reducing the gap between expert and lay models of risk. However, to achieve this there is a need to: a) add missing concepts; b) correct mistakes in risk analysis; c) strengthen correct beliefs; d) de-emphasize peripheral information.
2   *Calibration analysis.* This refers to communications that attempt to correct the systematic biases seen in recipient's beliefs about risk. In turn correcting such errors can lead to more appropriate decisions and actions.
3   *Value-of-Information analysis.* This is where communications seek to provide pieces of evidence that will have the largest possible impact on a pending decision. This term is a general one that covers a range of techniques that determine the sensitivity of decisions to different information.

They go on to suggest that the choice between these various methods, or combinations of methods, will depend on a variety of factors. These will include the amount of time available for the communication, how well the decisions are formulated and what scientific risk information exists. For example, they suggest that a value of information analysis may often be best when communicating information about risks in acute medical conditions, where patients are asked to give informed consent. Here patients will be given key information relating to probable outcomes (Merz, 1991; Fischoff, Bostrom & Quadrel, 1993).

Future Directions

A number of future directions in risk assessment suggest themselves from the discussion above. It seems clear that research and practice has until recently developed slowly. A number of reasons for this seem likely. Many of the behaviours of interest to forensic practitioners are of low frequency and are thus particularly difficult to predict effectively. However, other disciplines have made much greater strides in risk assessment of low-frequency events.

Another likely reason for the slow progress has been the failure to adopt a rational and systematic approach to areas that are often emotionally or politically charged. Notions such as 'dangerousness' have been enshrined in law but in fact have little utility for forensic practitioners. The use of more detailed specification of risk(s) and the relationship of these to a range of factors, seems a more promising route to improved decision making.

There is also a pressing need to undertake methodologically adequate studies of risk assessments in forensic contexts. As noted above, one of the priorities here is for studies of specific types of risk and effective predictors of these. In addition, there is a need for methodologically adequate studies of a wide range of interventions to reduce future risks (e.g. Willmot, 2000). Whilst this presents a number of ethical and practical challenges, there is evidently a great deal of learning to be had from looking at studies in other areas, a small number of which have been discussed above.

The outlined Cambridge model provides an integrated framework for assessing risk. As such it may also provide a useful tool for structuring future research and practice. In providing a logical structure for risk assessment it also has the potential to improve the communication of risk-related information.

There are a number of alternative approaches to this and similar models of risk assessment. These would include a range of actuarial assessments of risk, examples of which include the Psychopathy Checklist Revised (PCL-R: Hare, 1991), the Violence Risk Appraisal Guide (VRAG: Quinsey et al., 1998), the Sex Offender Risk Appraisal Guide (SORAG: ibid). All of these (although the PCL-R does not rely solely on historical data) provide actuarial assessments of the probability of the occurrence of specific types of criminal offending in the future.

Taking the SORAG as an illustrative example, this draws heavily upon the

notion of 'psychopathy', as defined by the PCL-R, as a measure of future risk
in sexual offenders. Advocates of this approach argue that a combination of
measuring 'anti-social' personality characteristics, the characteristics of the
victims of offences and physiological measures of sexual arousal[3] provides the
most accurate measures of future risk (ibid). Such approaches have been
shown to show moderate accuracy in predicting subsequent offending (e.g.
Hanson & Harris, 2000) and have also been shown to be superior to unstructured clinical judgement (e.g. Monahan & Steadman,1994; Monahan, 1997).
However, such approaches have been subject to a number of significant criti-
cisms.

Firstly, it needs to be said that a level of performance better than unstructured clinical judgements can be a very limited achievement. As noted above,
unstructured judgements, by 'experts' and 'non-experts' alike, tend to be poor.
However, such judgements can evidently be improved dramatically by introducing structure into the way in which such assessments are made (Douglas,
Cox & Webster, 1999).

Additionally, a number of the factors used in actuarial models are not independent of other social and economic factors. Such approaches draw heavily on items of historical information, which have been decribed as 'static'
predictors. A number of the 'static' predictors of risk used in the PCL-R and
SORAG are correlated with social and economic deprivation (Grubin, 1997,
1999). In stressing the role of past behaviour in predicting future risk actuarial models may also be seen, as Prins (2002) eloquently describes it, of
giving a 'therapeutic "counsel of despair"'. They may equally be seen as part
of a common attributional bias, whereby observers tend to overestimate the
role of 'dispositional factors' and underestimate the contribution of
'situational factors', particularly where negative outcomes are concerned
(see Jones & Nisbett, 1971). Grubin (1999) contends that the SORAG raises
issues concerning the generalizability of findings to different samples, the
extent to which judgements should be based exclusively on historical data
and the value of group data in predicting low-frequency behaviours in the
individual case.

The Cambridge framework is clearly not an empirical measure of risk. Rather
it is a logical framework for use by practitioners in conducting risk assessment
and risk management work. It does not, of course, preclude the use of empirical
measures as part of this process, quite the contrary. Such measures are seen,
though, as an adjunct to the risk-assessment process, an approach that is rejected by advocates of purely actuarial approaches (see Quinsey et al., 1998).
The framework aims, very clearly, to provide a working model for structured
but individual assessments of risk. The advantages of an approach based on
structured clinical judgement include systematization, flexibility, transparency
and relevance (Hart, 1998).

Summary

Risk assessment is a fundamental area of work for forensic practitioners. Many of the decisions made in forensic contexts, at an individual or systems level, relate directly or indirectly to issues of risk.

The area of risk assessment in forensic practice has been bedevilled by the absence of appropriate conceptual frameworks. This has held back both the development of good-quality pure and applied research and, related to this, effective practice.

In contrast there has been a substantial and growing amount of good-quality applied psychological research in a number of areas including medicine, engineering and meteorology. It is possible to draw directly and indirectly from such work, in order to inform the development of risk assessment and management in forensic contexts.

The Cambridge model for risk assessment outlined above serves to provide one possible conceptual framework, which in turn allows for the integration of a range of observations relating to risk. Such frameworks are likely to be an essential first step in forensic practice, as they have been in other disciplines, for achieving more accurate and useful risk assessments.

NOTES

1   The term 'client' is used throughout to mean the individual offender under assessment. It is acknowledged that the identification of precisely who the client is in the forensic field may not always be immediately obvious.
2   'Throughcare' refers to the planning of an offender's time in prison custody and under the supervision of the probation service in the community. It is a multidisciplinary system of assessment and management that aims to reduce levels of future offending.
3   The measure advocated for use with the SORAG is the Penile Plethysmograph (PPG). This records the degree of penile erectile response to sexual stimuli – usually in the form of pictures or sound recordings.

Chapter Five

The Management of Difficult Clients

Ruby Bell and Sue Evershed

Who Are the Difficult Clients?

This chapter aims to provide an overview of issues involved in working with difficult clients and some general strategies for managing and treating such individuals within a therapeutic framework. A manual of treatment interventions is not being offered. This area is so broad and diverse that it is not possible to be specific within the constraints of this chapter. The literature in this area is sparse. Most authors prefer to publish accounts of therapeutic success rather than failure. By definition, these clients demonstrate slow therapeutic progress and present threats and problems for clinicians and managers alike. However, it is possible to draw upon clinical experience, therapeutic approaches and empirical research that offer general guidance as how best to deal with difficult clients.

Most of the research evidence reviewed relates to offenders and mentally disordered offenders held within the criminal justice system or detained in conditions of high, medium or low security in mental health settings. This is not to say that difficult clients only feature in these two populations. Rather, these are two significant workplaces where forensic psychologists are employed.

Clinical experience and available literature suggest that the most constructive approach for working with difficult clients is to identify core themes, focusing on behaviours rather than diagnostic categories. It is the behaviours that cause the problems and that have to be dealt with, and these often cross diagnostic boundaries. Hence it is not possible to identify what makes a client difficult using only the diagnosis. However, many of the problem behaviours feature in the criteria for certain diagnoses, particularly the personality disorders. Thus the chapter draws heavily on work undertaken with clients who have personality disorder.

The two most widely used diagnostic classification systems) of personality disorder, DSM IV (American Psychiatric Association, 1994) and ICD 10 (World Health Organization [WHO],1992), and the British Psychological Society (BPS) all give similar definitions of personality disorder. The BPS recently referred to personality disorder as: 'an enduring pattern of personality organisation which significantly deviates from the norms of a culture; which leads to dysfunction in behaviour, emotional self-regulation and relationships with others, and is a stable pattern, resistant to change' (BPS, 1999, p. 2). Many studies indicate that the presence of personality disorder predicts poorer outcome for psychological interventions. Clients with personality disorder are frequently seen as more difficult to engage in treatment, requiring higher dosage and having higher drop-out rates (Reich & Vasile, 1993; Hardy et al., 1995; Lipsey, 1995; Goldstein et al., 1998; Blackburn, 2000). Thus it is useful to look at the literature on the treatment and management of personality disorder as a guide to dealing with difficult behaviour.

It is not suggested that only clients with personality disorder are difficult, nor is it the case that all difficult clients have personality disorder. However, estimates of the prevalence of personality disorders within prison and forensic mental health settings has been found to be high, although they vary depending on the assessment tools utilized (Bland et al., 1990; Singleton, Meltzer & Gatwood, 1998). In the USA, estimates for antisocial personality disorder alone, in the male prison population, vary between 50 and 80 per cent (Hare, 1983; Robins, Tipp & Przybeck, 1991), and Neighbors (1987) suggests that the prevalence rate for all the personality disorders could be as high as 90 per cent in the male prison population. Personality disorder is also common amongst mentally disordered offenders. Blackburn et al. (1990) demonstrated that 65 per cent of mentally ill clients at a High Secure Hospital had personality disorder. In the USA, Timmerman and Emmelkamp (2001) identified 86.8 per cent of forensic clients as having personality disorder.

All therapists are able to identify clients whom they perceive as 'difficult'. Our own professional strengths and weaknesses determine our ability to deal with certain client characteristics and therapeutic situations. There are however, some clients and some situations which pose problems for all therapists. For the purposes of this chapter, we will define 'difficult' as: behaviour(s) that places the client, therapist or therapeutic regime in danger; or behaviour(s) that so disrupts therapeutic systems and processes that they are rendered ineffective. Some examples of these behaviours will be explored, but it should be noted that the problem behaviours cited will not be an exhaustive list.

Parasuicidal and suicidal behaviours

Suicidal behaviours are defined here as those behaviours which convince others that the client is at high risk of imminent suicide, such as attempts to kill oneself, threats, planning and the expression of high suicidal intent. Kreitman (1977) introduced the term 'parasuicide' to describe non-fatal intentional self-injurious behaviour that resulted in tissue damage, illness or risk of death, or any ingestion of substances not prescribed or in excess of prescription, with clear intent to cause bodily harm or death. Whilst not necessarily aimed at causing death, such behaviour is dangerous to the patient. Research has shown that parasuicide is the best predictor of subsequent suicide (Stone, Stone & Hurt, 1987) and accidental death is not an uncommon consequence of parasuicidal behaviour.

The intention to harm oneself is incompatible with the goals of therapy, which are based on intent to help rather than harm oneself (Linehan, 1993). Ultimately, we 'can't treat dead patients' (Mintz, 1968). However, the management of such behaviour is problematic in that the therapist must achieve two, sometimes incompatible, goals: to keep the client physically safe, and to treat the client in such a way as to reduce the probability of subsequent suicidal behaviour. The focus of any ongoing therapy must shift to efforts to keep the patient alive. However, this shift can place too much emphasis on the first goal, at the expense of the second, with too much focus on making the client feel better, or avoiding distressing issues for fear of stimulating further suicidal behaviour. Whilst this may prove beneficial in the short term, it could result in more damaging consequences in the longer term.

Parasuicidal and suicidal behaviour also often drives an intense reactive response at a systemic level, which can distract from the main thrust of therapy. Frequently the clients' environment is severely restricted to keep them physically safe, further reducing quality of life, and responsibility is removed, reducing the ability to experience any sense of coping. Parasuicidal behaviour is resource intensive – being demanding of staff time in preventing self-injurious behaviour; treating injuries; and dealing with administrative work required particularly if an enquiry or investigation results. Other clients and other work can be ignored in order to deal with the client engaging in this behaviour.

Additionally, such behaviour proves extremely distressing to those involved in the therapeutic process and can lead to feelings of hopelessness and stress in the therapist (Goodman, 1997). Eventually clients repeatedly engaging in parasuicidal behaviour can engender negative feelings in the therapist, particularly feelings of anger and frustration which can lead to an urge to punish the client in some way (Fallon, 1983).

For many, the choice to die may be based on an informed, rational decision about their current and potential quality of life. The first dilemma facing the therapist is therefore an ethical one about whether to accept that the client should have the freedom to choose suicide, or whether to intervene against the client's wishes. For Linehan (1993) the choice is clear. The desire to commit suicide is based on the premise that life cannot improve. This is not true in many instances, where it is the nature of the psychological problems that leads to the feelings of hopelessness and poor quality of life. There are no data available about the relative quality of being that death brings about. Faced with this argument, Dialectical Behaviour Therapists take a stance against suicide, use therapy to improve lives but accept responsibility that some clients may live to regret this stance (Linehan, 1993).

Violent and destructive behaviours

Most forensic establishments contain at least a small group of clients who are chronically violent toward staff and peers, or destructive of their environment (Lion & Reid, 1983; Home Office, 1984). This behaviour will have a negative effect on therapeutic systems and any potential alliance. For these clients, it is not just the actual violence or destructiveness that causes difficulties. In fact these incidents are often rare events, but threats of violence or destructiveness can also be problematic. Flannery, Hanson and Penk (1995), in a psychiatric environment in the USA, found that whilst only 30 per cent of threats resulted in physical or sexual assault, many threats were as likely to cause psychological distress as actual violence. Often the unpredictability of violent or destructive behaviour can produce as many difficulties as the behaviour itself. Research on therapist and staff burnout (Lanza, 1995) shows that assaults on staff can be a significant source of extended psychological distress.

Inevitably, the real issues for these clients become fogged by the need to protect the safety and security of staff and other clients (Dubin & Lion, 1992). Clients become known as treatment failures, and can develop reputations of almost mythological proportions, which can be destructive to any possibility of further effective intervention. In effect, they can become barred from the very facilities and programmes that could help them.

Many writers feel that staff reactions to violent and destructive clients can exacerbate problems. Aggressive or defensive responses can lead to violence or set up cycles of escalating violence. In the USA, Rice, Harris and Quinsey (1994) demonstrated that assaults are often the result of the quality of staff interactions with clients and they developed a training course emphasizing interpersonal strategies, which led to a reduction in assaults. In England, Whittington and Wykes (1996) found that violence in psychiatric inpatient wards was preceded by aversive stimulation by staff (e.g. frustration, activity demand or physical contact) in 86 per cent of cases and concluded that staff interpersonal factors play a large part in client aggression.

Often, staff become restrictive as a means of managing violent and destructive clients, which can lead to a reduced quality of life for the client and to external criticism of the approach. This in turn can lead to stress and produce a defensive response within staff, which inhibits their ability to consider alternative approaches and the changing needs of the client. More importantly, it also limits the potential to help the client change the core issues underlying the aggressive behaviour: 'the dynamics of recurrent in-patient dangerousness have all the makings of long-term problems unless adequate interventions effectively break the cycle of aggression' (Maier et al., 1987, cited in van Rybroek, 2000, p. 158).

Seeking media attention

There is a dearth of material on how best to manage those individuals who seek and attract significant media attention. Such clients can present significant management and treatment problems. Having worked in a variety of prisons, high and medium secure settings, the authors have come across several examples of such clients and it is not difficult to cite names that appear regularly in newspaper and television articles. The difficulties posed are many and varied. If media coverage is wide then both clients and staff from the receiving establishment will already have formed opinions about the individual. Such information may put the client at risk and may engender feelings of fear, excitement or abhorrence in staff and peers alike.

All decisions about the treatment or welfare of the client are likely to be highlighted in the press with accompanying editorial comment and decisions about the management of such clients are inevitably affected by speculation as to 'what the papers might say'.

There are numerous examples of forensic clients having been elevated to cult or hero status, which again may result in management problems. The client may not engage in therapeutic interventions. They may view their detention as entirely political, regarding themselves as the victim, thereby shifting focus from their offending behaviour. The support received from peers and the public may reinforce any cognitive distortions held, as if justifying their crimes in some way. Positive media attention can result in feelings of jealousy and resentment in both staff and peers, which can have detrimental effects on therapeutic relationships and goals. In some cases where the clients are writing books, the organization and the staff may find themselves and their practice in the public arena. Research has demonstrated that threats to their perceived integrity are as, if not more stressful, than physical assault (American Federation of State, County and Municipal Employees [AFSCME],1982; Conlin, 1986).

Maier (Maier & Fulton, 1998) describes a hospital preparing for the admission of Jeffrey Dahmer, reporting the process as intense and 'destructive to the therapeutic milieu'. Managers were concerned that the client would receive thousands of letters and that someone might try to kill him by letter bomb. Checking the mail would utilize all existing resources and might require more. Additionally, there were plans to improve security at great expense, to prevent sniper attack. Ultimately, he was given a prison sentence but the fears expressed proved well founded.

Litigious behaviour

Some clients deal with their problems in a more acceptable, legally sanctioned way by becoming litigious. This is a more passive-aggressive form of difficult behaviour. Whist one would not wish to restrict a client's right to legal action, some individuals engage in protracted and often inappropriate legal arguments. Morowitz (1981) refers to this as 'jurisgenic disease'. In addition to the extra resources required in the establishment and system generally, it remains difficult if not impossible for the client to engage in any meaningful therapeutic work whilst the process is ongoing. It allows them to focus on the external world, with a feeling of 'moral righteousness', while distracting from the more internal, personal issues which may require more painful, therapeutic work.

Such legal actions can provide additional benefits – the client may be given higher status by their peers and may be requested to assist with other clients' legal arguments, again distracting from more personal issues. Miller et al. (1986) suggest that this litigious behaviour is a form of treatment resistance. Research by Chrzanowski (1980) focused on the concealed hostility of those clients identified as 'difficult'. Whilst the underlying dynamics appeared complex, those who engaged in litigious behaviour had greater feelings of helplessness with regard to authority.

Treatment-resistant behaviour

Difficult clients can engage in a variety of treatment resistant behaviours which Linehan (1993) placed into three categories: those interfering with the client receiving the therapy; those interfering with other clients benefiting from therapy; and those that burn out the therapist. These behaviours include any which contribute to the actual or potential failure of therapy.

In the first category there are a number of different types of difficult behaviour: Non-attending (e.g. not attending or dropping out of sessions); non-attention (e.g. attending sessions under the influence of a substance, daydreaming, or sleeping); non-collaboration (e.g. refusing to work in therapy, lying, not talking, emotionally withdrawing, arguing, distracting and digressing, and responding with 'I don't know/can't remember'); and non-compliance (e.g. failing to complete homework, failing to agree treatment goals, or not keeping to agreements made).

Silverman (1987) noted that silence can be employed as a strategy to resist therapy and can prove powerful in challenging the system. There may be more clinical explanations of such behaviour, such as 'elective mutism' whereby clients use silence as a means of restoring a perceived imbalance of power. This is frequently seen in children as a way of hiding abuse or dealing with frightening issues. These kinds of issues are also pertinent to all types of 'therapy interfering behaviour'. Choosing to be silent is dependent for its effectiveness on someone needing the client to speak. It is difficult to assess risk and dangerousness and engage in treatment if the client remains silent.

Behaviours that interfere with others benefiting from therapy include being openly hostile, verbally critical, expressing negative feelings toward others, whilst behaviours that burn out therapists include behaviours that push therapists' personal limits and decrease their willingness to continue with therapy. These latter behaviours are not always obvious to the therapist but can manifest within the social roles of the therapist and client. Clients may refuse to comply or may behave as if the therapist has limitless time, patience and therapeutic resources (Norton & McGauley, 1998). Also, they may be demanding of help in non-therapeutic issues, engaging in overly familiar ways. This can be seen in sexually provocative behaviour, infringing personal space and threatening harm. Other patterns involve threats to sue or complain or engaging in public rebuke.

What Works with Difficult Clients?

Although these behaviours may appear numerous and diverse, core functional themes can be identified and targeted to progress the therapeutic process. These arise within the literature pertaining to a variety of different treatment approaches. All of them draw on the traditional skills of clinical and forensic psychologists: the formation of a therapeutic alliance; a clear understanding of the behaviour, its origin, maintenance and function; and the systematic removal of internal and external factors that interfere with therapy.

Several innovative developments in therapeutic approaches to personality disorder have demonstrated some success. These include Dialectical Behaviour Therapy (Linehan, 1993), Cognitive Analytic Therapy (Ryle and Golynkina, 2000), Schema Focused Therapy (Young, 1994), Cognitive Behavioural Therapy (Davidson & Tyrer, 1996) and Therapeutic Communities (Dolan, 1998). There is also interest in applications of Attachment Theory (Holmes, 1993, 1996), and Interpersonal Theory (Benjamin, 1996, 1997). Many of the above incorporate a 'staged' model of treatment whereby different stages of progress are identified and operationalized. For those with personality disorders, these stages are likely to include building a therapeutic alliance and developing the motivation to engage as a first step. Later priorities include achieving physical safety and day-to-day emotional stability for clients by targeting violence and self-harm and teaching alternative coping strategies. The exploration and processing of difficult and disturbing events such as abuse or offending and the development of new approaches to achieve personal growth and improve the quality of life are also later priorities. Many of these approaches can be applied directly with difficult clients or adapted to suit their needs.

The therapeutic alliance

The first task in all clinical work, prior to any therapy being undertaken, is the building of a therapeutic alliance. Bordin (1979) defined a therapeutic alliance, notwithstanding the model of therapy, as the collaboration between a client and therapist based on their agreement about the goals and tasks of therapy.

Most of the new therapies (e.g. CAT, DBT, Schema Focused) place a great deal of emphasis on the therapeutic relationship. Morris and Magrath (1983) found that interpersonal warmth and friendliness were related to positive outcomes in psychotherapy. With difficult clients the building of the therapeutic alliance is possibly the central issue and poses particular problems. Many clients will have been through a therapeutic process before and often this will have been experienced as unsatisfactory. Issues of trust and fear of abandonment must be addressed and the formation of the alliance may be protracted. A central feature of these difficult clients is their poor interpersonal functioning. Many will have long histories of chaotic and abusive relationships dating back to childhood and so a strong therapeutic alliance is essential in providing possibly the first secure attachment. In addition it provides an arena in which the client can observe and practice new interpersonal skills.

Luborsky (1984) suggested that an alliance has two components: an attitudinal component, in which the client believes in the credibility of the treatment and therapist; and a relationship component, in which the client works in collaboration with the therapist. The therapist must generate optimism and instil confidence in the therapeutic process. Clients are likely to fear that change will mean relinquishing their means of coping or an important aspect of themselves. Communicating acceptance and understanding of these fears, of the clients themselves or their agenda is an important part of establishing the alliance. Expressions of respect and commitment by the therapist also set the scene for the building of a collaborative relationship. It is vital that the therapist relates to the client on a personal as well as a professional level. Clients with unhappy experiences of therapy are unlikely to relate easily to a therapist who hides behind their professional role. Above all else the therapist must be 'real'. Terms such as 'radical genuineness' are used throughout the therapeutic texts to describe this (Rogers, 1957). Livesey (2001) describes some of this when he recommends using empathy and validation rather than confrontation in the management of 'ruptures' to the alliance. He suggests that ruptures should be dealt with immediately, inviting the patient to express negative views and explore the problem. Livesey and other writers (e.g. Linehan, 1993) allow that therapist behaviour can also be 'therapy-interfering' and advocate that therapists should acknowledge any mistakes. This can be a powerful experience, which reduces defensiveness and encourages clients to reflect on their own behaviour.

Consistency in the therapeutic frame is also important with difficult clients. Most therapy texts recommend an explicit treatment contract specifying the goals and conditions of therapy (Linehan, 1993; Livesey, 2001; Ryle, 1997). To inform the contract, an open and honest discussion of boundaries and limitations (those of the therapist and those of the client) should take place, focusing on those issues that make clients difficult or which have led to therapeutic breakdown in the past. Discussion should include examining possible support for problems as well as the consequences of boundary or contract breaches. Once the contract is established, it should be adhered to and boundaries should remain firm to increase safe containment of the problematic behaviour. If breaches occur, the therapy should focus on those breaches. Linehan (1993) recommends a behavioural chain analysis to determine why the breaches occurred and to prevent recurrence. Whilst informative therapeutically, the analysis is likely also to be mildly aversive, avoiding any possibility of reinforcing problematic behaviour with attention. In addition to consistency in the treatment contract, stable treatment assumptions (the relative positions, the responsibilities and the approach to treatment) make the therapy less vulnerable to external pressures and promote predictability of response in the therapist. As previously stated, an empathic, supportive and validating approach is most successful.

Assessment of the problematic behaviour

Whilst the behavioural expression may be similar, Egan (2002) identifies reluctance and resistance as two major sources of difficulty. Reluctance refers to the client's misgivings about changing. Many are reluctant to discuss personal issues, especially as it is referring to a flawed aspect of themselves. Reluctance to engage may result from several issues, such as the fear of the process itself, trust issues, and the shame of self-disclosure. All patterns of behaviour are familiar and comfortable, however maladaptive, and any changes increase levels of discomfort and feelings of loss and helplessness.

Resistance is the reaction of clients who feel coerced, and can be either active or passive. This is perhaps particularly pertinent within forensic settings. There is a real and perceived imbalance of power and resistance is the client's way of fighting back (Driscoll, 1984). Those resisting therapy often feel abused and react by claiming no need for help, unwillingness to form a therapeutic alliance, and often sabotage the therapeutic process. Clients do not fit neatly into one or the other category and are likely to present with a combination of reluctance and resistance. For interventions to be effective, therapists need to find ways to help the client deal with reluctance and resistance.

For those who are reluctant, therapists need to support the client and contain their fears, offering patience, empathy, encouragement and challenge as required. A systematic approach will help with this. In dealing with resistance, therapists can experience many emotions, such as confusion, panic, irritation and rejection, resulting in unhelpful responses. Therapists need to recognize resistance as normal and accept and work with it. Clients' responses should not be taken personally, but at the same time therapists should recognize their own limits. In particular, care should be taken not to reinforce reluctance and resistance.

Within a therapeutic framework, the best way to work with these behaviours is to assume that they are maladaptive coping strategies. Before any change can take place, and the therapy progress, the therapist must be able to identify in behavioural terms the nature of the problematic behaviour. Whilst this might seem obvious, loose terminology such as 'manipulation' or 'aggression' is unhelpful. The therapist must be able to state precisely what it is that the client does that interferes with therapy, and if possible describe the frequency, duration, intensity and topography of the behaviour. In order to set change targets, the therapist then requires a comprehensive understanding of the pattern and function of the behaviour. What is maintaining the behaviour, where does it originate and what purpose does it serve for the client? Descriptions of behavioural chain analyses, functional analyses and formulations and similar methods can be found in the literature (O'Leary & Wilson, 1975; Bellack & Hersen, 1988; Linehan, 1993, Ryle, 1997). If possible, this process should be undertaken collaboratively with the client. Once the pattern and function of the behaviour has been established, it should be targeted for change using standard treatment techniques. Treatment should aim to significantly reduce the intensity and frequency of the difficult behaviour before progressing to previously identified treatment targets.

Removal of blocks to therapy

For many clients, motivational techniques or commitment strategies may be required to persuade them to enter therapy, to reduce the likelihood of drop-out and to change their difficult behaviours (Miller & Rollnick, 1991; Linehan, 1993; Egan, 2002). Lawrence Jones in this text provides a comprehensive account of assessment of motivation that should inform interventions. Ultimately the therapist should be aiming to promote self-efficacy. In order to help the client's initial commitment to therapy, targets for change should be cost-effective and appealing from the client's perspective. In negotiating therapy, the client should own the targets, and may require help with competing agendas. As therapy progresses, therapists should encourage and provide constructive feedback, model appropriate behaviour and reward success, and contain client fears.

For clients presenting complex and difficult behaviours, standard treatment packages are not likely to be effective at least in the initial stages. Individual case formulation – the design of treatment to fit specific individual needs – is recommended. Walsh and Murray (1998) found individual case management reduces violent and self-destructive behaviour in clients. However, there are some comprehensive packages, such as Dialectical Behaviour Therapy, which have been designed for use with certain types of difficult behaviour. Various adaptations have been made to the programme to treat clients in differing settings, including male high-secure forensic patients (Evershed et al., in review).

Notwithstanding the competing demands on therapy time and resources, for many clients with longstanding complex difficulties progress is likely to be slow, and targets should reflect this. To reduce client feelings of being overwhelmed and rejected, complex behaviours can be broken down into more manageable steps, but these steps should be reviewed regularly and renegotiated as appropriate. Later steps are often not clear in the early stages. In order to keep both therapist and client motivated, therapists need to expect, notice and acknowledge small improvements in behaviour (Hawton & Kirk, 1989), even if the overall behaviour is still inappropriate.

Many writers stress the importance of staying with the client throughout what is likely to be a long process (Linehan, 1993; Young, 1994; Benjamin, 1997). A realistic appraisal of the goals of therapy, and the likely time to completion should be undertaken at the outset. For entrenched behaviours, therapy is likely to last years (Linehan, 1993). However committed the therapist is to seeing the therapy to its conclusion, there will always be situations when this is not possible. Nevertheless, therapists should not offer their services unless they are sure that they can devote the time and energy to the client. Since working with difficult clients can be both tiring and stressful the therapist should also be firm about the number of difficult clients on their caseload. Whilst this decision will depend upon the skill and experience of the therapist and the severity of the clients, a guide can be taken from Linehan (1993) who recommends no more than four parasuicidal clients at any one time.

Environmental Issues with Difficult Clients

There are important differences between treatment and management. Treatment is the process by which a client explores feelings, thoughts and behaviours in a way that will enable change, self-acceptance and increased self-responsibility. It is an interactive process in which a trusting therapeutic alliance is built. Management is a one-sided interaction which does not require an alliance and does not always lead to personal change, merely a conformity to rules (Maier & Fulton, 1998). However, when working with difficult clients, supportive management can enhance individual treatment approaches. Manipulation of the environment in terms of policies and procedures, setting and staffing can exert a significant influence on client behaviour.

For example, Maier and Fulton (1998) suggest that a 'media treatment plan' in place prior to admission aids the management of clients who are the focus of media attention. Most forensic facilities have personnel available and policies in place to deal with the media. It is essential they are involved from the outset and can then work proactively with the media rather than reactively. Full briefing and preparation of staff when a difficult client is due to be accepted can help to identify fears or concerns, minimize any countertransference issues and can help to promote a consistent approach. (Ethical issues, such as confidentiality, prevent similar preparation processes with client peers.)

Clear policies and procedures and the communication of these to client and staff groups increases the consistency and reliability of client management, promoting clear boundaries for behaviour. This increases predictability, which reduces difficult behaviour. Loucks (1996) found that explaining proposed restrictions to individual liberty to prisoners before changes were introduced reduced the risk of unrest in a volatile situation. The milieu or management of establishments in which clients live also has a profound effect on violent incidents. A lax milieu and poor management with impaired structures, confused boundaries and poor leadership has also been shown to lead to an increase in such occurrences (Davies, 1983; McCorkle, Miethe & Drass, 1995; Flannery et al., 1996).

Controlling the mix of clients within an establishment and dispersing difficult clients can also help to reduce difficult behaviour. There is some research to show that aggressive and violent incidents can be reduced by the reduction in patient density or overcrowding, and better use of available space including more use of external activities (Davies, 1983; Brooks et al., 1994; Lanza et al., 1994). In addition Owen et al. (1998) demonstrated that the relative risk of violence increased as the number of violent or compulsorily contained clients rose, but decreased with the number of clients with substance abuse issues. This approach requires a high standard of pre-admission assessments, which include information on risk and protective factors.

Evidence from the Prison Service Special Units links a number of regime qualities to the reduction of difficult and disruptive behaviours: non-confrontational and non-punitive milieu; constructive occupation and a structured regime; consistency and fairness; key worker/personal officer approaches (Evershed, 1989; Bell, 1991; Evershed & Fry, 1992).

Several issues are raised when working with a forensic client group. For reasons described earlier, forensic clients do not always tell the truth about their behaviour or intentions, and their explanations of their behaviour can involve persistent denial and minimization. Even experienced psychologists can feel conned or manipulated by their clients, sometimes resulting in feelings of inadequacy or resentment. Staff first have to deal with their own views and emotions about the crime the client has committed. Clients can be viewed with either fear or anger, or seen as victims of their circumstances. (Gutheil, 1984). Staff must also adapt to what Maier and Fulton (1998) refer to as a 'mistrusting paradigm'. If they are unable to do this then it may result in their questioning their own professional identity.

Solutions for dealing with clients' chronically difficult behaviour require that staff recognize and understand their own emotional reactions and responses to the clients (countertransference). Whilst psychologists are trained to deal with offenders in a non-judgemental, objective and goal-directed way, those displaying difficult behaviours can test one's professional resolve and even lead to experienced practitioners reacting emotionally in the same way as untrained individuals. Generally, these clients tend to engender negative feelings of fear, frustration, anger and hopelessness (Winnicott, 1949). These feelings are understandable and real, given the behaviour of the client, but often staff lack awareness or consciously deny their existence. The subcultures within many forensic institutions serve to inhibit the healthy expression of such negative reactions. Those subcultures, which have an interest in promoting the staff as caring individuals, are wary of the expression of negative emotions because it appears contrary to their ideals. Other subcultures favouring a 'tough' containment approach fear the expression of emotion since it makes staff appear emotionally vulnerable.

The characteristics of this client group often result in their being perceived in a negative way, but it is not necessary to like a client in order to work with them. However, to be effective, therapists must be aware of their own feelings and prevent countertransference from interfering with the therapeutic process. Alternatively, clinicians can become frustrated with the criminal justice system generally, and then there is a real possibility that these views may become part of the clinician's countertransference issues either in relation to the system or the client.

Supervision is frequently used to work through these issues. More commonly used in health/clinical settings, it allows safe practice and facilitates practitioner development. (This is not the case in all forensic settings where often the dynamics of therapy are not addressed and supervision is regarded as a process whereby standardized and consistent practice is maintained). Faugier (1996) suggests that supervision (within nursing) is regarded as a continuum. At one end there is the personal psychotherapeutic process and at the other an appraisal system. When working with difficult clients, it is essential that there is a balance struck of the two extremes, encompassing personal growth and support and professional development (Tennant, Davies & Tennant, 2000)

If these feelings are not expressed and worked through supportively, they can influence every decision made concerning the client (Hansen & Berman, 1991) and can contribute to a spiral of increasingly difficult behaviour. At the very least they only promote 'here and now' solutions which may be successful in keeping people safe but which may strengthen underlying maladaptive behavioural patterns. The only way to move this negative cycle to a positive problem-solving process is by the introduction of regular and frequent meetings where all staff can discuss their difficulties and ventilate their feelings in a climate of trust and sensitivity. They can analyse their own part in contributing to the negative cycle of behaviour and explore and experiment with alternative interventions. Many of these interactions require an 'interactive shift' (Caldwell, 1994): the replacement of habitual practices with new and sometimes counter-intuitive treatment methods. This shift should be supported by high-level training in interpersonal/interactional skills.

Staff training, particularly training in interpersonal skills, can affect the frequency of difficult behaviour on two levels. Firstly, staff can serve as models in dealing with difficult situations and this promotes vicarious learning. Secondly, staff avoid escalating the violence. Corrigan et al. (1995) found that, after interpersonal skills training for staff, aggressive incidents decreased and staff were more likely to make further use of intervention programmes. Training in violence management (control and restraint procedures) also has a positive effect on the frequency and seriousness of violent behaviour and on promoting less restrictive regimes. Increases in staff confidence regarding dealing with violent episodes and a reduction in overreactions prior to or during an incident result from training. In addition there are fewer staff and client injuries, which reduces fear (Home Office, 1984; Gritter et al., 1995). However, violence-management training is varied across forensic establishments. Dowson, Butler and Williams (1999) found that there was poor documentation of violent incidents and deficiencies in training of violence management in ten English National Health Service trusts.

Programmes to reduce stress in staff, particularly those addressing psychological consequences of clients' assaults, have also led to declines in assault rates (Flannery et al., 1998). Risk-assessment training and the provision of opportunities for staff to communicate their assessments (both formal and informal) and observations have also been helpful in managing difficult behaviour. Doren, Miller and Maier (1993) found that systems to predict and forecast potentially dangerous events reduced overreactions in staff and increased effective management of dangerous events.

Staff-support mechanisms and frequent meetings to strengthen the team and prevent splitting and promote consistency of responding were central to the success of the Parkhurst Special Unit in reducing difficult and disruptive behaviour (Evershed, 1989, 1991; Bell, 1991, 1992). Indeed, prison staff themselves have cited the need for better communication and handover when managing clients with difficult behaviours (Loucks, 1996).

As forensic psychologists, we are judged on our success or failure with difficult clients, and change is often slow. Also, people are sometimes reluctant to perceive or accept positive change when it occurs because of the emotional reactions described earlier.

As this chapter demonstrates, there are effective approaches in dealing with the majority of difficult clients. However, there may be a small subgroup that remains impervious to all interventions offered. The skill of the psychologist lies in knowing when to withdraw from the therapeutic process. If we can be sure we have exhausted all avenues for helping the client manage their problems more effectively, then we must accept the client's right to choose not to change. At this point the psychologist's role may shift to helping to ameliorate the negative sequelae of the difficult behaviour and its impact on others. However, whilst some clients appear to be beyond help at this current time, the psychologist should review the situation at regular intervals. There may be a point when either the client wishes to re-engage or the therapist can provide a more effective approach to help the client move on.

Chapter Six

Intellectual Disabilities and Crime: Issues in Assessment, Intervention and Management

William R. Lindsay, Jacqueline Law
and Fiona MacLeod

The link between social policy, crime and intellectual disability goes back to the beginning of the twentieth century. It has to be said that the link has not always been benign, with both academics and social policy advisors interpreting theoretical and empirical research in a way that would prove restrictive and divisive for people with intellectual disabilities. The 1913 Mental Deficiency Act was developed against the framework of Darwinism and eugenics and drew on eight volumes of evidence collected by a Royal Commission from 1904 to 1908 in the UK and USA. The details of the research and subsequent legislation are described in Walker and McCabe (1973) but for the purposes of the present chapter, the important issue is that the link was firmly established between crime and intellectual disability. Unfortunately, the philosophical and scientific backdrop of Darwinism and the eugenics movement was influential. Craft and Craft (1983, p. 11) quote an example of these views in the writings of Terman (1916): 'There is no investigator who denies the fearful role of mental deficiency in the production of vice, crime and delinquency . . . not all criminals are feeble minded but all feeble minded are at least potential criminals'.

Political and research interest in the link between learning disability and crime has been maintained since this time. By far the most important recent development has been that of deinstitutionalization. Until the mid-1980s, many individuals who committed even relatively minor crimes were diverted to institutions, often for relatively long periods of time, for reasons of their intellectual deficit. This resulted in much of the research on crime and learning disability being conducted by psychiatrists and social policy researchers who had an interest in the practice and process of social and legal policies at the time. With the development of community care, many institutions have simply closed or been massively reduced in size and there are no longer the beds available to cater for large numbers of individuals who have committed crimes and who can be diverted for reasons of their learning disability. Over the last twenty years, psychologists have become increasingly involved with the assessment, treatment and management of offenders with intellectual disability both in the remaining institutions and in the community. The research base has grown correspondingly, with important developments in assessment, treatment, understanding of the process of the criminal justice system and determining prevalence.

Prevalence of People with Intellectual Disabilities in the Criminal Population

While there are a number of studies investigating the incidence of people with intellectual disability who commit crimes, the methodologies are so disparate that it is difficult to draw firm conclusions on prevalence. Three major variables will influence such studies. Firstly (and perhaps most importantly, since this chapter deals with intellectual disabilities), is the issue of inclusion criteria for the study sample. It is tautological, but nevertheless important, to remember that intellectual disability brings with it an increasing difficulty in understanding abstract concepts such as laws, societal rules and taboos. Therefore if one does not have the intellectual capacity to understand that (say) aggression towards others is not only an offence but is also against the mores of society, then if one acts in such a manner it cannot be an offence. However, it is difficult to determine the extent to which studies have included or excluded individuals who have IQs of less than 55 and would therefore fall in the ranges of moderate or severe learning disability. For example, in a survey of US prisons, Brown and Courtless (1971) found that around 1.6 per cent may have had an IQ of less than 55. Astonishingly, a tiny proportion of these individuals may have had an IQ of less than 25. Some studies would not include these individuals on the grounds already stated. At the other end of the range of intellectual disabilities, studies will explicitly include or exclude individuals in the range of borderline intelligence; this may also affect incidence (Noble & Conley, 1992).

A second major variable is the source of the sample. Incidence studies have been conducted in special hospitals, prisons, referrals to court, police stations and amongst social and health service referrals. These are very different populations and this will affect the figures derived. The third methodological variable is the method of determination of intellectual disability. Studies have employed a variety of methods including IQ tests, diagnosis of intellectual disability, scrutiny of prison records and educational history. In a study of offenders in Florida Spruill and May, (1988) noted that around 4 per cent of prisoners were identified as intellectually disabled. They then retested a sample of these individuals using the WAIS-R and found that slightly over 1 per cent had an IQ of less than 70. Murphy, Harnett and Holland (1995) found that no one in a sample of prisoners had an IQ less than 70. However, analysis of their data indicates that around 21 per cent had had some special schooling and therefore a perusal of their educational records may have provided the latter statistic.

In a study of approximately 57,000 individuals assessed for the courts in New York, Messinger and Apfelberg (1961) have found that about 2.5 per cent had an intellectual disability. On the other hand, Walker and McCabe (1973), in a study of individuals in special hospitals, found that 35 per cent were diagnosed as having an intellectual disability. Clearly, there is little relationship between these two populations although they both come under the rubric of forensic studies in intellectual disabilities. MacEachron (1974) reviewed the literature on prevalence rates for offenders with intellectual disabilities and found a range from 2.6 per cent to 39.6 per cent. In her own, more carefully controlled study, employing recognized intelligence tests, she studied 436 adult male offenders in Maine and Massachusetts State Penal Institutions. She found prevalence rates of intellectual disability of 0.6 per cent to 2.3. per cent. Hayes (1991), using intelligence tests and assessments of social and adaptive skills, reported that around 13 per cent of offenders in New South Wales prisons had an intellectual disability. In a similarly comprehensive study, Bucke and Brown (1997) reviewed 3,950 detainees across thirteen police stations in the UK and reviewed 12,500 custody records. They concluded that around 2 per cent of detainees were initially treated as mentally disordered or handicapped.

The importance of contextual factors is highlighted in work by Lyall, Holland and Collins (1995a, 1995b), who studied adults with intellectual disabilities who had been arrested. They derived their samples from two sources – people arrested and screened by the police and found to have been in a special school for children with mild or severe learning disabilities and, secondly, those adults living in residential placements for adults with learning disabilities who had been interviewed by police because of alleged offences. They noted that none of the latter sample appeared in court despite the seriousness of the offences. None of the sample received a prison sentence and none were diverted to the Health Services. They concluded that the tolerance levels of the relevant systems were extremely high and there was a lack of established links between the criminal justice agencies and other services.

Reviewing the various methodological issues involved and the range of studies, it would appear that two broad conclusions can be reached. Firstly, it would appear that there are several psychological variables that are relevant to the study of incidence of offending in people with intellectual disabilities. Secondly, as Holland (1991) concluded in an earlier review, 'There is little evidence to support any link between the presence of intellectual impairment due to a developmental disorder and a predisposition to criminal behaviour' (p. 123).

A further variable, already mentioned, which influences both the incidence of criminality and the way in which psychologists will engage with this population is the effect of social and public policy. Deinstitutionalization has been a major policy initiative across the Western world. Lund (1990) identified significant differences in criminal activity reported in individuals with intellectual disabilities. There was a significant increase in offenders with mild intellectual disability receiving a first sentence in 1984 compared to 1973. Day (1993) felt that this may be an early result of the influence of 'care in the community' policies. Rockoff (1978) found a reduction in the percentage of individuals with intellectual disability in Iowa prisons from 13 per cent in 1965 to 2 per cent in 1972. Again this was attributed to a change in sentencing policy. Colleagues working with people with intellectual disabilities across the length of the UK have indicated to the first author that there has been a dramatic increase in the number of offenders referred. It could be argued that there is in progress a major shift in social policy and referral patterns which is resulting in an increase in the number of offenders with intellectual disability remaining in the community and being referred for psychological assessment and treatment.

Characteristics and Patterns of Offending

A number of clinical studies have reported the characteristics of offenders referred to the respective authors. For example, Caparulo (1991), Day (1993) and Langevin and Pope (1993) have mentioned behavioural disturbance at school, poor ability to form relationships, poor impulse control, a history of family psychopathology and, for sex offenders, a low specificity for age and sex. However, the reader must be careful with clinical samples, since the characteristics may simply reflect the nature of referral patterns in that area. It may be that several or all of these features would be found in an appropriate control group. Leong and Silva (1999) found a high frequency of substance abuse amongst arsonists falling into a group typified by cognitive pathology (active psychosis or low intellectual capacity). However, Hayes (1991) and Lindsay and Smith (1998) have reported low levels of drug abuse amongst their samples of sex offenders. These differences may simply reflect referral patterns.

One variable investigated more frequently is that of mental illness in the cohort of offenders with intellectual disability. In a report on sixty-four patients admitted to a treatment unit for severe challenging behaviour, the majority of whom were under a section of the Mental Health Act, Xenitidis et al. (1999) noted a variety of characteristics. Psychotic illness was recorded in 48.4 per cent, non-psychotic illness in 18.8 per cent, autism in 17.2 per cent and epilepsy in 25 per cent of the chart, totalling 82.8 per cent. Part of the reason for referral for these individuals may have been mental illness and therefore the sample may be considerably skewed. Nevertheless it does indicate the importance of considering mental illness in this client group.

Day (1994) reported that 32 per cent of a sample of sex offenders with intellectual disability had suffered psychiatric illness in adulthood while W.R. Lindsay et al. (2002), in a study of sixty-two sex offenders and abusers with intellectual disability, also reported that 32 per cent were found to have significant mental illness including psychotic disorders, bipolar disorder and major depression. In a comprehensive study of offenders in Denmark, Lund (1990) reported on 274 offenders with intellectual disability, most of whom were under care orders. This was a longitudinal study which was not confined to individuals admitted to hospital and Lund reported an astonishing 91.77 per cent of this cohort had a diagnosed mental illness of which 87.5 per cent was categorized as behaviour disorder. This gives rise to questions about the inclusion criteria for mental illness across various studies. The most obvious methodological issue would be whether or not challenging behaviour/behaviour disorder is included as a mental illness or is classified separately in these studies. In the Day (1994) study and the W.R. Lindsay et al. (2002) study behaviour disorders were classified separately. Some individuals might have mental illness and behavioural disorder and were therefore reported in the mental illness group. However, those with behaviour disorder, in the absence of major mental illness were classified separately. Notwithstanding these methodological issues, there is little doubt that mental illness is an important characteristic when considering this client group.

Sexual abuse in childhood has been associated with sexual offences in adulthood. Thompson and Brown (1997) noted a high incidence of sexual abuse amongst a sample of abusers. However, Langevin and Pope (1993) and Briggs and Hawkins (1996) note that not all sexual abusers will have themselves been abused and it is not the case that all individuals who have been sexually abused will become sexual abusers or offenders. W.R. Lindsay et al. (2001) compared forty-eight sex offenders and fity non-sexual offenders with intellectual disability and found a significantly higher rate of sexual abuse in the sex-offending cohort (38 per cent v. 12.7 per cent) and a significantly higher rate of physical abuse in the cohort of other offenders (14 per cent v. 36 per cent). This finding is consistent with the House of Representatives report (1996) which concluded that 'The experience of childhood sexual victimization is quite likely neither a necessary nor a sufficient cause of adult sexual offending' (p. 14).

Winter, Holland and Collins (1997) interviewed adults with self-reported learning disabilities, charged with offences or in custody and compared their characteristics to a relevant control group. They found that the offenders were more likely to have a history of losing contact with their father, forensic contact in one or more family members, past homelessness, illicit drug use, an excess of recent life events, behavioural problems at school and childhood contact with the Police or Probation Services. All subjects had a history of repeated offending. However, it is notable with reference to factors considered earlier in this chapter, that only two of the subjects in the study had a full scale IQ of below 70.

In relation to fire-raising, Bradford and Dimock (1986) found that around 10 per cent of fifty-seven adults and forty-five juvenile arsonists were considered to have a learning disability. Raesaenen et al. (1994), in a study of seventy-two arsonists, found that 11 per cent of the sample had an IQ falling in the range of intellectual disability. Rix (1994), in a study of 153 adult arsonists, also found a prevalence of intellectual disability in 11 per cent of the sample. Leong and Silva (1999), in a smaller sample of thirty-two, found a prevalence rate of approximately 15 per cent. These figures are considerably higher than one would expect on the basis of the prevalence of intellectual disability in the general population. On the other hand, Puri, Baxter and Cordess (1995), again with a smaller sample of thirty-six arsonists, found a prevalence of intellectual disability of only 3 per cent. Walker and McCabe (1973) found that amongst arson and sexual offenders in special hospitals, there were extremely high incidences of intellectual disability.

Some authors have considered that people with intellectual disability are over-represented amongst sex offenders (Walker & McCabe, 1973; Hayes, 1991; Day, 1993). However, because of the methodological issues already mentioned, studies which have found that up to 50 per cent of offenders with learning disability have committed sexual offences (Gross, 1985; Bodna, 1987) should be treated with some caution. In a well-controlled study of 950 sexual offenders, Blanchard et al. (1999) found that sex offenders with intellectual disability were more likely to offend against younger children and male children. Several authors (Walker & McCabe 1973; Day, 1993) have written that sex offenders with intellectual disability are less likely to commit offences involving serious bodily harm, violence or death.

Noble and Conley (1992) report high rates (up to 38 per cent) of serious crimes among offenders with intellectual disability in a range of US prison studies. However, they state that more general studies, reviewing subjects across a range of secure hospital and community settings, often report lower rates of violent crimes and higher rates of misdemeanours in this client group.

In relation to characteristics, it should be mentioned that, as would be expected, offenders with intellectual disability are predominantly male. Noble and Conley (1992) report that only 8 per cent to 12 per cent are female. Day (1993) notes that the majority of female offenders have been detained for sexual misdemeanours or minor property offences (theft and larceny). McKerracher, Street and Segal (1996) found that in a high-security hospital, the main reasons for referral were attempted suicide, self-wounding and aggression to property or people. Again, the reader should be cautious about the source of the sample in this study.

Allen et al. (2001) report on the characteristics and successful treatment of five women with intellectual disability who have been involved with the criminal justice system because of serious assaults on others. Two had been sexually abused and three physically abused in childhood or teenage years. However, these authors felt that even after dealing with issues of sexual and physical abuse, there were residual issues related to personal control of aggression. Employing anger-management techniques, they report successful treatment with very low rates of reoffending up to seven years after initial conviction. This particular report is unusual because it is one of the only ones which comments on female offenders and all participants were treated while maintaining independent community placements or were discharged to independent living in the community.

What is to be made of these varied and sometimes conflicting findings? Where reports of characteristics are based on clinical samples, with no appropriate control condition, one cannot draw firm conclusions. For example reports on incidence of drug abuse are directly contradictory with some studies showing a high incidence and others a low incidence. Mental illness would appear to be a significant characteristic in consideration of offenders with intellectual disability. However, it is unlikely to be the pervasive feature which one might assume from the findings of Lund (1990). Sexual abuse in childhood is often cited as a predisposing factor in the development of men who go on to sexually offend. W.R. Lindsay et al. (2001) certainly found sexual and physical abuse to be significantly associated with those who go on to commit sexual and non-sexual offences respectively; however, it remained a minority of the samples who had been abused.

Glaser and Deane (1999) compared two cohorts of sexual and non-sexual offenders with intellectual disability and found no difference between the groups on age, educational history, family disturbance in childhood/adolescence or a history of contact with the psychiatric services. Even here, however, the issue of an appropriate control group is important. We do not know the extent to which either or both of these groups would differ from a matched group of non-offenders with intellectual disability. They did find that fewer sex offenders had abused drugs or alcohol and fewer sex offenders had served prior prison sentences. Although the evidence is not uniform, people with intellectual disabilities would appear over-represented amongst fire setters and sex offenders. Interestingly, Glaser and Deane (1999) found no differences between their two cohorts on number of previous sexual offences and concluded that 'for some disabled offenders, sex crimes are part of a pattern of impulsive and poorly controlled behaviour consistent with general psycho-social disadvantage rather than with any inherent propensity for sexual deviation' (p. 349). Such a hypothesis may account for an increased prevalence of both sex offending and fire raising.

Assessment

In general, assessment falls into four broad categories: investigating the characteristics of offenders, assessing competence and ability to consent, assessing individuals for treatment and assessing risk. The first of these has already been outlined and the last has not yet been systematically investigated in relation to offenders with intellectual disability. There is, however, published work on assessing competence and some preliminary work on assessment for treatment.

The main issues investigated in relation to competency are those relevant to the criminal investigation and ability to stand trial. It is now recognized that people with intellectual disability may be disadvantaged by the criminal justice process because of lack of understanding of the gravity of the situation, lack of support and lack of appropriate representation from early stages in the process. Gudjonsson (1992) and Gudjonsson et al. (1993) conducted a series of studies showing that people with intellectual disabilities are more vulnerable to false confession during interrogative interview due to heightened propensity towards acquiescence and suggestibility. Gudjonsson and MacKeith (1994) presented a carefully analysed case study to illustrate the way in which these psychological processes caused an individual to confess falsely to a double murder. There has also been a body of evidence indicating that people with intellectual disability have difficulty in understanding even a simplified caution (Hayes, 1996) and (in the US) are less able to understand their Miranda rights (Everington & Fulero, 1999). However, some evidence would suggest that only a minority of defendants with intellectual disabilities have been provided with appropriate assessment and support (Petrella, 1992).

Baroff (1996) has made the useful distinction between knowing that the criminal act is wrong and holding full responsibility for its commission. Of his clients, he writes that 'most of my clients know what they have done is wrong, however that does not mean that they should all be held fully responsible for their actions, rather we should consider issues of diminished or partial responsibility'. Here he seems to be saying that as professionals we are not making excuses for offenders with intellectual disability. They are not children who do not know right from wrong and most will recognize the illegality or 'wrongness' of their actions. However, the intellectual disability itself may lead to alternative considerations in what would be a proportionate response or outcome when it comes to trials, sentencing and management of those offenders with intellectual disability.

Clare (1993) and Seghorn and Ball (2000) have outlined some of the areas requiring assessment in relation to sexual offenders. Deviant sexual development and assessment of sexual knowledge may be especially relevant to these types of offenders but some of the other areas could be considered applicable to all offenders with intellectual disability. Interpersonal and communication skills are important aspects, both in relation to the development and nature of the offence and in consideration of appropriate treatments to prevent future offending. Assessment of mood and self-awareness with a view to identifying triggers for and patterns of individual offending are also important. There have recently been several developments in the assessment of mood in people with intellectual disabilities which are particularly appropriate for the assessment of offenders (Kazdin, Matson & Senatore, 1983; Helsel & Matson, 1988; W.R. Lindsay et al. 1994). These authors recommend the implementation of a visual analogue representing increasing amounts of the emotion being investigated. It has been found that people with intellectual disabilities have difficulty in understanding internal states such as anxiety and depression. However, with the help of a diagrammatic representation of increasing amounts of emotion, respondents can report reasonably reliably on their thoughts and feelings. Various means have been used to represent internal states of tension and most seem reasonably effective (W. R. Lindsay, 1999). Buckets from empty to full, walls of increasing height, even the client's own hands from clasped closed together to wide apart have all been used to represent increasing amounts of anxiety, depression, embarrassment, anger and so on. Normally it is easier to split each scale into two sections. First asking the client if they experienced the emotion or not, thereby establishing the first aspect of the scale; if they say they do experience the emotion then the response choices are offered in the form of a visual representation. This then becomes the medium through which the extent to which they experience the emotion can be ascertained.

Seghorn and Ball mention anger-management problems and there is no doubt that anger features significantly in offenders with intellectual disability. Law, Lindsay and Smith (1999) reported that up to 60 per cent of individuals referred for non-sexual offences were assessed as having problems with anger. Clare (1993) mentions that it is important to assess the extent to which the individuals understand the laws and conventions of society. This is particularly appropriate considering the intellectual disabilities and educational deficits of the individuals involved.

Case Examples

Ms D

Ms D was referred to the first author following an incident whereby she was charged with attempted murder. She had been staying with a number of friends and one evening had committed a serious assault with a knife on one of the males. He was taken to hospital with serious injuries and she was taken into custody and charged. Ms D's performance on the WAIS-III UK revealed an IQ of 70. She lived with her parents but had spent time living in flats on her own. She had held occupational placements through college in catering establishments and nursing homes with no apparent difficulty. She could use all public services and went out regularly with her friends on Friday and Saturday evenings. She was able to look after herself in terms of shopping, cooking, looking after her own flat and/or room and using public transport. There were no apparent deficits in adaptive behaviour. Therefore, it would appear that Ms D was functioning in the range of borderline intelligence just above the range of mild intellectual disability. Her knowledge of the legal system was assessed using the schedules developed by Everington and Luckasson (1992). These schedules cover several areas of understanding: aspects of court (a judge, a jury, prosecuting and defence counsel); understanding the legal system (being able to instruct your lawyer, understanding that you can disagree with witnesses if you feel they are not telling the truth); understanding sentencing (the meaning of probation, a prison sentence, etc.); understanding the meaning of the various punishment options available to the court; and ability to understand the illegality and consequences of a variety of criminal acts including the individual's own. Ms D appeared quite knowledgeable in relation to the legal system. Therefore in terms of intellectual ability and knowledge of court, it was quite clear that Ms D should stand trial.

Given the nature of the allegations against Ms D, it was decided to complete the following procedures: take a developmental history; ascertain her current personal and social relationships; make an assessment of anger and aggression, impulsivity, anxiety and depression. Apart from one or two incidents, Ms D's developmental history was unremarkable. She attended normal school and appeared not to receive any learning support or attend special educational classes. Rather than suggesting that her educational attainments were consistent with her peers, it seemed that this finding indicated that she was an easy-to-manage pupil who did not bring herself to the attention of her teachers. Ms D mentioned one or two incidents of aggression with peers at school but little of significance. She mentioned an incident five years previously when she had been sexually assaulted by one of her brother's friends. She did not report the rape at the time and did not wish to report it currently, but it was certainly significant in her account of the offence. She said that she had been sleeping on the evening in question when the man came over and sat next to her. Her account of the actual offence was somewhat vague but she said that he touched her, she had a flashback of the rape incident and she gabbed the knife and stabbed him. Why she was sleeping with a knife on this occasion, she has never been able to say, despite excellent treatment progress over the last year. Her current relationships appeared limited. She spent a lot of time with her mother, with whom she said she had frequent and fairly fierce arguments.

A series of structured assessments for emotion were administered, beginning with an assessment of anger and aggression which is based on Novaco's Cognitive Analysis of Anger (Novaco, 1986, 1994). This assesses anger in relation to situations involving disappointment, embarrassment, frustration, jealousy, anger towards self and direct provocation. In general Ms D reported low levels of anger in relation to these situations but did report some feelings of anger in response to situations where she was embarrassed and extremely high levels of anger in relation to direct provocation. It was particularly pertinent that she could think of no other response apart from extreme anger to situations of direct provocation and, to a lesser extent, embarrassment. The Zung Self-rating Anxiety Scale, adapted by Lindsay and Michie (1988) and the Beck Anxiety Inventory and the Beck Depression Inventory, both appropriately modified by Lindsay and Lees (2002) were administered. Ms D did not report clinically high levels of anxiety or depression on these scales.

The report indicated that there may be some particular difficulties in relation to impulsivity and anger, especially in situations involving direct provocation. This combined in this particular instance with flashbacks from a previous episode of sexual abuse to result in the serious assault. The fact that Ms D was in possession of a knife at the time suggested that she was worried about an assault. However, she herself did not confirm this and, as has been mentioned, is still unable to explain why she possessed the knife at that time. Indeed, it would have been easy for her to use such a fear as mitigation. Interestingly, in this case the defence had employed another psychologist and the two reports were broadly consistent. In the first author's formulation, sexual abuse and impulsive aggression towards a source of provocation received equal weight; the other formulation emphasized the consequences of sexual abuse. Both agreed on capacity to plead and understand court proceedings. Psychological treatment has been extremely successful, focusing on aggression and issues of sexual abuse and the formulation has been adjusted in considering that issues of impulsivity and aggression are somewhat more salient than originally thought. One should, of course, be careful about post hoc clinical impressions; it may be that had treatment focused primarily on aspects of sexual abuse, then the response to treatment and resulting impressions would have strengthened the formulation emphasizing sexual abuse.

Mr D

Mr D was referred following incidents of indecent exposure and was altogether a more difficult case in terms of capacity and ability to understand court proceedings. He had been brought up in England with his father and for the past twenty years had moved from town to town on his own, staying for three to four years and then moving on. He had lived locally for four years in his own flat. He said that when he moved to a new place he always rented a flat either from a private landlord or the council, preferring his independence to staying in hostels. Therefore he had lived completely independently for around fifteen years. He shopped for himself, he used public transport, looked after his own flat, cooked for himself, kept abreast of current affairs and had a range of social contacts. He kept up to date with current affairs and sports by watching television, reading the headlines from newspapers and reading all the football results. He attended adult education classes and had rudimentary reading skills and could read numbers up to ten. Mr D's performance on the WAIS-III UK revealed an IQ of 59, which places him towards the lower end of the range of mild intellectual disability.

As has been said, he had lived independently for fifteen years and compensated for any adaptive behaviour deficits to the extent that no significant deficits were apparent. When assessed on knowledge of legal proceedings, he had a broad and adequate knowledge of the various tenets and issues. In correspondence with the Procurator Fiscal Service in Scotland (the equivalent of the Crown Prosecution Service in England) it had been suggested that the defendant should have a broad understanding of the requirements of the legal service. It is not necessary that he or she have a detailed knowledge of each aspect of the court and legal system. Many of us would find it difficult to understand the procedures of a complex appeal but that does not mean that such an appeal would be denied.

Pertinent to this are the findings of Everington and Luckasson (1992), who compared three groups of individuals with intellectual disability on understanding proceedings of court. They compared twenty-four individuals for whom court proceedings had been conducted and for whom competency assessment had not been indicated, twelve individuals who had been referred for competency assessment and who had been considered competent and eleven individuals who had been referred for competency assessment and had been considered not competent. They found that the latter two groups with an average IQ of 59 and 58 respectively showed a very different level of understanding of legal proceedings. Group 2 (with an average IQ of 59) showed an understanding consistent with those in Group 1 who had an average IQ of 67, while Group 3 had a significantly poorer level of understanding despite having an average IQ consistent with Group 2. Therefore, there was a dichotomy in individuals with an IQ around that shown by Mr D (IQ 58–9), with some showing a high level of understanding of court proceedings while others showed a poor level of understanding. Mr D had no apparent significant deficits in adaptive behaviour, had lived independently for fifteen years and seemed to have an adequate understanding of the proceedings of court. There seemed little reason to divert the case in this instance.

Developmental history revealed Mr D had had frequent exclusions from school as a result of anger and aggression with both teachers and peers. Assessment using the anger inventory (already described) indicated that Mr D reported high levels of anger in situations involving embarrassment, frustration and direct provocation. Indeed, he said that he frequently got into fights and aggressive situations in public houses, although these had never been prosecuted. He seemed highly impulsive, in relation to his response on the anger inventory, saying that if somebody looked at him in a strange way in a pub, he would become verbally aggressive and then physically aggressive. His responses on the anger and depression inventories did not indicate clinically significant levels of anxiety or depression. Mr D was assessed on the questionnaire on attitudes consistent with sexual offending (Lindsay, Carson & Whitefield, 2000). This instrument is currently being developed to assess attitudes in sex offenders with intellectual disability in relation to rape, voyeurism, exhibitionism, dating abuse, homosexual assault, offences against children and stalking. There are now some preliminary data relevant to a range of reference groups and Mr D showed a high level of attitudes in relation to offending in the areas of rape, voyeurism, exhibitionism, dating abuse and stalking. These various findings were reported to the court and Mr D was given a suspended sentence which eventually lasted for two years as a result of supplementary reports. Therefore treatment lasted two years (as will be explained, there may be limited value in treatment of less than one year for this client group) and focused on both aggression and sex offending.

In this instance anger-management training was more immediately success-ful than treatment directed at sex offending behaviour and attitudes. Since sen-tencing, Mr D has continued to live independently in his own flat. After three months, he reported one further incident of aggression in a public house, but following that there have been no further incidents at three years follow-up. This information validates the regularly completed anger inventories over the nine months of treatment. Over the first year after conviction, there were a number of reports of inappropriate sexual behaviour on the part of Mr D to both women and teenage girls. One of these incidents involved following a fourteen-year-old and was reported to the police. Mr D was apprehended and charged, although the case was not prosecuted. This was not because Mr D was cur-rently receiving treatment; it seemed simply that the police did not consider that they had a sufficiently robust case. After one year of treatment, Mr D's attitudes and behaviour began to change and there have been no further inci-dents at three years follow-up assessment. This information again validates his responses on the questionnaire on attitudes consistent with sex offending and is also consistent with reports of progress published elsewhere (W.R. Lindsay et al., 1998a, 1999).

Clare and Murphy (1998) have emphasized the importance of assessment and identify a number of key issues which should be addressed and clarified. These include the reasons for referral, the available interventions, any ethical issues, the outcome of action taken following the offence, confidentiality and the role of relevant professionals in relation to treatment.

While these examples demonstrate some procedures which have been out-lined by various authors, it has to be said that there are, as yet, few available instruments with robust psychometric properties. Some of the problems are rel-evant to the intellectual disability itself. Many existing instruments are too lin-guistically complicated to ensure that the offender with intellectual disabilities has understood the requirements and items of the test. Therefore it is necessary either to develop new forms of assessment or alter existing assessment proce-dures so that they are appropriate. Either way, the psychometric properties of the schedule will have to be re-established. However, with the extension of cog-nitive therapeutic methods to populations with intellectual disability, it is now fairly well established that people with mild intellectual disabilities can respond to verbally presented questionnaires with some degree of reliability and validity (Kroese, Dagnan and Loumidis 1997; W. R. Lindsay 1999). Recently, cogni-tive distortions have been considered important variables for assessment in re-lation to both the perpetration of the offence and treatment. This is especially true in the areas of sexual offending, assault and arson, where it is felt that cog-nitive misconceptions may prompt the individual to commit offences and alteration of these misconceptions through cognitive restructuring may be a crucial aspect of treatment. Rose and West (1999) found that self-reports of anger and aggression were loosely but nevertheless significantly related to frequency of angry outbursts and assault. Taylor et al. (2002) reported a study of 127 intellectually disabled men with offending histories relating to anger and aggression. Using the Novaco Anger Inventory, they noted that clinically significant levels of assessed anger were associated with a range of offences related to assault. Lindsay, Carson and Whitefield (2000) described the development of a series of questionnaires dealing with attitudes consistent with rape, voyeurism, exhibitionism, dating abuse, homosexual assault, offences against children and stalking. Preliminary results indicate that the questionnaires may prove reliable, internally consistent, valid and will discriminate between sexual offenders, other offenders and non-offenders. Therefore, in the area of cognitive distortions related to offending, there are some promising current developments.

Treatment

Traditionally the most common treatments for behaviour problems (including offending problems) in clients with intellectual disabilities were behavioural. Plaud et al. (2000) write that they remain the most comprehensive treatment approaches in the management of sexual offending. They note that the goal of a behavioural treatment programme is to advance behavioural competency in daily living skills, general interpersonal and educational skills and specialized behaviour skills related to sexuality and offending. Grubb-Blubaugh, Shire and Leebaulser (1994) have employed a behavioural management approach in a closed unit to promote appropriate socialized skills in a group of offenders and abusers. Two comprehensive treatment regimes for sex offenders have extensively employed behavioural methods. Haaven, Little and Petre-Miller (1990) described a wide-ranging series of treatments including sex education, behavioural control, training on social responsibility, social skills training and specific programmes aimed at controlling sexual deviancy. Griffiths, Quinsey and Hingsburger (1989) described a similarly comprehensive behavioural management regime for sex offenders. Interestingly, they report no reoffending in over thirty cases. Social and personal skills acquisition and sex education are emphasized in the group treatment described by Swanson and Garwick (1990). They reported on fifteen individuals with a mean length of stay in the treatment group of fourteen months, and indicated that six (40 per cent) of the fifteen individuals treated had reoffended.

More recently, several authors have employed cognitive methods for the treatment of a range of offenders with intellectual disabilities. Black, Cullen and Novaco (1997), Rose (1996), Lawrenson and Lindsay (1998) have all employed anger-management training to treat individuals who have had assault-related offences. This is an essentially cognitive approach developed by Novaco (1986, 1994) which helps the individual understand the way in which they may misconstrue situations as threatening, helps them to develop realistic appraisals of anger-provoking situations and helps them to reduce arousal and control unreasonable aggression. In a controlled study, Rose, West and Clifford (2000) found anger management approaches to be successful when compared to a no-treatment control. The effects were also evident at nine months follow-up.

Clare et al. (1992) used a cognitive treatment successfully in a single case of an arsonist. However, in general, there are fewer reports of treatment of fire setters. Leong and Silva (1999, p. 532) note that 'For . . . mentally retarded individuals . . . there are generally inadequate resources to treat these individuals both while under the aegis of the criminal justice system if imprisoned and in the community when released from the jurisdiction of the criminal justice system'. They note that individuals who are both psychotic and intellectually disabled are amongst the most challenging to work with.

Cognitive treatments have also been employed with sexual offenders. O'Conner (1996) developed a problem-solving intervention for thirteen adult make sex offenders. She reports positive results from the intervention with most subjects achieving increased community access. W.R. Lindsay et al. (1998a, 1998b, 1998c, 1999) report a series of case studies on offenders against children, exhibitionists, stalkers and adolescent sexual offenders using a cognitive intervention in which various forms of denial and mitigation of the offence are challenged over treatment periods of up to three years. Consistently, across the studies they report changes in cognitions during treatment and low reoffending rates at least four years following initial conviction. Therefore there are some promising developments in treatment approaches in the area of cognitive and problem-solving therapies.

Brier (1994) reports on a controlled treatment trial for a comprehensive psychosocial intervention for older teenagers who had committed a range of offences. All of the individuals were considered to have a learning disability but it should be noted that the US definition of learning disability differs somewhat from the UK definition. Subjects had an average IQ of around 80. The goals of the intervention included increased problem solving, social, and moral reasoning skills, and the facilitation of vocational interests and job search techniques. The study period lasted twenty-four months; seventy-three subjects completed the project, eighty-five did not complete the project and a group of thirty-four constituted a matched, untreated control group. Based on official crime statistics, subjects who completed the project were found to have a significantly lower recidivism rate (12 per cent) compared to the non-completers (40 per cent) and to control subjects (38 per cent). The follow-up period lasted an average of twenty months.

Comprehensive inpatient treatments have also been developed to cater for the needs of people with intellectual disabilities who have severe challenging and offending behaviour. In reports of the MIETS Unit, Murphy and Clare (1991) Murphy et al., (1991) have described treatments for individuals with mental illness, assaultive behaviour, fire-setting tendencies and sexually abhorrent behaviour with a series of successful case descriptions. Xenitidis et al. (1999) reported on sixty-four patients admitted to the MIETS Unit. While 17.5 per cent had been admitted from community facilities, 84.2 per cent were discharged back to the community placements. There was also a significant reduction in the frequency and severity of challenging and abusing behaviours.

Outcome

Since there are few controlled studies in this area, it is important to consider studies which have simply reported reoffending rates in offenders with intellectual disabilities. Scorzelli and Reinke-Scorzelli (1979) reported reoffending rates of 68 per cent in their sample, while Klimecki, Jenkinson and Wilson (1994) found a reoffending rate of 41.3 per cent in previous prison inmates, two years after their release. In a study of ninety-one intellectually disabled patients on statutory care orders, Lund (1990) reported a reoffending rate of 72 per cent over ten years and Gibbens and Robertson (1983), in a study of 250 male patients with intellectual disability all on hospital orders, reported a reconviction rate of 68 per cent. Therefore there would seem no obvious difference in reoffending rates between studies of untreated offenders who have simply received a prison sentence and those of offenders who have been treated in hospital. It is, of course, difficult to compare studies, since subject samples may differ considerably.

Some outcome studies have already been mentioned, with Brier (1994), Xenitidis et al. (1999) and Griffiths et al. (1989) reporting excellent outcomes after treatment and at follow-up up to two years. However, it has to be acknowledged that outcome data are sparse and lacking adequate control groups.

One interesting finding in relation to outcome and length of treatment has been reported by a number of authors. Day (1988) found a positive correlation between length of stay over two years and better outcome. Walker and McCabe (1973) found that a shorter duration of institutional care was associated with a greater likelihood of reconviction or imprisonment. Lindsay and Smith (1998) found that sex offenders treated for less than one year showed significantly poorer progress and were more likely to be reconvicted than those treated for at least two years. Therefore it would seem that shorter periods of treatment may be of limited value for this client group.

Future Directions

Clearly, from the gaps noted in this chapter, although a number of studies have begun to look at issues relating to offenders with intellectual disability, there is much to be done in almost every area mentioned. There has been some initial work on incidence and descriptions of treatment approaches, especially for sex offenders and assault. Many of the papers cited have looked at the relationship between mental illness and offending.

Some of the initial, exploratory work has certainly been done and this gives us a clearer ideal of where clinical and research interest may usefully be targeted over the next decade. While there are a number of checklists and structured recording schedules for a variety of problems related to offending, there are few instruments, if any, which have robust psychometric properties and which are relevant to the population. This has important practical implications, since if someone has a high score on, for example, an arson inventory, we have little idea how this might relate to non-arsonists with and without intellectual disability. If they then move to a low score following treatment; again we have no reference to gauge the significance of the discrepancy. Development of a range of relevant assessments with known psychometric properties would seem to be a priority.

A series of case studies has indicated a range of promising therapeutic avenues, but case studies can be unreliable and even misleading. Some of the case studies have had long (four to seven years) and carefully conducted follow-ups. The control trials which have been conducted are promising but there is undoubtedly a requirement for a series of controlled trials across different problems related to offending. However, we have to recognize that there are practical difficulties associated with controlled treatment trials on people who offend when the treatments themselves are not established as therapeutically effective. Ethics Committees may be reluctant to sanction a no-treatment control for sex offenders (for example) since they may be uncomfortable in allowing a no-treatment condition for this high-risk group with the corresponding dangers of recidivism. Indeed, as psychologists, we may be uncomfortable in conducting such a trial and allowing an adequate follow-up period to compare reoffending rates. Therefore it may be that the best way forward is in comparison of alternative treatments or lengths of treatment time, as in the study of Lindsay and Smith (1998). Another possibility would be to employ the methodology of Rose, West and Clifford (2000), where they used the waiting list to form a control group. Brier (1994) collected information on treatment dropouts to make up a control group. Clearly, this does not attain the standard of a randomized controlled trial and is therefore deficient as an adequate control. However, it would meet the requirements of a substantive comparison better than the existing case studies.

Section Two

Working with Criminal Justice Personnel

Violent Police–Suspect Encounters: the Impact of Environmental Stressors on the Use of Lethal Force

Aldert Vrij and Jo Barton

Introduction

The legitimate use of force is a characteristic of police services worldwide. However, unlike many other countries, police officers within the United Kingdom remain predominantly unarmed. At present, approximately 5 per cent of the British police force are trained and authorized to carry firearms (so-called Authorized Firearms Officers [AFO]). In numbers, in 1998 a total of 6,411 officers in England and Wales out of a total of 126,814 police officers were licensed to carry firearms (Barton, 2000). These AFOs were involved in 11,005 operations in 1998, although only in seven of those operations were shots fired by police officers. Statistics from 1994 to 1997 revealed that the number of operations in which shots were fired varied from four (in 1997) to six (in 1994), whereas in those four years AFOs were involved in approximately 40,000 operations. In other words, although AFOs are frequently involved in operations, they rarely use their weapons. Although the frequency of shooting incidents in which AFOs are involved is rare, we should not underestimate its consequences. The use of excessive force may lead to the officer facing criminal charges, while the absence of a timely and accurate perception of, and response to, an armed confrontation may lead to psychological problems, physical injuries, or death of a member of the public, a colleague or themselves (Barton, 2000).

These potential negative consequences motivated us to conduct experimental research regarding police–suspect confrontations in the Netherlands and in the United Kingdom over the last decade. The theoretical underpinning and outcomes of these studies will be discussed in this chapter. Full descriptions of these studies are given elsewhere (Barton, 2000; Barton, Vrij & Bull, 1998, 2000a, 2000b; Vrij, 1996, 1998; Vrij & Morris, 1998; Vrij, van der Steen & Koppelaar, 1994, 1995a, 1995b).

American studies concerning shooting behaviour include laboratory-based studies aimed at examining officers' attitudes to the use of lethal force, and analyses of police agency statistics and national trend data from government records. These analyses of real-life statistics mainly focused on the frequency of lethal-force responses during confrontations with suspects (including the impact of officer and suspect characteristics on those statistics) and on marksmanship during those confrontations. See Barton (2000) and Barton, Vrij and Bull (2000b) for more details about this American research.

Decision Making to Use Lethal Force in Confrontations with Suspects: a Model

In confrontations with suspects three clusters of factors may influence police officers' decision making, namely (i) police officer characteristics; (ii) suspect characteristics; and (iii) environmental factors. Police officer characteristics include background characteristics such as age, gender and ethnic origin and personality aspects such as resistance to stress and field-independency. Our research (outlined below) focused on field-independency. Suspect characteristics include background characteristics (age, gender, ethnic origin), appearance (clothing) and demeanour. Our shooting behaviour research did not deal with suspect characteristics, although they are known to have an impact. For example, American research has shown that black people are more likely to be shot by police officers than white people (Barton, 2000), but it is not always clear why this is the case. Our own research, although not conducted in police officer–suspect confrontation settings, has revealed that black and white people tend to show different patterns of non-verbal behaviour, with certain patterns (such as making many movements, and having a narrower personal space) making an aggressive impression on white observers (Winkel, Koppelaar & Vrij, 1988; Vrij, 2000). Another suspect variable with a possible impact is colour of clothing. Research has shown that people who wear black clothes are seen as more aggressive than people who wear light-coloured clothes (Vrij, 1997).

Environmental factors are factors surrounding police officer–suspect confrontations, such as temperature at the scene of the crime, the presence of bystanders, the presence of noise, whether or not the police officer exerted physical effort before arriving at the scene of crime, whether or not the police officer drove at high speed to the scene of crime, and so on. The presence of environmental factors will often complicate police officers' decision-making processes, as they often result in increased physiological arousal (as will be discussed below). Because of this arousal-inducing aspect, we therefore will call them environmental stressors (Barton, 2000).

Figure 7.1 shows the relationship between environmental stressors and police officers' performance in potentially violent police–suspect encounters.

The theoretical model outlined in figure 7.1 attempts to integrate several social-psychological perspectives such as excitation transfer theory (Zillman, 1983), the cue-utilization hypothesis (Easterbrook, 1959) and social facilitation (Zajonc, 1965, 1980; Bond & Titus, 1983).

The presence of environmental stressors results often in increased arousal, especially if the task is difficult (Hockey, 1979; Loewen & Suedfield, 1992). The excitation transfer theory (Zillmann, 1983) states that individuals, being aware of this state of physiological arousal, try cognitively to explain this arousal. In principle, they can attribute this arousal to two different sources, to the environmental stressor (the environmental factors causes my arousal) or to the suspect (the suspect causes my arousal). In our studies we hypothesized that attributing the increased arousal to the environmental stressor or to the suspect will depend on the environmental stressor. Attribution of arousal to the environmental stressor is the most likely outcome when the police officer is fully

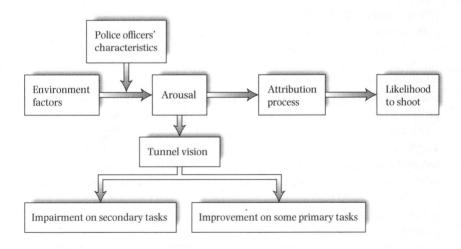

Figure 7.1   Distraction – performance relationship in police-suspect encounters

aware that the environmental stressor caused the increased arousal. This is likely to happen with environmental stressors that are clearly present before the confrontation takes place, such as the use of caffeine prior to the confrontation or the use of physical effort (for example, running) prior to the confrontation. Both the use of caffeine and the use of physical effort will result in increased arousal (increased heart rate, increased respiration and so on). Officers are likely to notice this arousal and will be aware that they are already aroused before the confrontation with the suspect takes place. It is therefore unlikely that they will attribute their arousal to the suspect. Disregarding the suspect as a source of arousal might result in an *underestimate* of the aggressive intentions of the suspect. It is therefore predicted that the presence of environmental stressors such as physical effort and the use of caffeine will make the suspect appear less aggressive, will lead to less aggressive feelings towards the suspect and will decrease the likelihood to shoot at the suspect.

Officers are likely to attribute the arousal that is actually caused by environmental stressors to the suspect if they do not fully realize that the environmental stressor caused the increased arousal. This is likely to be the case with environmental stressors such as high temperature at the scene of the crime, noise at the scene of the crime or high-speed driving before confronting a potentially dangerous suspect. Take as an example temperature. Temperature may increase police officers' arousal without the officer being fully aware that the temperature is the source of the arousal. Therefore officers may well attribute an increase in experienced arousal to the suspect rather than to the hot temperature. Disregarding the environmental stressor as a source of arousal may result in an *overestimation* of the aggressive intentions of the suspect.

It is therefore predicted that the presence of environmental stressors such as high temperature, noise and high-speed driving will make the suspect appear more aggressive, will lead to more aggressive feelings towards the suspect and will increase the likelihood to shoot at the suspect.

Attentional theories (Easterbrook, 1959; Broadbent, 1979) argue that arousal leads to a restriction in cognitive focus (tunnel vision) in which the individual attends more to cues that are most central to the task (or alternatively most central geographically in the display) at the expense of more peripheral cues. Tunnel vision therefore influences performance, as it impairs the performance on secondary tasks (tasks which are considered by the performer as not important), because someone will pay less attention to those tasks. According to Zajonc (1980) arousal will improve or impair the performance on primary tasks (tasks which are considered by the performer as important), dependent on the type of primary task. Arousal will improve the performance on well-trained tasks (such as shooting performance) but will impair the performance on tasks that are not well learned (such as taking cover). The reasons for this is that increased arousal will facilitate the 'dominant response', which is often the correct response in well-learned tasks but often an incorrect response in tasks which are not yet well learned.

A well-learned primary task is police officers' shooting performance. Most attention in police officers' shooting exercises is paid to shooting performance (so-called marksmanship training: Barton, 2000). It is also relatively easy to practise. An example of a primary task that is not well learned is taking cover. This is more difficult to practise as the decision to take cover and how to take cover depends on the circumstances during the confrontation with the offender. Not surprisingly, this so-called judgemental training occurs less frequently than marksmanship training in England and Wales (Barton, 2000).

This model predicts that environmental stressors lead to arousal. However, it could be hypothesized that personal characteristics determine the strength of this relationship. *Field-independent* people, for example, have the ability to understand complex situations very rapidly (Feij, 1976). They are also less rapidly distracted by features of a situation which are irrelevant (ibid). This implies that environmental stressors will cause less arousal in field-independent people, and as a result, their attribution processes (decision to shoot) and their performance on primary tasks and secondary tasks will be less affected by environmental stressors.

Empirical Support for the Environmental Stressor Performance Model

Experimental designs

Procedures

The experiments were conducted during regular shooting exercises. Police officers participated individually and their participation was voluntary. Table 7.1 gives some details about the eight studies that have been published to date. The experiments were carried out utilizing Fire Arms Training System (FATS, an American shooting simulator). The system uses video and laser disk plays to project scenarios on to a screen. The images are in full colour and are full size. The scenarios are as true to life as possible. The camera's point of view while the scenarios were videotaped was similar to the subjects' point of view. In other words 'the eyes of the camera are the eyes of the subjects'. As a result, what officers see and hear is what they would experience in reality. Participants in the experiments faced a scenario and were asked to act as they would act in reality. Their behaviour was videotaped and analysed afterwards. Following the experiment participants completed a questionnaire.

Table 7.1 Overview of the empirical studies

environmental stressor	n	country	% female	age	outcomes: the distraction group showed (compared to the control group):			
					arousal	irritation felt by officer	attribution for arousal to suspect	aggression towards suspect	tunnel vision
high-speed driving	58	UK	2	33	yes	more irritation	no significant result	less willing to shoot	not investigated
physical effort	40	Holland	12	29	yes	less irritation	less attribution to arousal to suspect	less willing to shoot	not investigated
physical effort	40	Holland	16	28	yes	less irritation	less attribution of arousal to suspect	less willing to shoot	not investigated
temperature	38	Holland	21	27	ni*	more irritation	more attribution to arousal to suspect	more willing to shoot	not investigated
voice in background	52	Holland	15	36	yes	not investigated	not investigated	more willing to take weapon	tunnel vision
caffeine	52	UK	20	29	ni*	not investigated	more attribution of arousal to suspect	more willing to shoot	not investigated
loud music	51	Holland	18	28	yes	more irritation	not investigated	no significant effect	tunnel vision
sound of a drill	49	Holland	11	33	yes	more irritation	not investigated	no significant effect	tunnel vision

* not investigated

Scenario

Different scenarios were used in different studies. The following scenario was shown to the subjects in a physical effort study (Vrij & Dingemans, 1996). The participant (the camera's point of view) and a female colleague are patrolling in a shopping centre. Suddenly, a waiter runs to them and asks them to come with him to a Chinese restaurant because a customer is causing trouble. Both police officers join the waiter and walk to the Chinese restaurant. When entering the restaurant they see the back of a man who is shouting to a waitress that she has to give him her money. The participant's colleague walks towards the man and calls, 'Hey, what are you doing?' The man turns around, kicks the colleague in her stomach (she runs away to the left, out of sight of the subject), takes his firearm and points it at the participant. The waitress runs away (behind the man), and the man shoots at the participant. The scenario lasted one minute, the period between taking his firearm and shooting at the participant lasted 3.5 seconds.

Independent Variables

Different independent variables were introduced in different experiments. In the high-speed driving study (Barton, Vrij & Bull, 2000a), police officers drove for fifteen minutes in a marked car to 'the incident' either at high speed (110 mph on the motorway) or at patrol speed (70 mph on the motorway). In the physical effort studies (Vrij & Dingemans, 1996), prior to the exposure to the scenario, participants either had to cycle quickly on an exercise bike for one minute or they had to walk for one minute. In the temperature study (Vrij, van der Steen & Koppelaar, 1994), the temperature in the room where the experiment took place was either 27 degrees Celsius or 21 degrees Celsius. In the voice in the background study (Vrij, van der Steen, Koppelaar & Vermaas, 1994), 'a colleague' (whom the officers could only hear) talked in the background or said nothing to someone who had just been shot down. In the caffeine study (Vrij & Morris, 1998), the participants either ingested three caffeine tablets (50 mg each) or ingested three tablets of vitamin C prior to the study. In the loud music study (Vrij, van de Steen & Koppelaar, 1995b) there was either loud music coming out of the pub (85 dBA) or no sound of music (the scenario took place in front of a pub). In the sound of a drill study (Vrij, van der Steen & Koppelaar, 1995b), the sound of a drill was either present (85dBA) or absent (the scenario took place in a car park).

Dependent Variables

Most variables were measured via a questionnaire, which was filled out after the scenario has finished. *Arousal* was mostly measured with items such as 'Did you feel nervous during the task?' Answers could be entered on seven-point scales, ranging from certainly not (1) to most certainly (7). The *irritation felt by the officer* was measured with items such as 'To what extent did you feel irritated by the suspect?', 'To what extent did you feel annoyed by the suspect?' and 'To what extent did you intend to shoot at the suspect?' Answers could be entered on seven-point scales, ranging from certainly not (1) to most certainly (7). *Attribution of arousal to the suspect* was measured with items such as 'To what extent did the suspect make an aggressive impression?', 'To what extent did the suspect make a dangerous impression?' and 'To what extent did the suspect make a nervous impression?' Answers could be entered on seven-point scales, ranging from certainly not (1) to most certainly (7). *Aggression towards the suspect* was measured within the questionnaire with one item 'To what extent were you willing to shoot the suspect?' (certainly not [1] to most certainly [7]), or alternatively, it was noted down whether or not the police officer did shoot the suspect. *Tunnel vision* was measured by asking participants to recall central details (such as details about the weapon used by the suspect or the physical appearance of the suspect) and peripheral details (for example details about bystanders).

Results

Do environmental stressors increase arousal?

The results clearly support the expected link between environmental stressors and arousal: the presence of environmental stressors leads to arousal. See also table 7.1 for an outline of the findings of each of the eight studies.

Do caffeine and physical effort make police officers less willing to shoot?

We found evidence of our predictions that caffeine and physical effort make police officers less willing to shoot. This may well lead to an underestimation of danger, as we found in one of our physical effort studies. In this study, officers were confronted with a suspect in a Chinese restaurant who pointed a gun at them and eventually shot at them (scenario has been described above in detail). The appropriate action for the police officer in this scenario would be to shoot at the suspect (before he shoots at them). All police officers in the no physical effort condition actually shot the suspect, whereas only 80 per cent of the officers in the physical effort condition shot the suspect.

Do high temperature, street noise, and high speed driving result in excessive use of force?

The results are mixed concerning the relationship between temperature, noise, high-speed driving and the willingness to shoot. The temperature study showed most support for this prediction: high temperature made the officer feel more irritated, made the suspect appear more dangerous and resulted in a greater willingness to shoot the suspect. In this study, officers were exposed to a suspect who held a crowbar in his hand. More officers (62 per cent) in the high temperature condition than in the low temperature condition (45 per cent) shot at the suspect. The voice in the background study did not reveal a significant difference in shooting behaviour; however, more officers in the voice condition (69 per cent) than in the control condition (31 per cent) had their weapon ready to fire. The loud music and sound of pub study did not reveal differences in shooting behaviour either, although police officers felt more irritated in the environmental stressor conditions than in the control conditions. In other words, officers seem to become more irritated as a result of the presence of these environmental stressors, which might result in finding the suspect more dangerous, but this does not necessarily lead to increased willingness to shoot the suspect.

Do environmental stressors lead to tunnel vision?

We found empirical support for our assumption that the presence of environmental stressors leads to a better description of central details. For example, in the loud music study, a man stood next to the entrance door of a pub with something in his hand, although it was not clearly visible what it was. More officers in the loud music condition (44 per cent) than in the control condition (19 per cent) noticed that he held a knife in his hand.

Do environmental stressors lead to improved marksmanship?

We did not find evidence that the presence of environmental stressors leads to improved marksmanship. In two studies in which we investigated marksmanship, the percentage of hits (percentage of shots that hit the target) were 31 per cent (in the loud music study) and 28 per cent (in the sound of a drill study). The percentages seem low but the task was difficult. The officers had to react quickly, there was a reasonable distance between the officer and the suspects (about 10–15 metres) and the suspects were moving. We believe that the lack of support for the improved marksmanship hypothesis could be due to a ceiling effect, that is, a hit rate of 30 per cent is the optimal score for police officers in these difficult situations (Vrij, van der Steen, & Koppelaar, 1995b).

Do environmental stressors lead to impairment in primary tasks which were not well learned?

We found strong evidence for the prediction that performance is impaired in primary tasks which are not well learned. For example, in the loud music study, more officers in the environmental stressor condition (96 per cent) than in the control condition (73 per cent) reacted too late and shot at the suspect after the suspect shot at them. In the sound of a drill study, two suspects started shooting simultaneously at the officer. The noise of a drill resulted in more officers 'forgetting' to take cover in this scenario: fewer officers in the environmental stressor condition (14 per cent) than in the control condition (37 per cent) took cover first before they started firing back at the suspect. In a physical effort study, the officers were confronted with a suspect who had a knife in his hand and eventually tried to stab the officer with it. The appropriate action would have been to 'step aside' in order to avoid the stabbing. More police officers in the physical effort condition (32 per cent) than in the control condition (18 per cent) failed to do this. ('Failing to step aside' might also be considered as an underestimation of danger: see above).

Are field-independent police officers less affected by environmental stressors than field-dependent officers?

We investigated the impact of field-independency only three times (Vrij, van der Steen & Koppelaar, 1995b; Barton, Vrij, & Bull, 2000a, 2002b). The sound of a drill study (Vrij, van der Steen & Koppelaar, 1995b) showed beneficial effects of being field-independent. Compared to field-dependent officers, field-independent officers were more accurate in describing the suspect, showed better marksmanship (38 per cent hits compared to 22 per cent) and took more cover (47 per cent compared to 18 per cent). However, Barton, Vrij and Bull's (2000a, 2000b) findings are less conclusive. For example, as predicted, field-dependent officers who drove fast to the incident found the suspect more dangerous than field-independent officers who drove at patrol speed to the incident. We further expected that field-independent officers would not be influenced by the high-speed driving. In reality, however, they were. Field-independent officers who drove fast to the scene of crime found the suspect *less* dangerous than those who drove at patrol speed. It might be that field-independent officers recognized that high speed driving had increased their levels of arousal, and consequently did 'overcompensate' for this by attributing the arousal mainly to their driving. This may entail that field-independent people are at risk of underestimating the danger. Indeed, field-independent officers were less willing to shoot the suspect than field-dependent officers, although the suspect used excessive force against them.

Conclusions

Our studies have shown that environmental stressors cause arousal and that this arousal might have an effect on police officers' decision making in confrontations with suspects. We therefore believe that police officers should if possible avoid potential environmental stressors. That is, do not rush to the scene of crime if it is not necessary to do so, do not ingest excessive amounts of caffeine while on duty as an AFO, and so on.

Obviously, many environmental stressors (such as temperature) can not be influenced by police officers themselves. One way of handling environmental stressors is to recruit officers who are known to be less influenced by them. Unfortunately, our research concerning field-independency does not provide conclusive results. We were expecting that field-independent officers would be less influenced by environmental stressors than field-dependent officers but the findings do not fully support this assumption. There is some evidence that shows that field-independent officers tend to overcompensate, and attribute their arousal mainly to the environmental stressor. This may put their lives in danger. However, given the conflicting results and given the fact that only a few studies have addressed the impact of field-independency/field-dependency on police officers' decision-making processes, we believe that more research concerning this issue is needed.

Another way of dealing with environmental stressors is to train police officers how to 'resist' them. In other words, interventions could be incorporated in AFO training to reduce the impact of environmental stressors. It should be plausible to suggest that the more frequently officers are exposed to environmental stressors in their firearms exercises, the less they will be affected by these environmental stressors (as they will get used to them or will learn how to cope with them). However, to our knowledge no research has been conducted to test this hypothesis. We believe it is important to further investigate this issue. This future research should also address a possible relationship between personality and dealing with environmental stressors, that is, whether some people can be trained more effectively to disregard the influence of environmental stressors than others.

Chapter	Eight

Enhancing Eyewitness Memory: Developments in Theory and Practice

Pam Newlands

'The criminal justice system recognizes that eyewitness testimony in general and eyewitness identification in particular play profoundly important roles in the apprehension, prosecution, and adjudication of criminal offenders.'

(Cutler and Penrod (1995), p. 6)

The recognition of the importance of eyewitness information by the criminal justice system has been largely due to the contribution psychology has made to this area since the beginning of the twentieth century, when *On the Witness Stand* (Munsterberg, 1908) was published. Since then, the proliferation of research in this area testifies not only to its theoretical interest but also its practical value in relation to the investigative process. Sanders (1986) demonstrated the importance of eyewitnesses by asking New York State sheriffs' deputies and detectives what they considered to be the central and most important feature of criminal investigations. The majority replied 'eyewitnesses'. A number of other researchers have also found the role of eyewitnesses to be acknowledged as crucial among those involved in the investigative process. For example, the report of the Rand Corporation in 1975 (Rand Corporation, 1975) found that the completeness and accuracy of the eyewitness account was the main predictor as to whether or not a crime was solved. Kebbell and Milne (1998) investigated police officers' perceptions of eyewitnesses and found that most respondents believed that the major leads to an investigation were usually provided by eyewitnesses. Such findings serve to emphasize the importance not only of the process of gathering eyewitness information but also the manner in which it is done to maximize its usefulness in an investigation.

The success with which an eyewitness can perform the key role s/he plays in investigative proceedings relies on the witness's accurate encoding, storage and retrieval of the witnessed event. At each of these stages, there is a vast range of factors that can influence the witness (Cutler, Penrod & Martens, 1987). The research regarding eyewitness performance can be divided into two major areas: firstly, research identifying variables that affect the accuracy and completeness of eyewitness memory and, secondly, research seeking to identify how certain variables may be modified in order to enhance eyewitness memory, primarily concerned with enhancing retrieval. Research on the former of these areas has dwelt, for the most part, on the negative aspects of eyewitness performance and has sought to establish the conditions under which eyewitness memory is most susceptible to error (e.g. Bull & Clifford, 1979; Loftus, 1996). The type of variables that have been the focus of this type of research have been estimator variables, distinguished from system variables by Wells (1978). Estimator variables occur at the time of the event, their effects can only be estimated and they cannot be manipulated post-event, for example whether a weapon was used (Loftus, Loftus & Messo, 1987; Cutler, Penrod & Martens, 1987). Shapiro and Penrod (1986) discuss the effects of a number of estimator variables in their meta-analysis of witness, target and situational factors that influence eyewitness memory (also see Cutler, Penrod & Martens, 1987; Narby, Cutler & Penrod, 1996). System variables, however, occur after the event hence, unlike estimator variables, can be controlled by the criminal justice system. Thus system variables have the potential to be manipulated to help improve eyewitness memory, and Wells (1978) argued that they should be the focus of future eyewitness memory research.

Another distinction between the two main areas of eyewitness research described above can be made in terms of the stages of memory at which they occur. Estimator variables occur at the encoding and storage stages, whereas system variables occur at the retrieval stage. Fisher and Geiselman (1992) point out that despite considerable knowledge concerning the encoding and storage phases of memory, it is really only at the retrieval stage that strategies to enhance witnesses' recollection can be employed. Since a crime usually happens unexpectedly, witnesses have no time to adopt any kind of encoding strategy, as they are generally unprepared for the event. The process of storage of the memory is also not under a witness's conscious control. Therefore, like knowledge about estimator variables, knowledge about encoding and storage cannot help improve eyewitness memory, and attempts to do this should focus on the retrieval phase of memory which, unlike the other two stages, is mostly under the witness's conscious control. Thus manipulation of system variables at the retrieval stage of memory seems the most promising way to enhance eyewitness memory.

The importance of eyewitness testimony was stressed at the beginning of this chapter, and particular attention has focused upon identification evidence. Clifford and Davies (1989) identified three major phases of an investigation during which identification evidence is employed by the police. The first is the 'descriptive phase', which will usually be the first stage, where identification information will be elicited from the witness as a verbal description and/or a pictorial image, either using a sketch artist or a computerized facial composite system. Following this, there will be a 'search phase' in order to attempt to identify possible suspects, using the witness's information and/or criminal records. The third phase is defined as the 'identification phase', where the eyewitness may be required to attempt identification of the perpetrator, usually by viewing an identification line-up. The role of the eyewitness is particularly crucial in the descriptive and identification phases of an investigation. This chapter will be concerned with research that has investigated methods of manipulating system variables within each of these phases in order to enhance adult eyewitness memory and will address research developments from a number of selected areas within these phases from both theoretical and practical perspectives.

The Descriptive Phase

Eyewitness recall:verbal description

Recall difficulties in relation to an eyewitness providing a verbal description of an event, and particularly description of a perpetrator's face, are well documented[1](Ellis, 1986; Sporer, 1992; Shepherd & Ellis, 1996) and can occur for a variety of reasons. According to Phillips (1978), faces are represented visually in memory and recall requires translating the visual image into a verbal form, which will be of poorer quality. However, other researchers, for example Christie and Ellis (1981), have refuted such a claim. Recall difficulties in relation to providing a verbal description, again particularly of a face, could also stem from a witness lacking a comprehensive enough vocabulary to describe the face effectively. Much of the research on the effects of misleading information (see Loftus, 1996) has also contributed to awareness of circumstances under which eyewitness memory, as manifested by verbal recall, can be distorted, supporting a view of eyewitness recall as 'incomplete, unreliable, partially constructed and malleable during the questioning procedure' (Fisher, Geiselman & Raymond, 1987, p. 177). The problem of inaccurate and incomplete eyewitness reports, and the need to improve these, has been acknowledged not only by psychologists but also by police and legal professionals.

The problem of how to improve eyewitness recall was specifically addressed in 1984 by psychologists in the USA, whose application of psychological techniques led to the development of an eyewitness interview technique called 'The Cognitive Interview' (Geiselman et al., 1984). The Cognitive Interview (CI) may be considered the first 'psychologically based interview package' to attempt to improve the accuracy and completeness of eyewitness recall in terms of trying to improve a controllable system variable, the police questioning technique. The focus here on recall should be noted, as attempts to improve eyewitness identification accuracy using a guided memory procedure involving context reinstatement had been made before (Malpass & Devine, 1981). The theoretical underpinnings of the CI technique are based on two generally accepted cognitive psychological principles of memory. Firstly, that the memory trace is composed of several features (Bower, 1967; Underwood, 1969) and the effectiveness of a retrieval cue is related to the amount of feature overlap with the encoded event (The Encoding Specificity Principle, Tulving & Thompson, 1973). Secondly, there may be several retrieval paths to the encoded event so that information which cannot be accessed by one retrieval cue may be accessed by a different cue (Tulving, 1974). The CI can be described as one of the most successful developments in the area of enhancing the verbal description elicited by eyewitnesses. As originally devised, it consisted of four memory retrieval mnemonics, based around the two psychological principles of memory described above. The first two mnemonics serve the purpose of increasing the feature overlap between the encoding and the retrieval of information, while the second two encourage the use of several retrieval paths. Each of the four mnemonics and the theoretical rationale for each will now be discussed briefly.

Reinstate the context

The Instruction.   The interviewee is requested to try and mentally reinstate both the physical context (i.e. the environment) and also the personal context (i.e. the feelings, thoughts and reactions) that existed at the time of the event. This mnemonic attempts as vivid a mental reinstatement as possible, incorporating and encouraging both mental reinstatement of physical environment and of mood.

The Rationale.   As indicated above, the theoretical rationale behind this mnemonic stems from the Encoding Specificity Principle (Tulving & Thompson, 1973). Context reinstatement as a process to enhance memory has received considerable research in its own right (Godden & Baddeley, 1975; Davies & Milne, 1985; see Malpass, 1996, for a review). The finding that mental context reinstatement can be as beneficial to memory as physical context reinstatement

(Smith, 1979) is particularly important in the case of witnesses to crimes, since often it may not be possible to return to the scene of the crime, or the scene of the crime may have changed, thus precluding physical context reinstatement taking place. Accordingly, mental reinstatement of context formed one of the original main techniques of the CI and it has been argued that it is the most important mnemonic of the CI technique (Memon & Bull, 1991).[2]

Report everything

The Instruction. The interviewee is instructed to report everything s/he can remember about the event, even partial information, regardless of the perceived importance of the information or confidence associated with it.

The Rationale. While this instruction may seem an obvious one, Geiselman et al. (1984) identified that witnesses frequently do not report everything, as they often edit from their accounts information that they do not perceive as important, but that may, in fact, be relevant to the investigation. This editing by eyewitnesses may also occur if they do not feel certain about some of the information that they recall (Geiselman, 1992). However, the unreliable nature of the relationship between confidence and accuracy (Wells & Lindsay, 1985) suggests that witnesses should not only report information about which they feel certain. By instructing witnesses to report all they remember regardless of the perceived importance of the information or the confidence that they have in the information, the 'report everything' mnemonic attempts to elicit any extra information which the witness may be editing from their report.

Report events in different orders

The Instruction. The interviewee is instructed to recall the event in different sequential orders, for example chronologically, in reverse order, or from different starting points (e.g. from the part of the event that made the most impact on him/her).

The Rationale. Research has demonstrated that memory for information from different sequential positions can be affected by changing the order in which an event is recalled (Mingay, Dennett & Bekerian, 1984; Geiselman & Callot, 1990). Models of memory which postulate description formation, such as those of Norman and Bobrow (1978) and Tulving (1983), predict that this should be the case. These models suggest that changing the order of recall should enable the use of a different retrieval description, thus making new information available. The rationale for the change of order mnemonic is also based on schema theory, and in particular the assumption that prior knowledge, expectations and the application of schemata influence the retrieval of information from memory. Bellezza and Bower (1982) found that recall of schema-consistent information was facilitated by forward recall of a schema-based text, while Geiselman and Callot (1990) found that reverse-order recall facilitated the recall of more information incidental to a schema. Geiselman and Callot (1990) explained this in terms of reverse-order recall disrupting script usage by facilitating data-driven processing of non-schematic information, and suggest that the incidental information generated using this technique may be valuable to the police in linking crimes. Thus a forward recall attempt followed by a reverse-order recall attempt may elicit more information than two forward recall attempts. In addition, reverse-order recall, through being a less schematic retrieval process, may also reduce intrusion errors.

Report events from a different perspective

The Instruction.   The interviewee is instructed to recall the event as if s/he were viewing it from another person's position. For example, the interviewee might be asked to report the event as if s/he were the victim, instead of a witness.

The Rationale. As in the case of recalling the event in different orders, the change perspective mnemonic leads to the recall of new information by the occurrence of a change in the retrieval description, with models of memory such as that of Norman and Bobrow (1978) again providing the theoretical rationale for this. This mnemonic, however, stemmed more directly from a study by Anderson and Pichert (1978) that demonstrated that recall could be influenced by a change in perspective. The aim of the Anderson and Pichert (1978) study was to investigate the influence of a change of schema on memory and Bekerian and Dennett (1993) have argued that it was the individual's conceptual perspective which was changed, not their perceptual perspective, which is what the CI instructs interviewees to change. This technique requires particular care when it is used, especially in the case of child witnesses, due to concerns that it may elicit fabricated details through the use of words like 'imagine' or 'pretend' in its instruction[3] and it tends to be less frequently used by police officers (Clifford and George, 1996).

   Since the CI was originally devised, it has undergone a number of revisions (Fisher et al., 1987; Fisher & Geiselman, 1992). However, as pointed out by Bekerian and Dennett (1993), the revisions have not so much affected the cognitive components of the interview as the communicative elements. Research investigating real-life police interviews suggested that, as well as incorporating the cognitive mnemonics, police interviews would also benefit from enhancement of the communicative aspects of interviewing (Fisher, Geiselman & Raymond, 1987). Such techniques have included the following.

Focused retrieval

The strategy of focused retrieval attempts to facilitate eyewitness recall by instructing the witness to concentrate on the mental images s/he has of the event while describing what s/he remembers, having already reinstated the context of the event. Using this technique, the interviewer will try to elicit as much information from the witness's conceptual image code as possible and will encourage a high level of concentration on the part of the witness in order for him/her to be able to achieve this.

Extensive retrieval

This principle of the enhanced CI combines the recall in different orders and recall from different perspectives components of the original CI. The interviewer should encourage the witness to make as many retrieval attempts as possible, employing strategies such as changing orders and perspectives, since continued retrieval attempts in general lead to more information being recalled (Roediger & Payne, 1982).

Witness-compatible questioning

Once again relating to the mental representation the witness has of the event, this principle addresses one of the main problems found in Fisher et al.'s (1987) analysis of real-life police interviews, namely that the interviewers did not take the witness's mental representation for the event into account during questioning. The interviewer should structure the interview around the way in which information appears to be organized in the witness's mind, gauged from the witness's initial narrative of the event, and contiguous questions should relate to the same mental picture.

Rapport building

As well as addressing witnesses' memory and cognition processes in recalling the event, the enhanced CI also addressed general issues of communication and the social dynamics between the interviewer and the interviewee. Rapport building is an important part of this enhanced communication strategy that aims to try to put witnesses at ease. This part of the interview can also be used to 'transfer control' to witnesses by explaining to them that they will need to work hard at their recall and, in fact, control the interview, as they have all the information (Fisher & Geiselman, 1992). This process can be particularly important with child witnesses to make it clear to them that they alone have information about the event and that the interviewer does not know the answers to the questions they are asking, since repeated questioning may lead a child to be-lieve that s/he has not given the correct answer the first time.

In addition to these refinements, the enhanced CI provided guidelines about the sequential structure of the interview, beginning with establishing rapport, then progressing through stages of explaining the aims of the interview, initiat-ing free recall, questioning, using varied and extensive retrieval, before finally summarizing and closing (see Fisher and Geiselman, 1992; and Milne and Bull, 1999, for detailed descriptions of the structure of the CI and how it has been incorporated into police training packages).

Since the CI was devised, research has investigated it within a wide range of eyewitness contexts. The majority of studies have investigated it in relation to its original aim of enhancing the verbal description a witness is able to pro-vide in a police interview. The results of a number of empirical research and field studies (see Köhnken et al., 1999, for a meta-analysis of forty-two stud-ies) led to the CI being incorporated in a Home Office Investigative Interview-ing Package in 1992. Since then, the CI has remained an important research area in relation to enhancing eyewitness report. There have, in addition, been some theoretically and practically interesting research developments concern-ing its effects at other stages of the investigative process. The eyewitness report is only one part of one phase of the investigative process, and the role of the eyewitness in assisting police to create a pictorial likeness of the suspect or to identify accurately the suspect from an identification line-up can also be crucial. In terms of CI research, early research concentrated on the descrip-tive phase of the investigation, and within this phase on verbal description rather than pictorial representation, with the identification phase receiving far less research attention. Taking a broader perspective of the investigative process, it is important to establish any effects that use of the CI at this initial stage may have on eyewitness performance during later stages of the investi-gation, such as constructing a pictorial likeness of the suspect or attempting to identify the perpetrator from a line-up. These issues have been subject to an increasing body of research and will now be discussed both in terms of CI research and research on other factors that may be manipulated to enhance eyewitness memory at these stages.

Face composite construction

A facial composite task, although usually discussed as an eyewitness recall task, combines elements of both recall and recognition. When first describing a per-petrator, the witness must recall the appropriate mental image and verbally convey this information to the composite system operator. However, from the point at which an initial image is constructed and shown to the witness, the task becomes one more of recognition as the witness attempts to match the image on the screen to his/her mental representation of the perpetrator. When the witness assists in creating a facial image, either sketch or composite, a verbal description is initially required. In these tasks, however, the verbal description is used as the basis for creating the image and it must be effectively communicated to a second party, either the artist or the composite operator. It is this extra stage in communication that it has been argued may pose another area of difficulty on recall tasks of this nature (Shepherd, Davies & Ellis, 1978; Cohen, 1989). Cohen (1989) refers to such recall tasks as 'second hand', in comparison to recognition tasks where no transfer of information has to be made. This difference between the two types of tasks may, in part at least, account for the superiority of recognition over recall.

Technology has now become sufficiently advanced so as to provide highly developed computerized facial composite systems, although early research in this area used the Photo-fit system (launched in 1970) to investigate this aspect of facial memory. Accuracy of identification from Photo-fit studies has been found to be very low (Ellis, Shepherd & Davies, 1975; Davies, Ellis & Shepherd, 1978). However Davies, Milne and Shepherd (1983) and Gibling and Bennett (1994) have pointed out that findings of the lack of sensitivity of Photo-fit in leading to correct recognition may represent the poor enhancement skills of the operator as much as weaknesses of the system. Gibling and Bennett (1994) found that when the basic Photo-fit was artistically enhanced by a skilled operator using a variety of techniques, identification accuracy was significantly increased. Despite this finding, Photo-fit has been superseded for some time by computerized facial composite systems, such as the Electronic Facial Identification Technique (E-FIT). E-FIT was developed jointly by the Home Office Scientific Research Group and Aberdeen University, though it has undergone further development by Aspley Ltd, who currently market the package. E-FIT composites are constructed from specially edited photographs of volunteers, providing over 1,000 exemplars of facial features which have each been coded using a set of descriptors based upon those developed by the Aberdeen group working on facial databases (Shepherd, 1975, 1986). There are a number of important improvements in composite production using E-FIT compared to Photo-fit. For example, E-FIT always presents features in the context of a complete face, whereas Photo-fit involved selecting facial features separately from a printed array of isolated features. E-FIT creates an 'average' face by default, thus if a witness cannot provide a description of a certain feature then E-FIT provides an exemplar of that feature which fits in with the other selected features. This is advantageous, since face recognition involves a combination of the processes of recognizing the individual features along with their combination in the face

(Diamond & Carey, 1977). In addition, E-FIT allows a far greater opportunity to make adjustments to the configuration of the face and reduces the search task of the witness by making use of the witness's verbal description to select a range of appropriate features. As technological advances are made, Gibling and Bennett's (1994) finding that appropriate skill and training can enhance Photofits would most certainly also hold for images created using the newer computerized systems. Therefore the training and skill of the operators, not simply in the technical operation of the system but in the relevant psychology as well (such as interviewing techniques), are of paramount importance.

Findings that the CI increased likeness ratings of a facial composite, the features of which had been selected in the context of a face rather than in isolation (Luu & Geiselman, unpublished, cited in Fisher, McCauley & Geiselman, 1994), coupled with Davies and Milne's (1985) finding that instructions to recreate the original viewing conditions enhanced facial composites, led Fisher, McCauley and Geiselman (1994) to suggest the possibility that some variant of the CI might be employed successfully to improve facial composites. If this is the case, the use of a composite system such as E-FIT, which manipulates features within the context of the face in a holistic manner, may have the potential to improve composite quality, and hence recognition, when used with the CI. However, in a study comparing E-FIT composites created using a cognitive interview with those created using a structured interview, Newlands (1997) found no significant difference in ratings of likeness to the target face. The effects of the CI on facial composite production using E-FIT have also been explored by Clarke (2000) and this research has more specifically addressed use of the interview in face composite construction. The process involved in creating a facial composite involves a number of stages. Firstly, the witness is interviewed to gather information about the suspect. The interview and the manner in which it is conducted are, therefore, crucial parts of the facial construction process. The resultant information is then entered into the computer by selecting the relevant descriptors from the description fields. An example of the descriptors for the feature 'face shape' is shown below.

Face shape: oval, round, triangular, square, angular
Chin shape: oval, rounded, pointed, squared, angular
Fleshiness: gaunt, lean, average, chubby, fleshy
Length: short, average, long
Width: narrow, average, wide
Forehead: low, average, high
Dimpled chin: no, yes
Age: young, adult, middle-aged, old
Heavy jowls: no, yes

Double chin: no, yes
High cheekbones: no, yes
Dimpled cheeks: no, yes
(From the E-FIT package, Aspley Ltd.)

Witnesses usually do not view the process of entering the descriptors, due to the potential provision of leading or misleading information during this process. The reason that this could occur is because the descriptor categories for each of the features are of a forced choice design, that is, they provide a set number of descriptor options for each part of the feature from which the operator must choose the ones that best fit the witnesses' descriptions. The example of the face shape descriptors shows the descriptor choices for each part of the face shape description. If witnesses were to view these, they might be less likely to provide a description in their own words, being led by the descriptors provided. Once all the descriptors have been entered, the computer searches for the closest match in all of the description fields and an initial image is revealed. The witness is shown this image and, depending on its likeness to the witness's memory of the suspect, s/he has the opportunity to change as many of the individual features as required in order to improve the likeness of the image, which can also be enhanced using a paint package. While the witness is involved in this process, the usual procedure is to reinterview the witness.

Similar to the CI, the whole E-FIT process is very witness-centred and Clarke (2000) comments that the operator brings nothing to the process apart from interviewing skill, familiarity with the system and artistic ability. Of course, each of these aspects is very important in its own right to the success with which the process can be conducted. For example, as mentioned earlier, previous research using Photo-fit has established the importance of using artistic enhancement to enable more identifiable composites to be created (Gibling & Bennett, 1994). The questions that Clarke (2000) addressed were: 'What procedures were operators adopting in the field?' and 'What effect was the interview as a part of the facial composite process having on the resultant composites?' In practice, it was found that some operators found it helpful to use the descriptor fields at the initial interview stage and in general there was considerable variety in how the production process was instigated, particularly concerning the use of description boxes and the practice of reinterviewing after the initial image had been revealed to the witness. At present, police practice, as taught to operators, is to pre-interview, not show the description boxes during construction of the initial image and then reinterview during refining of the image. However, Clarke (2000) found that a higher number of correct composite identifications resulted from use of the description boxes while constructing the composite with no reinterview during the process of refining the initial image. Clarke (2000) suggests the derogatory effects found regarding reinterviewing could perhaps be due to interference between the mental processes involved in recall during the interview and the processes of recognition when viewing the image on the screen.

Follow-up research from these findings is investigating what effects the pre-interview may be contributing. It is possible, for example, that interference with the witness's visual image through verbal overshadowing may occur at this stage. Verbal overshadowing refers to the process by which verbally describing a stimulus that is difficult to translate from a visual code to a verbal representation (e.g. in the eyewitness context, a face) impairs subsequent identification accuracy of the stimulus (Schooler & Engstler-Schooler, 1990). This phenomenon will be discussed in more detail later in the chapter.

Another factor that has been identified as being useful to consider in face composite construction is feature saliency (Turner et al., 2001). In a study that manipulated the order in which features within the composite were selected and adjusted, it was found that using the feature saliency order, as determined from the witness's initial description of the perpetrator, may lead to more accurate composites than the present (unordered) way in which features are selected during facial composite construction. The facial composite research discussed so far has been conducted using full-face images on E-FIT. However, research using the package PRO-Fit (developed by ABM UK) has addressed use of three-quarter views of the face (Ness et al., 2001). In facial recognition studies of unfamiliar faces, accuracy has been improved by using three-quarter views rather than full or profile views of test faces (Logie, Baddeley & Woodhead [1987], cited in Ness et al., 2001). The use of the three-quarter view may also be valuable in cases where a witness has seen the perpetrator, but only from the side. The PRO-Fit system allows both the construction of three-quarter views and the generation of three-quarter views from full-face views. Initial research using this system (Ness et al., 2001) found that three-quarter views were recognized as well as full-face views and, in addition, that presentation of both views increased recognition accuracy.

The present police practice of having only one witness construct a facial composite, in cases where there are multiple witnesses, has also been questioned by research (Kemp, Pike & Brace, 1999; Bennett et al., 2001). Problems with this current procedure arise for two main reasons. Firstly, the police cannot be certain which witness is able to provide the most accurate composite and, secondly, research has demonstrated that identification accuracy rates are improved by showing multiple composites produced by different witnesses compared to a single composite (Bennett et al., 2000). It has also been suggested that a more accurate composite could be constructed by generating one that consists of the most accurate features from a number of composites, as judged by witnesses (Bennett et al., 2001). The emerging research on multiple witnesses, multiple composite views and the development of 3D composite models poses new challenges both for research in this area and for police training and practice.

As previously mentioned, the effects of the use of techniques such as the CI are important not only in relation to their direct effect on processes such as eyewitness recall but also in relation to the effects they may have on subsequent tasks in which eyewitnesses may be involved. For example, if an inaccurate composite is created, then this may interfere with subsequent recognition accuracy. This effect was demonstrated in a study by Jenkins and Davies (1985), who found that composites that were misleading as to the appearance of the target led to significantly lower identification accuracy and the tendency for participants to select distractors which embodied the misleading features. Therefore, the importance of non-biased procedures at the descriptive phase of the investigation is emphasized in order to enhance accuracy at the identification stage, to which I shall now turn.

The Identification Phase

Clifford and Gwyer (1999) have conducted extensive research in the area of the CI, context reinstatement and eyewitness identification performance. They have emphasized the importance of considering encoding and retention factors when investigating context-manipulation effects and their research has suggested that the CI mnemonic of mental context reinstatement may be capable of enhancing eyewitness identification in target-present line-ups in circumstances where encoding the event has been difficult or there has been a reasonably long retention interval. There are a number of explanations that have been proposed for the CI, and context reinstatement in particular, not being as successful in enhancement of identification as in enhancing recall. For example, differences between recall and recognition processes are often cited (see Sporer, 1989, for discussions of differences between these memory processes). The outshining hypothesis is another explanation proposed for the inability of context reinstatement to enhance recognition (Smith, 1988). The suggestion here is that more powerful cues at the time of retrieval moderate or 'outshine' the effectiveness of a context reinstatement cue, for example the presence of the perpetrator in an identification line-up. An explanation suggested by Fisher et al. (1994) to explain the CI's lack of ability to improve identification accuracy is that the CI facilitates accessing specific features, but face recognition is mediated by holistic information. Another possible reason for the CI being unable to enhance identification accuracy is the occurrence of verbal overshadowing (described above in relation to composite production). Schooler and Engstler-Schooler (1990) have suggested that a more detailed examination of verbal overshadowing is long overdue. Given the central role of the interview in gathering eyewitness information, the possibility of a link between the interviewing of witnesses and subsequent inaccuracies in identification performance is too important to ignore. Research should seek to identify the circumstances under which the least interference occurs to the witness's representation of the perpetrator.

A series of experiments relevant to this was conducted by Finger and Pezdek (1999). They noted that previously published studies that had investigated the CI in relation to identification accuracy had found no difference in participants' performance between a CI and a standard interview. The interviews in these studies were administered forty-eight or ninety-six hours after the face had been viewed. Finger and Pezdek (1999) argued that there would already be degradation of the memory in this time and, therefore, they interviewed participants immediately after they saw the target face. The interview was followed with a recognition task and participants in the CI condition were found to be significantly less accurate in their identifications compared to those in the standard interview condition. In terms of descriptive information, those who were inaccurate in the facial identification task provided significantly more descriptive information about the target, both accurate and inaccurate. Thus there appeared to be a trade-off between accurate recall and accurate identification. In follow-up experiments, Finger and Pezdek (1999) hypothesized that introducing a delay between the interview and the face identification test would lead to a reduction or elimination of the verbal overshadowing effect and, hence, more accurate face identification. The theoretical rationale for this hypothesis follows from the findings that qualitative differences between visual representations and verbal descriptions of faces (Ellis, 1984) led to faces being easier to recognize from the visual representation of them. However, if at the time of the identification task the verbal description is more prominent in memory than the visual representation, then this will be detrimental to identification performance. The inclusion of a delay between the interview and the identification task should allow time for the verbal description to fade from prominence. Findings from Finger and Pezdek's (1999) studies supported this prediction, with the insertion of a delay of one hour removing the disadvantage of the CI found previously. Furthermore, there was no significant difference in identification accuracy found between the CI and a no-description condition with only a 24-minute delay between the interview and the identification task. Finger and Pezdek (1999) argue that delaying the recognition test reduced the extent of retroactive interference and that the findings also suggest that the original visual memory for the target face is not permanently degraded. Evidence from Schooler and Engstler-Schooler (1990) has also supported this in their findings that giving participants less time to think about their identifications overcame the effects of verbal overshadowing. The problem of verbal overshadowing, therefore, would appear to be a problem of accessibility. Results from a meta-analysis of the verbal overshadowing effect (with twenty-nine effect size comparisons) have provided further support for the above findings, with overshadowing effects being more likely to occur when the identification task immediately followed the description task (Meissner & Brigham, 2001). However, Meissner and Brigham (2001) also found that if participants were given instructions intended to elicit an elaborative description of the target face during the description task rather than a standard instruction, such as free recall, verbal overshadowing was also more likely to occur.

In real-life terms, such findings have important implications for how witness interviews are conducted, and the factor of delay is particularly relevant in the investigative process. In circumstances where a witness is interviewed about a crime immediately afterwards and there is then a delay before s/he is required to attempt to identify the suspect, then the above findings suggest the CI will not impair subsequent identification. The rationale behind this research contrasts with that investigating the outshining hypothesis in relation to context, which has suggested that the memory trace needs to be impaired for context reinstatement cues not to be outshone by a cue such as the presence of the target (Smith, 1988). In many investigations this opportunity for the memory to be impaired is a realistic one if, for example, a witness only came forward after a delay to be interviewed, by which time their original memory would already be impaired. Thus scenarios such as those introducing a delay before the context reinstatement may in some circumstances be more realistic forensically. Future research in this area may investigate a scenario combining these identification studies, whereby there is a delay before the interview, then a further delay between the interview and the identification task. However, there is evidence to show that certain individuals may be more susceptible to verbal overshadowing than others, with individuals whose general perceptual abilities exceed their verbal abilities being more likely to succumb to the effects of verbal overshadowing (Ryan & Schooler, 1998).

The CI is not the only system variable that has been investigated in relation to enhancing eyewitness identification accuracy. The identification lineup has received considerable attention in relation to improving the procedures surrounding it in order to help improve the chances of identification accuracy. The method of presentation of visual information in a lineup has been one of the variables that have been successfully manipulated to enhance eyewitness identification ability. Sequential presentation of photographs has been found to result in significantly higher levels of eye-witness identification accuracy than simultaneous presentation (R.C.L. Lindsay et al., 1991). Not only did sequential presentation significantly reduce false identifications in target-absent line-ups compared to traditional simultaneous line-ups, but also it significantly reduced the impact of biased instructions. Within the sequential presentation procedure, there are ways to enhance identification accuracy even further. For example, research by Lindsay and Bellinger (1999) suggests that the risk of false identifications in sequential line-ups can be reduced further by the line-up being control-led by the police officer rather than the witness. This research stemmed from the finding that in order to adhere to psychological recommendations re-garding blind testing (i.e. the officer running the line-up should not know the identity of the suspect to remove any risk of the witness's decision being influenced), police officers were adapting the sequential procedure in prac-tice by leaving witnesses alone to make their decisions and hence effectively control their own viewing of the line-up (R. C. L. Lindsay, 1999). Witness control of a line-up in the study by Lindsay and Bellinger (1999) resulted in witnesses comparing line-up members in an inappropriate way and using relative judgements rather than absolute ones, leading to higher rates of false identification. Lindsay and Bellinger (1999) suggest that advances in computer technology will enable more control of sequential line-ups, through allowing witnesses to work through the line-up on their own but preventing them from violating line-up instructions by making comparisons. This is a valuable area for future research with very important implications at a practical level.

Areas for Future Development

More recently, research attention has begun to focus on the people involved in the interview rather than on the interview process itself. For example, by combining competency research from areas of occupational psychology, research has addressed the question: what makes a good interviewer? (Clarke & Milne, 2000). The approach adopted to try to answer this question has assumed that, similar to many other skills, cer-tain competencies will be particularly important in skilful witness inter-viewing and some people will possess these skills to a higher level than others. Devising a competency framework could be helpful in creating a selection tool to identify officers who might be better suited than others to perform good interviews or respond most to interview training. In relation to the interviewee, recent research has been attempting to address the issue of individual differences between witnesses, investigating the relationship between witnesses' cognitive style and the effectiveness of context reinstatement in improving event recall (Emmett, Gwyer & Clifford, 2000). Initial results revealed differences between the performance of field-dependent and field-independent participants in relation to the effects of context reinstatement on free and cued recall. In free recall, context reinstatement improved the performance of field-dependent participants but not field-independent participants, and in cued recall the opposite was true. When identification accuracy was examined, it was found that field-dependent participants were significantly more accurate in target-present line-ups than field-independent participants (Emmett, Clifford & Gwyer, 2001).

Within the area of identification accuracy, research attention has also been directed towards the older eyewitness in light of the increasing numbers of those in the population who are aged sisxty-five and over. Previous research in this area has found that older adults are more likely to misidentify a stranger's face (Searcy, Bartlett & Memon, 1999) and are also more likely to be susceptible to misleading post-event information (Cohen & Faulkner, 1989). Building on these earlier findings, Hope, Gabbert and Memon (in press) have investigated age in conjunction with the system-variable mug-shot inspection to ascertain whether older eyewitnesses are more likely to make false identifications when they have viewed a book of mug-shots before line-up identification. Line-up accuracy was indeed found to be impaired by prior exposure to mug-shots, though the detrimental effect of such interference could be reduced by instructions to reinstate the context of the video prior to identification. In relation to individual differences between older eyewitnesses, it has been found that negative performance on a line-up task can be predicted by positive performance on measures of verbal recall and metamemory (Searcy et al., 2001). Specifically, high levels of memory self-efficacy and verbal recall were correlated with false identification in a target-absent line-up.

The research on individual differences, as well as that on interviewer skills, represents interesting new developments in eyewitness research. As stated at the beginning of this chapter, in the process of information gathering, the witness has a vital role in the investigative process. As developments in forensic science continue, evidence gathered by scientific means can provide crucial information about a perpetrator and carry considerable weight with a jury. Psychological research has contributed greatly to our understanding of eyewitness memory and to enhancing eyewitness performance. It continues to do so and to inform practice and policy within the criminal justice system as a result.

NOTES

1   It should be noted that field research in this area such as that of Yuille and Cutshall
    (1986) has found high levels of accurate person description, contrary to laboratory
    findings. See Sporer (1996) for discussion of potential reasons for this difference.
2   However, much research on context reinstatement has also focused on its effect on
    identification, with mixed results (e.g. Krafka & Penrod, 1985; Cutler et al., 1986).
    In addition, reinstating the context of traumatic events was found to be detrimental
    to recall by Loftus, Manber and Keating (1983).
3   However, Milne (1997, cited in Milne & Bull, 1999) has found that five- and six-
    year-old children seem able to understand this instruction when it is explained care-
    fully to them.

Chapter Nine

Occupational Stress and the Criminal Justice Practitioner

Jennifer Brown

Introduction

Occupational stress has been the subject of much research effort since the 1950s, because of lost productivity and financial costs incurred through sickness absenteeism and premature medical retirements (Brown & Campbell, 1994). Since then literally thousands of research papers have been produced, although only in more recent times has attention been directed at the field of criminal justice practitioners.

This chapter will focus largely on the experiences of United Kingdom practitioners, although similar analyses are evident from practice abroad. It will also concentrate on the uniformed criminal justice services, as they share some distinctive elements and differ in their interactions with client groups compared with, for example, members of the judiciary. This is not to say that lawyers, judges and other criminal justice professionals do not suffer stress, but space precludes a thorough discussion of the context in which they work, analysis of stressors and their impacts on these groups.

Police, Prison and Probation Services have experienced considerable operational and organizational changes in recent years, often stemming from some key critical event such as the Brixton riots in 1981 or the Strangeways prison riot in April 1990 and their associated influential reports (Scarman and Woolf respectively), or in the aftermath of tragedies such as the Bradford football stadium fire or murders committed by mentally disordered offenders. In the subsequent fallout from such events, stress of personnel has been implicated in contributory causes, and features in subsequent consequences, of the traumatic events experienced. Thus discussions about occupational stress often begin with potential post -traumatic stress disorder (PTSD) suffered by operational officers and recognition for professional clinical or counselling interventions for staff. Thereafter, other sources of stress have been identified with a commensurate range of additional supportive and preventative counselling services being developed together with a flurry of research activity. The Home Office initiated a number of workshops that identified key sources of stress for Police (Manolias, 1983) and Prison Services (Cox & Smith, 1990). Both research and stress interventions were extended to examine and ameliorate routine organizational and operational sources of stress or daily hassles. In addition, research also identified vicarious or secondary stress, the spillover from exposure to victims of distressing experiences. More recent research attention has looked more specifically at stress impacts of organizational change and shifted in focus from the operational officer to criminal justice managers. This chapter will reflect this chronology and will outline some key definitions and processes identified in the research literature, examine some of the problems when interpreting findings from that literature, describe some of the commonalities and differences between Police, Prison and Probation Services and then discuss sources of stress, reactions to stress, interactions and interventions.

Definitions and Concepts in the Stress Process

There are probably almost as many definitions of working concepts related to the area of stress as there are papers researching the topic. The term stress does, however, have a connotation of commonness and for many, being 'stressed' is a recognizably adverse state. It is also a truism that a certain amount of stress can enhance performance e.g. pre-performance nerves can enhance an actor's delivery of the part but 'stage fright' can completely inhibit a rendition.

More technically the interactive approach to stress has tended to dominate definitions and conceptualization of stress (Schaufeli & Peeters, 2000). They take job stress to be a particular relation between the employee and his or her work environments and concentrate on the adverse consequences following from an individual's incapacity to cope with external demands made upon them. Conceptual distinctions tend to be made between job stressors and stress reactions or strains. Stressors are the factors identified as being potential sources of adverse reactions and, as identified by Cooper (1986), include those that are intrinsic to the job (e.g. work overload, time pressures and deadlines); role in organizations (e.g. ambiguity or conflict); career development (e.g. promotion, job rewards); relationships at work (e.g. with supervisors, delegation); organizational structure and climate (e.g. participation in decision making, consultation). Stress reactions have been described in a number of ways. Firstly, there is a suggestion that a subjective element is present and has been identified as felt stress by Brown and Campbell (1994). Secondly the concept of strain has been described which relates to more objective identifiable symptoms. Schaufeli and Peeters (2000) include physiological distress (such as heart palpitations, high blood pressure) psychological distress (e.g. job dissatisfaction, burnout, anxiety) and behavioural strains (e.g. quitting job, substance misuse). In addition Wilkinson and Campbell (1997) suggest that stressed individuals may also suffer some cognitive impairment in terms of ability to concentrate or organize thoughts. As a result they may be unable to follow instructions or may misread information. These effects were noticeable from the report by Sir John Woodcock following the Whitemoor escape (Woodcock, 1994) and from a Prison Governors Association survey of governor stress (Duncan, 1995), in which 81 per cent of respondents claimed not to be able to absorb what was being read or being unable to listen when stressed.

Burnout as a stress reaction has received particular attention. This is considered to be a response to chronic stress, the result of long-term exposure to routinely occurring stressors and particularly likely in professionals who have intensive interactions with people on a regular basis. Maslach and Leiter (1997) define the evolving stages of burnout and associated states: imbalance between resources and demands resulting in the depletion of emotional reserves; development of negative attitudes resulting in a detachment from, and cynicism towards, recipients of one's services (depersonalization); this distancing represents a poor coping adaptation, resulting in a cycle of increasing distress and decreasing professional effectiveness. Edelwich and Brodsky (1980, p. 14) describe a disillusionment model of burnout defined as a progressive loss of idealism, energy and purpose comprising four stages: enthusiasm, stagnation, frustration and apathy. Hellesøy, Gronhaug and Kvitastein (2000) suggest that certain burnout components may be profession-specific. Thus, where there is a high demand for close contact and interactions with clients, and where there is a sense of having to perform and where professional norms do not allow for 'ups and downs' in performance, burnout is particularly prevalent. This is further compounded if there are exit barriers within the job context. As will be discussed later, these characteristics do apply to the criminal justice practitioners under review.

Single exposure to traumatic incidents may result in post-traumatic stress disorder (PTSD). This is defined by DSM IV (American Psychiatric Association, 1994) in terms of witnessing or experiencing or being confronted with an event or events that involve actual or threatened death or serious injury or threat to the physical integrity of oneself or others. Symptoms include intense fear, helplessness or horror, recurrent intrusive and disturbing thoughts and images, persistent avoidance of thoughts and feelings regarding that event and increased arousal. For police, exposure to major public-order events such as the Bradford football stadium fire or Hillsborough disaster or their involvement in shooting incidents may result in officers suffering PTSD. Involvement in prison riots, escapes or hostage situations provide operational exposure to traumatic incidents for prison staff. For probation staff, managing the violent or mentally disordered offender could also result in PTSD.

Reactions to extended exposure to the distress of others can result in a distinguishable stress reaction termed secondary traumatic stress or secondary victimization by Figley (1995). Symptoms such as re-experiencing traumatic material, avoidance of reminders of the traumatic event and persistent arousal, typical in PTSD, have been found by therapists dealing with the survivors of sexual abuse (Coppenhall, 1995) and researchers of distressing experiences (Pickett et al., 1994). Martin, McKean and Veltkamp (1986) found examples of both primary and secondary exposed victims in a police sample. Twenty-six per cent of the sample (N = 75) reported symptoms meeting criteria for PTSD following exposure to psychologically traumatic on-the-job events relating to either their own victimization or working with victims of rape, spouse abuse or child abuse.

Research has also attempted to delineate the importance of particular strategies employed by individuals and organizations to minimize negative impacts of stress. Social support has been implicated in both alleviating and exacerbating stress reactions (Brown & Grover, 1998). In other words, social support may have both positive & negative effects. Cooper, Cooper and Eaker (1988) distinguish between adaptive and maladaptive coping strategies. The former includes recognition of limitations and talking about problems, whilst the latter includes avoidance, distractions and substance abuse. As levels of demand build up, a person may have certain resources at their disposal to manage the pressures. Coping resources may relate to individual factors such as disposition, knowledge and ability and external factors such as money. Financial resources may, for example, allow a person to pay for domestic help if demands of job and home are excessive. Psychological coping has been divided into problem-focused and emotion-focused. Wilkinson and Campbell (1997) describe the former as coping that involves individuals evaluating stressful situations and engaging in strategies to manage or change elements of the stressful situation. The latter involves attempts to reduce the anxieties attached to the problem but not necessarily dealing with the problem itself. Emotion-focused coping can include repression or denial, where there is an attempt to exclude or ignore the external reality, and displacement, projection or rationalization, where the individual devises strategy to relocate the source of the problem.

Research Problems

A number of researchers in this area comment on the difficulties in drawing firm conclusions from the emergent literature. Schaufeli and Peeters (2000) note with respect to prison officers that much research is drawn from the United States, with significantly fewer European studies available and those mostly deriving from Britain, Sweden and the Netherlands. Brown and Campbell (1990) make a similar point with reference to research on the occupational stress experienced by police officers. Comparative studies of the criminal justice systems that compare agencies or countries need to take into account the differences in practice and systems to draw any firm conclusion about the consistency and sustainability of findings. For example, McKenzie (1993) notes that numbers of police officers and police organizations differ considerably between the United States and Britain and, together with differences in the arming of officers, makes comparisons of stress findings problematic. Schaufeli and Peeters (2000) indicate that the population of a prison can be as much as 1,500 in the United States, compared with 250 in the Netherlands and Sweden, which, together with differences in ratios of officers to prisoners and different recruitment and selection polices, make comparison of correctional officers' experiences problematic.

Methodological variability also presents problems is assessing the viability and generalizability of research findings with respect to prison officers. Schaufeli and Peeters (2002) indicate that studies are frequently cross-sectional, self-report, with small convenience samples. Prospective, multi-method, large-sample studies are rare. Brown, Fielding and Grover (1999) suggest that with respect to research into the occupational stress of police officers much of the published output is descriptive and research samples are hard to recruit and are often modest in size. Theoretical and practical constraints often mean that (with a few notable exceptions) studies are limited by opportunity, cross-sectional sampling strategies and relatively unsophisticated statistical analyses.

Occupational stress within the three criminal justice agencies under present scrutiny has received variable levels of coverage, with the police probably having the greatest research output, followed by the Prison Service, with probation being the subject of least scrutiny. There are relatively few studies utilizing a common research instrument and time-frame to compare the three services. Thus assessing the similarities and differences between the three occupations can be problematic because of different sampling strategies, different measuring instruments and different research questions employed. Notwithstanding these difficulties, there are some striking parallels between uniformed criminal justice practitioners, possibly because they share some common elements of occupational culture and all have been subjected to organizational changes influenced by new public-sector management (NPM) initiatives.

Organizational Context

In a recent review, Armenakis and Bedeian (1999) propose that receptivity, resistance, commitment, cynicism, stress and related personal reactions are clearly relevant factors when considering planning and implementing organizational change. They suggest that stress is particularly associated with a stage in the change process where individuals deny or resist the new direction that the organization is taking. The public sector generally and criminal justice agencies in particular have been subjected to much change in recent years in terms of remit, public expectations, accountability, performance measurement and customer satisfaction.

Brown, Cooper and Kirkcaldy (1999) point out that the Police Service was subject to a number of management innovations under the rubric of NPM. For the Police Service, Home Office Circular 114/83 (Home Office, 1983) established some of the principles of good management, which included increased civilianization, better use of information technology and devolved financial responsibilities. The work of the Audit Commission, established to monitor and promote economy, effectiveness and efficiency in the public sector, meant that the Police Service found itself subject to the scrutiny of a new (non-police) body of professional accountants, who not only took a much more critical examination of management practices than the HMI inspectors but also published their reports. The Audit Commission's police investigations brought about significant changes, such as the introduction of civilian administrative support units and changing the philosophy of the territorial command through the basic command unit (BCU) concept (Audit Commission, 1990). The setting of publicly accountable targets for the effective and efficient delivery of services, and the requirement to measure performance, create new tensions for managers and frontline delivery of service.

There were, too, ranges of organizational innovations that resulted in significant changes to traditional management practices within the service and with which senior officers had to come to terms. Working hours were subject to variation through the introduction of more flexible shift patterns which brought about changes in the traditional eight-hour shift rotation. These were more difficult to organize and manage. Operational commanders were required to take a more proactive role in managing sickness absence within the officers and civilian staff whom they managed. Equal opportunities policies, which had previously been largely ignored by the Police Service, became a reality in the aftermath of a number of high-profile tribunals involving ethnic minority and women officers (Gregory and Lees, 1999). The introduction of part-time working and job-sharing arrangements were major challenges to managing police working arrangements.

Brown, Cooper and Kirkcaldy (1999) show that, against such a background, change itself and the (mis)management of change were sources of stress within the Police Service. Senior officers in particular, promoted on the basis of their operational knowledge and skills, found themselves increasingly being required to move into a more explicit managerial role. The Prison Service faced similar radical changes described by Bryans (2000a). For H.M. Prison Service the seminal document was Circular Instruction 55 of 1984, which laid out much the same agenda for the Prison Service as HO 114/83 had for the Police Service. Schaufeli and Peeters (2000) suggest that underpinning much of the change occurring within the prison sector was a demand for a more sophisticated professionalization of the role of prison officers. In particular, they noted the following pressures within the prison system: growing size and changing composition of inmate populations; increase in the numbers of drug addicts, mentally ill and aggressive prisoners; introduction of a new raft of rehabilitation programmes; liberalization of regimes for prisoners such as conjugal visits and access to facilities such as telephones; introduction of new treatment specialists such as forensic psychologists managing sex offender treatment programmes; middle-level supervision and new career structures within the service; better-educated officers; financial cutbacks and reduction of staff.

The Audit Commission (2001) notes that the British Probation Service faces changes with respect to purpose (with attention being refocused on punishment and rehabilitation of offenders; organizational structure (the existing fifty-four local committees being reworked into forty-two local boards with a national directorate); governance arrangements (new boards being accountable to Parliament via the Home Secretary); management arrangements (with the introduction of the European Excellence model); financial arrangements (with the service moving from local to central government financial rules); and professional practice (with 'what works' initiatives introducing accredited programmes for working with offenders). In effect, these changes are bringing significant alterations in the operational environment, with greater multi-agency and partnership working. The Commission recognizes the pressures that these changes are placing on Probation Service managers and frontline staff.

British government polices have echoes elsewhere. The Probation Officers Association of Ontario (2001a), in a presentation made to the Minister of Finance in February 2000, noted that the current government has positioned itself as being 'tough on crime' and its initiatives 'have had and continue to have a profound impact on our profession'. Tin (1999) describes changes impacting on the Singapore Probation Service which reflected a switch from retributive to restorative justice programmes. As with the Police and Prison Services, the Probation Service faces a changing role and clientele. Lowry (2000) notes that the role of the USA probation/pre-trial services officers has changed from predominately one of a social worker to one of an enforcement agent of the court. There has, too, been a shift to more dangerous caseloads and new activities which increase risks to officers. Changes in offender populations, especially drug abusers and sex offenders, present potentially difficult and dangerous individuals with whom the officers have to interact.

Changes in policy, reorientation of operational practices and new expectations of service quality impact not only on line officers but also those who are responsible for managing change. Uniformed criminal justice agencies share elements of occupational culture, which suggest there to be strong rank and file solidarity, an 'us and them' mentality and a resistance to change. There are also some differences such as the gender balance of the Police and Prison Services compared to probation. Nonetheless, sources of and reactions to stress can be linked to aspects of organizational culture.

Sources of stress

Launay and Fielding (1989) argue that prison officers suffer two broad categories to stress: staff–inmate confrontations and communication difficulties between management and uniformed staff. Schaufeli and Peeters (2000) elaborated sources of routine organizational stressors that impact upon prison officers. These include high workload, especially when demand peaks: at times when there is much to do in too little time, with little time for recovery. They argue that within the Prison Service this job pressure is exacerbated by a lack of autonomy. Schaufeli and Peeters explain that prison officers have relatively little discretion in performing their tasks and correspondingly have fewer feelings of personal accomplishment. Staff often feel under-utilized and they point to research evidence from Sweden that shows an association between under-stimulation and higher rates of sickness absence. Hay and Sparks (1991) suggest that prison officers are often left to their own devices to figure out how to manage good relationships between themselves and prisoners, so tensions are evident because of the lack of direction and training, which then undermines the professional status and self-esteem of prison staff.

A further type of stressor noted to impact upon prison officers is role problems. These can be divided into role ambiguity (lack of adequate information enabling job to be done well) and role conflict (tension between custodial and rehabilitation demands of incarceration). Changing correctional philosophies and institutional practices have exacerbated these problems. Bryans (2000a) discusses this in relation to the problems faced by governors as follows: 'For some governors, the managerialist culture does not fit readily with their caring and reforming ideas as they perceive that it has attempted to change their orientation, value base and ways of working' (p. 26). This is exacerbated by policy shifts from softer, more constructive engagement with prisoners following from Woolf's recommendations to a return to harsher alternatives following political rhetoric to crack down hard on criminals. Role ambiguity and low levels of control in decision making are predictors of burnout. Schaufeli and Peeters (2000) suggest that estimates of burnout vary and report research that finds between one-third and one-quarter of prison staff are affected. When compared to other occupational groups, prison staff are found to be more alienated, cynical, pessimistic, sceptical and powerless. Rates of premature retirement also vary within jurisdictions (Israel is amongst the highest at 50 per cent and the Netherlands the lowest at between 4 and 5 per cent). More rigorous selection criteria and a better match between job experiences and expectations account for this difference.

Robinson (1992), in a study of 658 Canadian corrections staff, found that one-fifth felt ashamed to tell people that they worked in prisons. Over half felt frustrated and angry by their job and 45 per cent agreed that they usually felt that they were under a lot of pressure when at work. From follow-up interviews, 26 per cent of staff felt little or no stress, 37 per cent medium, 28 per cent high and 10 per cent very high stress. Over a fifth felt stressed through fear about their personal security, poor communication, workload, annoyance from inmates, poor promotion prospects, lack or waste of resources and problems caused by their immediate supervisor.

Bromley and Blount (1997), reporting the results of American research, found that significant stressors for prison officers were management ambiguity, problems with inmate contact, poor communication, fear of inmates and lack of participation in decision making. Interestingly, when Bromley and Blount (1997) compared the stressors of police and probation officers, they found out that for the latter most derived from the organization itself, whereas for the former much derived from job-related tasks. This finding tends not to be supported by research literature for police occupational stress hailing from Britain and Australia. Biggam et al. (1997); Crowe and Stradling (1993); Brown and Campbell (1990); Hart, Wearing and Headey (1995) report that organizational stressors seem more likely sources of stress than operational duties. A possible explanation for this is linked with the high levels of discretion and relatively low levels of street supervision that frontline operational police officers enjoy compared to prison staff. Moreover, operational tasks, even if distressing, are associated with higher levels of job satisfaction and pride of accomplishment.

Brown and Campbell (1994) itemize the five most significant sources of organizational stress self-reported by police officers to be staffing shortages; shift work; working with civilian staff; time pressures and deadlines; and lack of consultation and communication. Brown, Fielding and Grover (1999, p. 318) suggest that operational tasks which police officers self-report as being stressful can be divided into high-frequency, low-impact deployments such as dealing with victims or routine missing persons; low-frequency, high-impact traumatic incidents such as handling the death of a colleague, child or multiple road fatalities; and having to deal with sexual offences, which they describe as vicarious stressors, in that the officer is exposed to the fallout of traumatic events (not their own) and may suffer PTSD-type symptoms. The occupational culture of the police has been described by Reiner (2000) as deriving from officers' sense of mission and need for action and as infused with cynicism, pessimism, suspicion, conservatism and machismo. In such an environment it becomes difficult to admit feeling overwhelmed by the difficult or distressing, and the informal culture operates to alleviate stress by socializing and drinking when off duty.

Corbett and Harris (2000), in reviewing the research literature on stressors identified to impact upon Probation Service staff, found evidence for organizational factors such as boredom, role ambiguity and conflict and inadequate participation of line personnel in decision making. Moreover, the rank and role of probation officers made a difference. Managers, who, it was suggested, had greater direct input into decision making and whose work was more challenging, were less likely to suffer burnout compared with frontline staff. Simmons, Cochran and Blount (1997) found that senior staff and specialists were less likely to express thoughts of leaving the Probation Service compared to entry-level officers, who had a greater propensity to express a desire to resign. Thomas (1988) reported that probation staff found unnecessary paperwork and lack of time to accomplish tasks as the two most frequently cited sources of stress. Thereafter, officers indicated financial concerns, uncertainty about retirement benefits and family–work tensions. Thomas (1988) noted the political pressures of the job and dangers faced by officers were additional stresses. Slate, Johnson and Wells (2000) suggest that probation staff also suffer from stresses generated by the organization itself and include unnecessary paperwork, lack of time to accomplish tasks, and pay and conditions. Bromley and Blount (1997) report the results of several studies into sources of probation officers' stress. These are found to be poor pay and status, role conflicts and ambiguity, client–officer interactions, excessive paperwork, performance pressures and job risks.

A new operational concern for criminal justice practitioners has been the increasing workload in relation to sex offenders. Lea, Auburn and Kibblewhite (1999) compare practitioners' responses when dealing with these offenders. They indicate that in Britain sixty sex offender treatment programmes have been established within the last five years. They found that attitudes towards sex offenders differ between members of professional groups. Thus probation officers and psychologists tend to have a more positive attitude than prison or police officers. Sex offenders are reported as being viewed as more dangerous, harmful, violent, tense, unpredictable, aggressive and irrational compared with other offender types. Their findings reveal what they term the 'professional personal dialectic'. This is defined as the tension between the need for the professional to develop a relationship with the sex offender whilst simultaneously managing a desire not to enter into a relationship because of abhorrence of the offences committed. This tension results in degrees of stress and is coped with by separating personal feelings from professional role. However, such a coping strategy may result in the professional being unable to empathize with the offender and impeding either an investigation or treatment intervention. There are dangers of colluding with offenders in an attempt to establish rapport. As well as these dilemmas, practitioners feel stress from their responsibilities towards public safety from sex offending. The professionals' sense of responsibility is compounded by stress associated with the notion that sex offenders have a poor prognosis. A further source of stress was identified to lie with the very character of sex offenders because of their propensity to deny or minimize the impact of their offences. Findings reported earlier indicated that the best predictor of stress experienced by police officers working with victims of sexual offences was their own earlier victimization. It may be that a similar dynamic is operating with prison staff who volunteer to work on the sex offender treatment programmes. This is a topic that requires more research investigation.

Research findings suggest there to be some practitioner-specific hazards. For prison officers this has been taken to include riots, attempted intimidation or being taken hostage. A study of hostage victims by the Correctional Service of Canada (online, n.d.) noted that fifty-two members of staff had been taken hostage between 1985 and 1995. Twenty-seven survivors took part in the study. Most (63 per cent) were female and incidents ranged from a few minutes to over sixty hours. Weapons figured in 85 per cent of incidents. The study reported that ten (37 per cent) suffered severe distress and disjunction. These were officers who had experienced the longest periods of captivity and symptoms included: feelings of powerlessness; shock; fear; and isolation. Hostage survivors also reported feelings of embarrassment, critical reactions from fellow officers and lack of management support. Survivors were asked how they coped and comments included remaining calm and thinking clearly; use of interpersonal skills; knowledge of institutional procedures; and resourcefulness.

The Probation Officers Association of Ontario (2001b) highlights a particular problem faced by their managers given shifts in criminal justice polices. They note that, with community mental health programmes, people previously detained in psychiatric hospitals may be released without adequate supervisor programmes to support them. They argue this may place frontline probation officers at special risk and question the adequacy of present training in terms of symptom recognition and violence-diffusion techniques. Similarly, clients with poor anger-management skills and limited tolerance of administrative process may also place the officer at risk, and he/she must also attempt to balance increased caseloads, meaningful client interactions and bureaucratic demands for performance monitoring and accountability. Littlechild (1997) looked at risk of violence towards British probation officers. This research found that Probation Service staff were less at risk than social workers. By and large rates were under-reported (about one in three reported being subject to threats of violence) because of concerns about what colleagues might think.

Police officers face the possibility of violent assault involving the use of firearms. Brown and Campbell (1994) review research that suggests about a third of officers suffer a severe reaction after having to shoot someone in the line of duty, about a third suffer a moderate reaction and a third report minimal impact. Typically, the first days after the incident is the time for greatest impact, with an average time of about twenty weeks for officers to report 'getting back to normal'. Most commonly reported symptoms include flashbacks, sleep problems and concern over legal proceedings.

Interactions

As discussed above, the occupational culture of organizations has been implicated both in contributing to stressor exposure and in helping (or hindering) practitioners in coping with stress responses (Bar On et al., 2000; Martin & Jurik 1996). Bar On et al. (2000) suggest that occupational culture defines the latitude permitted for emotional expression, a significant feature of which is the role played by colleagues and informal support. From the police research literature there is some indication that officers do talk things through with friends or colleagues (Alexander & Walker, 1994). Yet according to Stephens, Long and Miller (1997) the sharing of emotional experiences is an aspect of support that is not always found in police culture. They report research findings from samples of Australian and British police officers that displays of emotion were perceived as personally weak and occupationally hazardous. Fear of not performing well in the eyes of peers leads to blocked feelings in stressful situations. They conclude that these attitudes actually hinder the therapeutic responses appropriate for recovery from the possible adverse consequences of exposure to traumatic episodes. Brown and Grover (1998) suggest that under conditions of low stressor exposure, social support did not necessarily buffer the police officer from potential adverse effects. They propose that the solicitousness of family or colleagues may be more of a hindrance than a help. However, under conditions of high stressor exposure, social support did seem to be important in modifying possible ill health. Stephens, Long and Miller (1997), in their study of trauma amongst New Zealand officers, found that support from peers in talking about negative aspects of police work was associated with beneficial outcomes, but that other aspects of social interactions between colleagues may actually be burdensome and result in poor health outcomes.

Schaufeli and Peeters (2000) suggest that group solidarity and collegiality are weakly developed amongst prison officers because they only interact occasionally. The organization emphasizes individual rather than team responsibility and this results in an individualistic culture. This may not be so within the British prison system and will depend on where the officer works. Staff on special units may develop a stronger sense of cohesion. Nevertheless, as with the Police Service there is a strong sense in which asking for social support may be considered to be an expression of incompetence. The Canadian Corrections review of the experiences of prison officers who had been taken hostage indicated that where there had been previous close supportive relationships with fellow officers and good relationships with managers, survivors recovered more quickly. Survivors who had had previously unsupportive colleagues who made critical judgements about the hostage taking experienced revictimization and this was more likely to impede recovery.

A number of commentators make the point that law enforcement is male-dominated with women only relatively recently making serious inroads into its ranks (Hurst & Hurst, 1997; Martin & Jurik, 1996; Brown, 1998). Heidensohn (1986, p. 289) describes the gendered nature of approaches to justice. She defines a male approach as: rational, clear-thinking and procedurally competent where justice is achieved through laws and the courts within a model of legal equity. The feminine approach on the other hand is described as caring and personal, relying on responsibility and co-operation, achieving justice through more informal means and networking. These underpinning differences are contained within an informal culture that is supportive of the male (and mostly white) norms and informal values. Thus off-colour humour, off-duty drinking and socializing can involve sexist (and racist) comments that are supportive of the majority and exclude minority groups. Hurst and Hurst (1997) note that male prison officers are more likely to depersonalize inmates and use confrontational coping strategies, whereas women officers are seen as more prone to violence from inmates and to engage in suppressive coping or utilize social support. However, they found no differences in male and female prison officers' burnout scores. Schaufeli and Peeters (2000) suggest that gender, ethnic and age differences in experiences of stress amongst prison staff are difficult to substantiate and propose that the roles of these characteristics are more subtle. They report that minority male prison officers show greater efficacy in working with inmates and this is associated with lower job stress. For white female officers, higher levels of job satisfaction are mediated by quality of supervision. For younger prison officers, role conflict and increased inmate contact contributes to their emotional exhaustion, whereas for older officers, emotional exhaustion is associated with decreased inmate contact. It is likely, then, as Wilkinson and Campbell (1997) point out, while personal resources are differentially distributed and influence capacity to cope; operational exposure and style of supervision are influenced by group membership of staff. Britton (1997) suggests that despite gender-neutral rhetoric, training within the Prison Service assumes men's prisons as the model and exaggerate risks of violence. She contends that assignments are seen as safe or unsafe with the latter taken to involve more inmate contact and greater contact with potentially violent prisoners. Women are deemed less fit to deal with unsafe assignments by both men and women prison officers.

Martin and Jurik (1996) describe changes within the corrections environment in the United States following the Civil Rights movement of the 1970s. More women entered the Prison Service and, together with changing penal philosophies, they were supposed to prompt more humane treatment of inmate populations. Yet, as with the Police Service, a combination of paternalistic protectiveness and rivalry for promotion opportunities allowed sexual harassment to flourish.

A fair amount of research is now available examining gender differences in the stress experiences of police officers (Brown & Fielding 1993; Brown, Fielding & Grover 1999). Again the conclusion of this research is that the effects of gender differences are interactional and somewhat subtle. There are relatively few differences in exposure to organizational stressors except with respect to a greater level of discrimination and harassment experienced by women officers compared to men. Women police officers are more likely to have a direct involvement in the policing of sexual crime, where often the victims are women or children, and this does seem to add to their stress burden. Brown, Fielding and Grover (1999) link this to women's approach to victims and justice and resonates with the dichotomy pointed out by Heidensohn described earlier. Brown, Campbell and Fife-Schaw (1995) found from a national survey of policewomen that they experienced fewer 'dangerous' deployments, were less satisfied with their promotion opportunities and suffered sexual harassment when compared to male colleagues.

There is little research available examining gender differences in terms of stressor exposure and adverse reactions within the Probation Service. Bar On et al. (2000) compared police officers with various caring professions having a social service orientation which may be analogous to the Probation Service. They argued that care workers have an informal culture that expects to recognize, defuse and handle distressed or potentially violent clients. Whilst policing is male oriented, care work tends, traditionally, to have employed more women. Under these circumstances men as a gender minority may experience greater difficulty in meeting and managing expectations about more feminized versions of justice. Their study found no significant gender/occupational interactions in care workers' or police officers' ability to respond to stress.

Age has been found to be associated with reported occupational stress levels (Smith et al., 2000). They indicate that those at either end of the working age spectrum (18–35 and 55-plus) were less likely to report stress. This relationship has also been found amongst police and probation officers but not for prison officers (Patterson, 1992). Explanations offered to account for this finding include the 'disenchantment hypothesis'. This is when officers realize that they have little impact on crime and their ideals seem removed from the reality they experience. Early career enthusiasm is replaced by mid-career cynicism. As officers enter the final phase of their career there is a renewed emphasis on personal rather than work-oriented goals and this can have the effect of reducing stress levels. As officers near retirement, their stress levels are said to decline even further as they contemplate the 'good old days' and become less concerned with the demands of the job or fear of failure. An alternative explanation is the 'reference group' theory. Patterson (1992) describes this as follows: the least experienced officers (rookies) may perceive the most experienced (veteran) as a reference group, i.e. not the group to which they belong, but the group to which they aspire. The lower stress levels of rookie officers is attributable to modelling themselves on veteran officers who appear less stressed and more in control. Schaufeli and Peeters (2000) propose the 'healthy worker' hypothesis, whereby those who survive their law-enforcement careers are healthier and less stressed, with more susceptible personnel having left or prematurely retired from the service.

Patterson's (1992) finding that stress levels tend to increase for longer-serving prison officers was associated with exposure to more demanding work and greater challenges from inmates as the officers' experience increased. Brown and Blount (1999) found that psychologists working as sex offender programme treatment managers within prisons suffered different foci of stress depending on their years of experience. Inexperienced staff were more concerned about their personal safety; intermediate levels of experience were associated with concerns about supervision and others delivering the programme effectively. The longest-serving managers had greater bureaucratic concerns and worried about the accreditation of their programme. These and related findings suggest that interventions may need to be developed to fit the years of service profile of practitioners rather than assuming a homogeneity of stressor exposures and impacts being evenly distributed throughout the workforce.

Interventions

In a recent review, Cooper and Cartwright (1997) point out that evidence for the success of occupational stress interventions has been equivocal. Briner (1997) states the case even more strongly: 'while a number of different stress management interventions (SMI) techniques are routinely adopted within organizations and the flourishing stress management industry continues to make extravagant claims for their benefits, there is surprisingly little evidence that supports the value of SMIs' (p. 61). Briner argues that few organizations undertake assessments as to whether an SMI is necessary or suitable. Often interventions have not been designed on the basis of much detailed analysis of the problem and are, in themselves, incomplete or inadequately maintained. Cooper and Cartwright (1997) identify three major strategies available for dealing with the problems of stress in police officers: primary, secondary or tertiary interventions. The first seeks to eliminate or reduce sources of stress and recruit those who may be more stress resistant; the second mitigates the possible consequences of exposure through training and protective equipment; the third provides support in the form of counselling or psychiatric services to the stressed personnel. Primary interventions should be preceded by some type of stress audit to identify specific stressors. Secondary prevention is concerned with prompt detection and management of stress by increasing awareness and improving stress management skills. Tertiary prevention is concerned with rehabilitation and recovery and often includes the provision of professional programmes. Brown and Campbell (1994) point out some of the inhibitors that can impede the success of stress interventions: those that focus on equipping workers to cope better with stressors rather than eliminating or reducing sources of stress; limited scientific basis for intervention means less precision is possible in matching a solution to the problem; logistic and financial constraints associated with the organization's willingness to change its procedures and structures; minimalist or legalistic attitudes in meeting obligations to staff.

Health and safety regulatory authorities draw attention to the legal obligations of employers to ensure the well-being of staff with an emphasis on requirements for risk assessment (Cooper & Cartwright, 1997). They point out that assessment of physical hazards is well established but that assessment of psychosocial factors relating to health is not only newer but is also substantially different. The Health and Safety Executive (HSE) has produced a number of reports that describe basic principles for risk assessment, which is defined as a careful examination of what could cause harm at work and whether existing preventative steps are sufficient for eliminating or reducing harm. The five-step approach (recommended by the HSE) involves: examination of hazards that could reasonably be expected to result in significant harm; identification of who might be harmed (paying particular attention to inexperienced staff or those working in isolation from other staff members); scrutiny of whether the present preventative measures are sufficient; fully documentating findings; a review and revision of precautions to control hazards.

Given commonalities in the stress exposures of uniformed criminal justice practitioners and greater tendencies towards multi-agency partnerships there is scope for some common remedies. Bromley and Blount (1997) identify similar external stressors impinging on Police, Prison and Probation Services which include frustration with the judicial system; lack of support or negative public attitudes towards criminal justice practitioners; negative or biased media coverage; rank and file dislike of administration; and outside agencies' scrutiny of law enforcement functions. Organizational stressors such as paperwork, poor communication, lack of manager/supervisor support, role ambiguity or conflict also seem common experiences. It is in the area of operational tasks that the different practitioners may find themselves exposed to different stressors which may require more tailored stress interventions.

Schaufeli and Peeters (2000) suggest two types of stress interventions: organizational and individual. The latter are designed to help the individual cope better and suggestions include avoidance or palliative strategies (listening to music, talking to family members, reading and exercise). Training interventions designed for individuals relate more to enhancing job-related skills and include relaxation techniques, stress inoculation and cognitive restructuring. Organizational strategies relate to the infrastructure and work environment. Here improvements in human resource management (such as better recruitment and selection practices, in-service training and career development can be invoked to improve the staff member's resistance to stress. Active stress prevention can be incorporated into performance appraisals, stress audits, burnout checks, exit interviewing and closer monitoring of absenteeism. Job enrichment can improve the variety of work and devolve levels of decision making. Better communication with and support from management, fostering coaching styles of leadership are also suggested.

Increasingly, criminal justice practitioners are being offered employee assistance services (Bromley & Blount, 1997). They suggest asking three questions before offering such services to personnel: what are the sources of stress affecting the employee? How does the agency take steps to reduce stress created by its own policies and practices? What will encourage targeted practitioners to use the services offered? They suggest an organizational strategy be adopted that includes: a survey/review of the organization itself in order to identify internal sources of stress and developing plans for needed change; encouraging upward communication and pushing autonomy down; ensuring openness and fairness in discipline, performance evaluation and promotion. The most successful employee assistance programmes are ones in which the assistance on offer is seen as professional, independent and confidential. Generally services are more successful if located away from the organization and available to provide 24-hour emergency cover.

Mitchell and Bray (1990) describe a systematic approach to debriefing following exposure to traumatic incidents, termed critical incident stress debriefing (CISD). This relies on trained and primed support personnel from the organization concerned who conduct debriefing sessions through group meetings at strategic intervals after the incident. Mitchell (2000), in an evaluation of CISD within the Police Service, suggests that it has a function in providing information and an opportunity for group discussion but that there is little evidence to support a role for CISD in preventing acquisition of PTSD or reducing sickness absence.

Plant (2001) reviews the use of critical incident debriefing for emergency personnel and points to its wide adoption even though some doubts have been expressed as to its efficacy. Plant concludes that it is unlikely that a single, standardized procedure applied in a mechanistic fashion is likely to produce universal benefits given the diverse nature of trauma and idiosyncratic processes involved in individual traumatization. She suggests that a comprehensive approach be adopted in designing interventions that are task orientated, educative and psychosocial. The first includes more comprehensive recruitment and selection of staff in the first place, providing a general educational input to staff, periodically refreshed in which symptoms of traumatic exposure can be explained and procedures to address them identified. Pre-incident preparation can be structured to help create socially cohesive working teams so that those who have to deal with the difficult or unpleasant work do so in a context which is supportive and where staff are accustomed to discussing difficult cases and their emotional responses.

Cox and Smith (1990) propose that stress be thought of as the experience of demands and pressures that are difficult to manage or are perceived as unmanageable. They found from their workshops with prison officers a cycle in which organizational demands, lack of clear objectives, low morale and motivation increased levels of absenteeism, substance misuse, and had the knock-on effect of adversely affecting relationships with prisoners and increasing lapses and mistakes and serving further to lower morale and motivation. Their prescription was to improve the occupational culture by management being more willing to encourage flexibility and try new ideas, valuing good relationships between people and departments and having clear roles and objectives. Hay and Sparks (1991) state this as follows: 'if (prison) staff are to be equipped to resist being worn down and burned out by the demands of the job, or co-opted into regressive sub-cultures, then they must be offered a clear and viable vision on what being a prison officer means at the outset of their training'. These sentiments might be echoed by police and probationer colleagues.

Conclusion

The world of the criminal justice practitioner has been subject to considerable change in recent years, with new demands on managers and frontline officers. Greater behavioural and financial accountability, greater demand for professional competence and higher public expectations for quality of delivered services add to the extant operational tasks that may potentially expose practitioners to occupational stressors. Police, Probation and Prison Services share a number of features in that they have all been subject to organizational and operational change and so it might be expected that the pattern of stressors arising from the nature of the respective agencies may be similar. This indeed appears to be the case, with common stressors being poor communication, role ambiguity, unusual work patterns, inadequate support from supervisors, paperwork and limited career development. Organizational prescriptions to improve human resource management may translate across organizations and indeed, given increased multi-agency co-operation, there may be scope for sharing experiences and the burden of costs amongst agencies.

The Health and Safety Executive provides some general principles for good stress management: take occupational stress seriously; develop an understanding attitude towards people who admit being under too much work pressure; encourage managers to have an open attitude towards stressed staff; ensure staff have the skills and training needed to do their jobs effectively; vary work tasks; treat people fairly and consistently; indicate that bullying and harassment are not tolerated; encourage two-way communication, especially at times of organizational change.

More recent research within the Police and Prison Services (Brown, Cooper & Kirkcaldy, 1996; Bryans, 2000a) finds that senior management suffer occupational stress as a consequence of attempting to manage change. Senior staff find the importation of private-sector management practices difficult to reconcile with duties of care and legal requirements for which there is no direct commercial parallel. Political pressures, greater financial accountability and public scrutiny into probity of practice place greater pressure on criminal justice managers. So as well as managing change well to buffer operational staff from stress, senior managers also need training and support.

There are some operational tasks which may expose officers to specific risks given the point of entry of the practitioner within the criminal justice system. Thus police officers may face violence from suspects avoiding apprehension or vicarious exposure to the distress of victims of sexual assaults. Prison staff can also face violence and may run the risk of being taken hostage. Probation staff interact with released offenders and face public opprobrium when attempting to reintegrate former prisoners within the community. There may be a need to design bespoke programmes to deal with agency-specific stressors of this type. Critical Incident Stress Debriefing has a growing number of critics as the best intervention following some traumatic exposure. Better preparation for possible exposure and more effective support in the aftermath of exposure are likely to be more effective.

Chapter Ten

The Contribution of Job Simulation Assessment Centres to Organizational Development in HM Prison Service

Keith Baxter, Kirstin Davis, Eliot Franks and Sonia Kitchen

Introduction

Since the early 1980s the pace of change in organizations has increased dramatically. Calls for improvements in efficiency have resulted in flatter management structures and the introduction of staff profiles set at levels that precisely meet organizational requirements. As a result, higher expectations are being placed on smaller workforces to achieve increasingly demanding performance targets. So-called 'lean organizations' rely heavily upon the employment of competent personnel who perform consistently at, or above, the required level. Additional staff resources simply do not exist to compensate or cover for under-performing personnel.

The idea that 'people make the place' (Schneider, 1987) is axiomatic in the workplace. This is evidenced by the phenomenal growth in the field of human resource management and the central role now being played by recruitment, selection and career development in corporate strategies. All business-focused organizations are keen to select the right people for available jobs. Failure to do so is not only disruptive but expensive too. It is clearly a waste of valuable resources to recruit, train and retain unsuitable personnel. However, dismissing them or 'moving them on' can be a precarious process fraught with industrial relations and legal pitfalls.

Traditional methods of selection such as unstructured interviews are inexpensive and easy to organize but they are also unfair and fail to predict subsequent job performance (Feltham, 1989). With the introduction of ever more stringent equal opportunities and health and safety legislation they are no longer a viable option. For example, employers have a legal obligation to provide a reasonable level of care for their employees' physical, social and psychological well-being (Cooke, 1995). If personnel feel that they have been inappropriately selected for job roles that they lack the skills or potential to fulfil, and experience psychological stress as a result, they may be justified in seeking compensation for the negligence they have suffered.

The selection method increasingly being used to recruit, evaluate and develop personnel is the assessment centre (Shackleton & Newell, 1991; Spychalski et al., 1997). Well-designed assessment centres rest on the foundation of a rigorous job analysis that has identified the particular skills required for a target job role both now and in the foreseeable future. Unlike unstructured interviews, they have an impressive and proven ability to predict subsequent job performance (Gaugler et al., 1987). Moreover, they tend to receive enthusiastic support from both assessors and participants. Woodruffe (2000, p. 13) states:

> The assessors see how people behave in the centre and can place a lot of faith that this is a good preview of how the person would behave in the job. In addition, if used for selection, participants come through the centre feeling that the organization has treated them fairly and that it has obtained sound evidence for its decision.

Assessment centres have been used most frequently to select managers (Hunter & Hunter, 1984) but they can just as readily be applied to other roles. One organization where they are being used extensively to select and promote personnel at both managerial and non-managerial levels is the Prison Service.

Role of the Prison Officer

Two decades ago the May Report on the UK Prison Service (May, 1979) described the relationship between prison officers and prisoners as key to the humane and effective management of prisons. This message was echoed by HM Chief Inspector of Prisons, Sir David Ramsbotham. He introduced the concept of the 'healthy prison', where prison personnel are expected to demonstrate positive attitudes and develop relationships that encourage prisoners to adopt pro-social behaviours.

Prison officers are obviously key to this process as they routinely interact with prisoners at both procedural (e.g. searching) and more complex interpersonal (e.g. welfare assessments) levels on a daily basis (Bagshaw & Baxter, 1987). They have to respond flexibly to meet the subtly changing balance of care and control demands of each unfolding situation, maintaining supportive relationships with prisoners while simultaneously dealing with transgressions and remaining alert to security threats. Sometimes prison officers need to be assertive, without becoming aggressive, and at other times they need to be helpful and understanding without becoming emotionally enmeshed and susceptible to manipulation (Bagshaw & Baxter, 1987). The interpersonal demands of the job are clearly quite sophisticated and demanding.

Shepherd (1993), writing about investigative interviewing for the police, proposes the concept of ethical conversation management which presumes an inclusive relationship founded on empathy that communicates respect for the person and signals that the speaker is also human and has rights. He states:

> An ethical conversationalist converses with two-sided logic, with self and other in mind, evidencing verbally and non verbally a commitment to co-operative talk by: using appropriate conversational style; consciously orienting the other person as to the reason for the conversation (to avoid the guessing game and to signal no hidden agenda); to work at making the exchange mutual by sharing the talking turn and talking time, balancing assertions (questions, statements, observations and comments) with responsive listening; striving not to talk disruptively (over talking, interrupting, minimally responding and rapidly changing the topic); and not bringing the exchange to an ill-considered or inconsiderate close. (p. 45)

This statement provides a powerful and succinct definition of the type of interpersonal performance required of prison officers and other personnel working in the Prison Service. It requires them to transcend the seemingly contradictory care and control aspects of their role. Personnel who cannot do this may experience feelings of frustration, helplessness, cynicism and even hostility (Shamir & Drory, 1982). Moreover, where such feelings are pervasive amongst staff, the prison regime is likely to be based on authoritarian interactions that have been shown to be ineffective as they merely provoke resistance and hostility from prisoners (Lovibond, Mithiran & Adams, 1979).

The emphasis placed on prison officers' interpersonal skills seems to be supported by the wealth of emerging research into 'emotional intelligence'. Goleman (1995), who popularized this concept, defines its five component elements as self-awareness, self-control, motivation, empathy and social skills. The research clearly indicates that highly effective interpersonal skills are dependent on an awareness of one's own feelings. Goleman suggests that emotional intelligence is at least twice as important at cognitive and technical ability, which he states contributes less than 20 per cent to successful performance in most jobs. Higgs and Dulewicz (1997) researched these ideas from personal and competency data collected on 100 management and business leaders. They data tracked their career advancement over a seven-year period and found that emotional intelligence was more highly related to success than cognitive ability alone.

An Overview of the Prison Service's Job Simulation Assessment Centre (JSAC)

A simulation represents the essential elements of a real-world phenomenon (Robson, 1997) and may be used to train, assess proficiency or carry out research (Patrick, 1997). Job simulations are work-related role-play exercises that match, as closely as possible, important aspects of a job. They are the most effective way of 'test driving' individuals in realistic but safe conditions and it is in this context that the Prison Service introduced them in the late 1970s to develop and assess hostage negotiation and command skills. McClelland (1973) makes a clear case for the use of simulations: 'if you want to know how well a person can drive a car, sample their ability to do so by giving them a driver's test'.

This rather obvious approach to assessment is, perhaps unsurprisingly, also one of the most accurate. In the mid-1990s the Police Services in England and Wales began using simulations as an integral part of their assessment of candidates seeking promotion to the ranks of sergeant and inspector (Bligh, 1994). Shortly afterwards, in 1996, the Prison Service developed its first Job Simulation Assessment Centre (JSAC) to select new prison officers. It has subsequently been extended to assess personnel for promotion to senior officer (first line manager), operational manager and senior operational manager.

A continuous process of consultation with key stakeholders in the organization informs the design of role-play simulations prior to each JSAC. The ability to keep pace with the changing skill requirements of the Prison Service is a key feature of the JSAC process, which only selects and promotes those who can demonstrate behaviours consistent with its strategic vision, goals and values.

At a JSAC candidates are expected to participate in up to eight consecutive role-play simulations that vary in time and complexity depending on the level of skills being assessed. For example, the simulations included in the senior officer (first line manager) JSAC are longer and more demanding than those included in the prison officer (basic grade) JSAC.

All JSAC simulations are based on a rigorous job analysis and are therefore realistic. However, it is important that candidates are given every opportunity to demonstrate the required skills so they are designed with consideration to their previous experience.

Job analysis techniques used in the development of JSACs include:

Repertory Grid: individuals at the appropriate level are asked to think of a good, average and poor worker and express how they differ from each other.

The Critical Incident Technique (Flanagan, 1954): descriptions of behaviours that result in good or poor job performance are sought from knowledgeable personnel at appropriate positions in the organization. For example, line managers are asked to record behaviours of staff that greatly influence their performance.

360° feedback: information is gathered about the target job role from significant others such as people already working at that level, subordinates and superiors, etc.

On entering the JSAC candidates attend a verbal briefing where they receive an information pack designed to structure expectations and reduce anxieties about the pending assessment process. All candidates' performances at a JSAC are videotaped. This offers the following benefits:

If an assessor is uncertain about a candidate's performance, he or she can review it on video before making a final decision.

Assessors can be independently monitored to ensure that predetermined marking standards are applied equally and fairly to all candidates.

Role-players can be independently monitored to ensure they deliver their scripted roles in a consistent manner to all candidates.

The videotape can be used to facilitate JSAC performance feedback to candidates. (Note, written feedback is offered to the candidates who have attended the senior officer promotion JSAC but personal [one-to-one] feedback is given to operational manager and senior operational manager candidates.)

If, or when, disgruntled candidates appeal against JSAC decisions, videotapes may be used as evidence of their performance at any subsequent adjudication meetings or tribunals.

On completion of the JSAC candidates are individually debriefed. This provides them with an opportunity to unwind and raise any concerns they may have about the assessment process.

The whole of the JSAC design and delivery process is transparent and therefore open to scrutiny. Unsuccessful candidates can, if they wish, challenge the assessment process but the high level of monitoring and independent checking undertaken during and after each JSAC usually ensures that assessment decisions are fair, valid and defensible. Most unsuccessful candidates accept this, particularly when they receive evidence-based performance feedback, which helps them to acknowledge and address their identified training and development needs.

The Prison Officer JSAC

The JSAC designed to select new entrant prison officers mainly assesses skills required to meet the interpersonal demands of the role. The following skills, defined by observable behavioural indicators, were assessed on the prison officer recruitment JSAC introduced in 1996.

> *Calming*: use of pacifying and soothing skills to calm a person down enough to listen to explanations.
> *Influencing*: use of assertiveness to correct the way people are behaving.
> *Taking criticism*: accepting accountability and agreeing action plans to rectify a problem.
> *Giving constructive criticism*: use of listening and assertion skills to influence the behaviour of someone else.
> *Dealing with requests for help*: use of listening skills and showing empathy.
> *Listening with a purpose*: use of questioning and listening skills to establish the facts of a situation.
> *Written and analytical skills*: analysing information and preparing clear, concise and relevant reports.

The Senior Officer JSAC

The senior officer is a first line manager responsible for championing effective working relationships between staff and with prisoners. It is the only management grade represented in the prison at all times and therefore plays a pivotal role in developing and maintaining a 'healthy prison'.

Prior to the first senior officer JSAC a comprehensive job analysis of the role was conducted to distinguish it from the job roles immediately below (prison officer) and above (principal officer) it in the organizational hierarchy. The following critical responsibilities were identified:

> Managing poorly performing staff.
> Acknowledging good staff performance.

Dealing with personal problems from both staff and prisoners.
Briefing.
Dealing with an incident.
Representing staff fairly.
Dealing with manipulative prisoners.

Critical incident interviews informed the design of role-play simulations. These were piloted and videotaped using a cross-section of incumbent senior officers from different types of establishment. The videotapes were then used to design scoring guides that enabled assessors to discriminate between acceptable and unacceptable candidate performances.

Operational Manager JSAC

The operational manager is a middle-management grade. At this point personnel wear civilian clothes instead of the black and white Prison Service uniform. This has symbolic currency in the organization where such a transition represents a significant step towards senior management responsibilities and status.

A job analysis of the operational manager role revealed the following distinguishing, and critical, managerial responsibilities:

Being a significant point of reference to staff and a key decision maker.
Acting as a cantilever between policy and practice.
Taking a legal responsibility for prisoner care.
Trouble shooting.

The role also involves substantial analytical and written demands. In view of this an examination has been introduced to sift applicants to the operational manager JSAC. This comprises three work sample tests that closely match the type and level of analytical and written work normally completed at this level. Candidates are required to analyse statistical information and establish trends, draft a letter of reply to a complaint from a member of the public, and draft an operational report.

Core Management Skills (CMS)

A content analysis of the simulations used at the different levels has revealed three main skill clusters required for working in the Prison Service (figure 10.1).

As indicated by figure 10.1, the use of analytical and written skills increases progressively as one moves up the management hierarchy whereas the use of

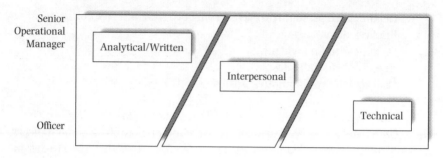

Figure 10.1   Prison service: required skills

technical skills decreases. (Note, technical skills are defined as prison-specific physical, procedural and professional skills). The relative importance of interpersonal skills remains constant at every level of the organizational hierarchy. In view of this, it is essential that JSACs assess analytical, written and interpersonal skills, whereas trainable technical skills do not need to be assessed but must be incorporated into successful candidates' personal training and development objectives.

A more detailed analysis of the skills required at the different levels assessed by the JSAC has revealed eleven Core Management Skills key to operational performance in prisons. These are:

1   Briefing
2   Inquiring
3   Caring
4   Developing
5   Acknowledging achievement
6   Giving constructive criticism
7   Persuading
8   Managing conflict
9   Completing written work
10   Analysing written information
11   Incident management

The Core Management Skills relate to the management of others from prisoners up to senior managers and are required by all staff except those whose work does not entail incident management or direct involvement with prisoners. The depth and breadth of responsibility, as well as the complexity, of the Core Management Skills increases at each consecutive management level.

Figure 10.2 illustrates the requirements at each managerial level for the Core Management Skill of 'Caring'.

Competencies, Skills, Behaviours and Micro-behaviours

The terms competencies, skills and behaviours are often used interchangeably in the assessment literature. This can be very confusing. In order to remedy this problem the JSAC process has established a hierarchical classification system comprising four levels of observable behaviour. This provides a common language that aids communication between the JSAC design and delivery teams and the wider Prison Service organization. The four behavioural levels are:

Competencies

Competencies are broad behavioural statements of Prison Service requirements used to identify the general skill demands of specific jobs. Figure 10.3 outlines the Core Competence Framework for the Prison Service.

Officer	Senior Officer	Operational Manager	Senior Operational Manager
Dealing with prisoners with personal problems	**Dealing with prisoners with personal problems**	**Dealing with prisoners with personal problems**	**Dealing with prisoners with personal problems**
	Dealing with staff with personal problems	*Dealing with staff with personal problems*	*Dealing with staff with personal problems*
		Dealing with managers with personal problems	*Dealing with managers with personal problems*
		Fostering a supportive approach to staff with personal problems	Fostering a supportive approach to staff with personal problems
			Dealing with senior mamagers with personal problems
			Taking action which supports the organization's duty of care

Key: **Primarily operational**; *Will do occasionally but not primary task*; Primary task.

Figure 10.2   'Caring': requirements at each managerial level

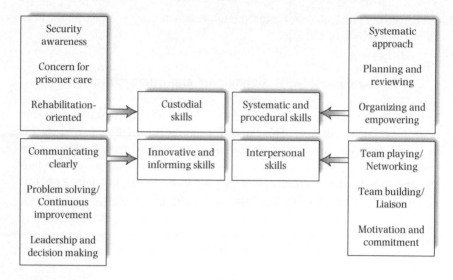

Figure 10.3 Prison Service Core Competence Framework

Core Management Skills

Core Management Skills are cumulative in that they build upon existing skills that are then applied to increasingly complex situations requiring greater breadth and depth of responsibility at each consecutively higher level in the organization.

Behaviours

Behaviours contribute to the successful performance of each Core Management Skill (CMS) and form the basis of assessment. It is necessary to describe what behaviour looks like in order for the assessment to be as objective as possible. For example if untrained assessors were asked to rate a candidate on 'caring' they would each have slightly different ideas about the behaviours that underlie this activity. However, by describing the kinds of behaviour sought, assessors who have been trained and accredited have a common anchor point to refer to which helps to ensure that their assessments are reliable and objective.

Micro-behaviours

Micro-behaviours are a further breakdown of behaviours. For example, non-verbal skills consistent with effective listening break down into a cluster of behavioural indicators such as eye contact and posture. These behavioural descriptions form an integral part of the training of assessors.

Research and Development of the JSAC Process

The JSAC process is an ever-evolving one and subject to constant research and development. Following research, the new entrant prison officer JSAC has now been brought into line with the CMS. From the CMS five core behaviours were identified that were pertinent to successful execution of the prison officer role. These were:

> Exploring and clarifying.
> Listening.
> Suspending judgement.
> Assertion.
> Showing understanding.

Rather than observing behaviour in a simulation and candidates receiving a score for each simulation, the JSAC now assesses in terms of behavioural indicators culminated over the course of the assessment centre. This subtle change from simulation measurement to behavioural measurement results in a more refined assessment, and the ability to pinpoint strengths and weaknesses in behaviour. This is true of all the JSACs run by the Prison Service.

The prison officer JSAC is currently piloting a way of testing for desired 'diversity' attitudes. Although currently not used in the accreditation process research is being carried out to identify if this can be incorporated into this particular JSAC. Currently at the promotional JSACs, assessment is made on whether a candidate will uphold Prison Service Principles related to policies such as Race Relations and Equal Opportunities. This is also undergoing rigorous research and development.

In November 2001 a new sift for the senior officer JSAC was introduced. This replaced the Prison Officer Promotion Exam (POPE) and brought the senior officer promotion in line with the operational manager and senior operational manager promotions. Like the operational manager stage one its aim was to identify those prison officers who had the written and analytical skills required by senior officers. This sift was designed in consultation with senior officers, operational and senior operational mangers and was bench-tested past current serving senior officers. The results identified it to be an effective sift.

Organizational Climate

As in most organizations, status is important in the culture of the Prison Service, where there is intense competition for jobs and promotion. However, this desire for enhanced status can cloud applicants' objectivity about their current ability and potential, which results in very few selecting themselves out of the JSAC process. Line managers appear to collude with their subordinates' self-deception as they tend to be unwilling to convey an honest report of their unsuitability for promotion on the JSAC application form. Research suggests that this phenomenon is quite common (Kane et al., 1995) and it is not, therefore, unique to the Prison Service. However, when line managers lack frankness this merely encourages failing candidates to rationalize that the JSAC has misrepresented their ability and is therefore unfair. In order to alleviate this problem guidelines are now given to line managers to assist their assessment of candidates' suitability for a JSAC against the Core Management Skills. This procedure is intended to clarify what is required of aspiring managers.

Audit Criteria

Common principles underpinning the design and delivery of all JSACs have been identified and incorporated into the following checklist of audit criteria:

> Core Management Skills form the basis of all JSACs and simulations are developed in consultation with personnel who have an appreciation of the type of critical situations encountered at the target job level.
> Simulations are piloted and validated.
> Core Management Skills are broken down into behaviours that are directly observable and amenable to reliable assessment.
> Behaviours are defined on a bipolar five-point marking scale.
> There is multiple assessment of each Core Management Skill across simulations to provide cumulative evidence of ability.
> Performance on each simulation is independently assessed without cross-referencing to performances on other assessments.
> The logistics of the assessment centre are managed efficiently and effectively.

Assessors are trained and accredited on the basis of their ability to assess performance objectively against behavioural indicators.

Role-players are trained and accredited on the basis of their ability to adhere to the role specification.

All assessors and role-players receive Equal Opportunities Training.

Assessors and role-players are quality controlled throughout the JSAC.

Candidates are comprehensively briefed, debriefed and sensitively treated.

All aspects of the JSAC are continually monitored and reviewed for possible unintended discrimination.

Written feedback is given as a minimum and, where ever possible, one-to-one feedback using the videotape of performance.

Each candidate's overall performance is measured as a profile of their ability to perform each of the CMSs.

The profile of results indicating a competence, and therefore success, is determined for each JSAC and applied equally to all candidates.

Each JSAC receives operational sponsorship from a senior member of the Prison Service who takes overall responsibility for the integrity of its design and the management of its delivery.

This audit checklist has now been used to design and deliver a newly introduced JSAC for promotion to operational manager.

Predictive Validity

The allocation of resources given over to the development and operation of the JSAC process is justified by the return on investment through the cost savings it achieves for the organization. These come from reduced recruitment and training costs, because fewer of those selected fail to make the grade. They also come from appropriately skilled recruits and promoted staff contributing to improvements in the overall performance of the Prison Service. However, establishing the predictive power of the JSAC is not a straightforward process. It requires that the subsequent work performance of a large cohort of selected candidates be objectively, reliably and accurately measured. This is hindered in the Prison Service context, where, as stated previously, many managers are reluctant to formally criticize their subordinates' performances.

A further, and perhaps even greater, obstacle to establishing the predictive power of the JSAC is the fact that a proportion of selected personnel are invariably placed into unreceptive prisons. The skill set being assessed at the JSAC is consistent with an emerging culture, defined by the leadership, that is far from the current norm across the Prison Service. Among the rank and file of staff, as in any organization going through change, there are those who cling to the familiar and resist the adoption of the new skill set. Therefore, the skills demonstrated by newly recruited and promoted personnel may not be valued or supported, and may even be undermined, by the cultural context in which they work. Some may be subjected to such intense social pressures from colleagues that they find themselves having to decide between fighting to pursue their beliefs, looking for a way to escape to a more 'healthy prison', or giving in and conforming to the status quo. In these circumstances it is obviously very difficult, if not impossible, for selected personnel to display the level of job performance that they are capable of.

In view of this, the predictive power of the JSAC must rely on support from research elsewhere and validation studies to show that, where the required behaviours are being deployed, they are producing the desired outcomes. This research is long-term and ongoing.

Adverse Impact

Adverse impact occurs when a person seeking a job is judged on criteria that their group membership makes it especially difficult to meet and which is irrelevant to effective performance of the job. It may also occur when membership of a particular group makes it more difficult to produce a representative performance in the assessment procedure, which could occur if they were are treated in a way that produces psychological discomfort or increased stress (Body, 2001).

Given the rigorous design of the JSACs, adverse impact on any particular group should not be possible and has not been evidenced. Even if an assessor or role-player does have a concealed malicious intent against some group at a JSAC, their opportunities to distort the assessment are severely restricted. This is so particularly because the distribution of assessing responsibility for each candidate is spread across several people and a number of checks and balances are built into the process. The facility to replay and therefore reassess candidates' performances ensures that assessment standards are adhered to and maintained.

Careful attention was paid to the possibility of adverse impact when the JSAC process was used in Northern Ireland. The release of prisoners from the Maze Prison following the Good Friday Agreement greatly reduced the requirement for prison officers in the Northern Ireland Prison Service. An early retirement and redundancy scheme was introduced but was over subscribed resulting in the loss of 44 per cent of the incumbent managers at or below middle-management levels. In 2000 the Northern Ireland Prison Service utilized the JSAC process to promote suitably skilled staff into the management vacancies. Statistical analysis revealed that the pass rates at this JSAC did not differ significantly between the community backgrounds of the applicants.

The Role of the JSAC in Human Resource Development and Organizational Change

'It is attention to employees, and not work conditions per se, that has the dominant impact on productivity.'   (Peters and Waterman, 1987)

The JSAC process is a tool for planned organizational change. It primarily operates as an aspect of the Prison Service's human resource strategy by facilitating the achievement of the following four key goals:

To deliver professional personnel services.
To bring in and bring on staff.
To reward good performance and effectively manage poor performance.
To value staff and provide a good working environment.

However, the wealth of data collected at JSACs can also be used to analyse and diagnose the organizational culture of the Prison Service. It is, for example, currently being used to identify 'healthy' and 'unhealthy' prisons. Over a period of two years approximately 2,500 prison officers were assessed on the senior officer JSAC. Analysis of the performance profiles of candidates from particular prison establishments with a very low success rate highlighted quite specific performance trends. One trend indicated that candidates from an identified prison generally performed well on *incident management* but performed poorly on *dealing with prisoners with personal problems, talking to prisoners to gain information* and *giving constructive criticism to staff*. When these results were reported to the prison's senior management team, they recognized this profile as an accurate 'snapshot' of staff deficiencies. They also felt it was indicative of the cultural problems they were currently experiencing.

Changing structures and reorganizing work are generally accepted methods of improving organizational effectiveness and efficiency. However, Peters and Waterman (1987) suggest that nothing much is likely to change if these are the only measures implemented. Their research indicates that any intelligent approach to improving organizational effectiveness and performance must encompass, and treat as independent, at least seven variables. Structures, systems or strategy, described as the hard s's, form only part of the contribution to effective performance. Equal cognizance should be given to the soft s's: staff,

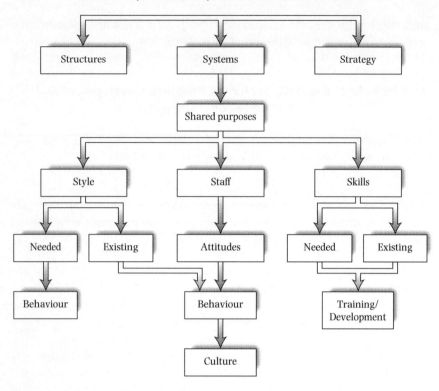

Figure 10.4   The Seven s's for organizational and cultural development in the prison service

skills and style (i.e. the way staff are expected to behave). Shared values are the link between the hard s's and the soft s's. This model has been developed to illustrate some of the cultural and organizational development issues for the Prison Service. Figure 10.4 makes explicit how behaviour and attitude affect culture.

The Core Management Skills reflect how the Prison Service expects its staff to behave towards other staff and prisoners. However, as performance trends indicate, a noticeable gap exists in some prisons between this expectation and the reality of what actually happens in practice.

Conclusion

Research has shown that the use of carefully selected job-related simulations is one of the most effective methods of predicting the future job performance of candidates. In view of this the Prison Service initially developed the JSAC process to be a valid and fair method of selecting appropriately skilled prison officers. It has since been extended to select, promote and develop personnel at several other key levels in the organization. The JSAC process is now an integral and important aspect of the Prison Service's human resource strategy, where it is valued as a versatile tool for organizational change and development.

Chapter Eleven

Design and Evaluation of Training

David Boag

Introduction

One of the most rewarding and influential ways in which a forensic psychologist can make an impact upon the criminal justice system (CJS) is through the training of staff. Since the purpose of training is to improve the work performance of individuals and/or organizations (Goldstein, 1993; Robinson & Robinson, 1995; Kirkpatrick, 1998) forensic psychologists trained in the skilled application of psychological knowledge and possessing the appropriate attitudes to impart that knowledge can operate at the very heart of the CJS. Through their qualifications, training and experience they are uniquely placed to offer added value to the organizations that employ them.

Let me illustrate my point with one or two personal examples. There have been several occasions in the past when I have had to apply my skills, knowledge and experience at a very practical level, for example, in the opening of new prisons and special units. Having the opportunity to contribute to the design of the regime and the training of staff to operate that regime has had several benefits. As well as applying the attitudes, skills and knowledge that I have developed in my own training, I have been able to influence the attitudes, skills and knowledge of others to the extent of becoming a key player in the organization. It is a truism that people always remember their trainer. An important spin-off from this is that, because of the high degree of rapport that is established between the forensic psychologist and the staff during training, the staff become more receptive to helping the forensic psychologist in future research projects and developments that the psychologist is involved in. A specific example is when a new prison was being opened and officers were being drafted in from all over the country to staff it. The governor was faced with the dilemma that the various staff brought with them disparate methods for dealing with the same issues and he came to me with the problem. I suggested training as a way of bringing the staff together to identify with the new prison. Subsequently, an intensive training initiative was undertaken. The initiative was successful. Not only was an ethos developed for the prison, but my subsequent job as head of psychology was made much easier because of the rapport I had established with the staff. I have applied the same strategy on three other occasions, always having the same result.

Another example is where a manager asks me to train his/her staff in a specific topic, for example 'stress management'. In such situations I do not automatically think of a training solution to the problem. Just because a manager indicates that he or she has a preferred solution to the problem does not mean that is the only solution. Before launching into the costly exercise of designing, delivering, and evaluating a training package, I suggest strongly that the problem is investigated applying a DOT analysis.

Essentially in a DOT analysis the following questions of the problem are asked.

> Can the problem be designed out?
> Can the problem be organized out?
> Does the problem have to be trained out?

Designing out the problem

When I examine the design aspect of the problem I consider the physical environment. For example the 'stress' in the case described above was being caused by staff attempting to resolve conflict, caused by dealing with difficult prisoners in an 'open regime'. Many of the most fraught encounters took place in the wing manager's office, where prisoners would attempt to dominate the space through vocal displays that frequently included other prisoners entering the room and joining in. It was important that the pattern did not continue. The solution was to rearrange the furniture in such a way that opportunities were created to reduce tension in the staff–inmate interactions and to reduce the size of the area so that the prisoners had less room to remonstrate. A chair was introduced into the area so that the staff having to deal with the angry prisoner could invite him to sit down and discuss the problem; then interpersonal skills could be applied appropriately and effectively. In this case moving around a few desks and chairs created a safe system of work and thus the issue of 'stress' was designed out. There are many other ways in which problems can be designed out of the workplace through practical steps such as installing extra lighting, cameras, armoured plated glass, and staff wearing clip-on ties.

Organizing out the problem

When investigating organizations, I ask the following: does the job need to be done this way? Can it be done another way? A good example of organizing out the problem which caused a 'stress' reaction (anger) is when Post Office counter operation changed from 'parallel' queuing to the 'snake' queue, which is demonstrably much more efficient and is perceived by customers to be to be fairer. A personal example is when I was asked by the Vehicle Inspectorate to offer interpersonal skills training to staff who were being harangued by lorry/coach owners/drivers regarding the process of MOT testing of their vehicles. It only took a phone call to the appropriate authorities to reorganize a relevant procedure, avoiding the frustrating delays that were at the root of the problem. The situation was resolved and costly training was avoided.

Training out the problem

Lastly, if the problem cannot be designed out, or organized out, then we consider training as a solution. However, bear in mind that training is costly and the evidence suggests that only 10 per cent of training actually transfers to workers' jobs (Baldwin & Ford, 1988; Detterman & Sternberg, 1993). Training must be thoroughly well designed and evaluated. To undertake this task most effectively I suggest the application of the Systematic Approach to training (Prison Service Training Planning Unit, P6 Division, 1990a).

Methods

The Systematic Approach to training is based upon the premise that training is a purposeful activity that should be targeted on explicit outcomes. Training effectiveness is targeted on job performance and job performance is defined and assessed by line managers, the job holder, senior managers, and the trainer. Training, therefore, should be a systematic process with a high degree of planning and control in contrast to random learning from experience. It should be concerned explicitly with changing attitudes, skills and knowledge of people treated both as individuals and as members of groups with the intention of improving both present and future job performance. As such, the overriding goal of training is to have a positive, and lasting, impact on the effectiveness of the organization (Prison Service Training Unit, P6 Division, 1990a).

There are nine stages to the design, development and evaluation of training.

1 Conduct a job analysis.
2 Identify training needs.
3 Determine SMART objectives.
4 Devise training content.
5 Deliver training.
6 Validate training.
7 Evaluate training.
8 Modify and update training.
9 Start again.

Conduct a job analysis

The first stage concerns an analysis of the job. A job may be defined as a coordinated group of responsibilities and activities, which together are capable of achieving a specific task (Prison Service Training Planning Unit, P6 Division, 1990b). There are several techniques that can be used to analyse the job. These are:

> observation of either the task or the behaviour of the individual undertaking the task;
> interviewing of the job holder, identifying 'good' and 'poor' performers via staff appraisal;
> interviewing the manager of a job holder;
> critical incident technique (Flanagan, 1954);
> repertory grid technique to draw contrasts between 'good' and 'poor' performers with regard to specific tasks;
> standard instruments of job analysis including the Position Analysis Questionnaire (McCormick, Jeanneret & Mecham, 1972) or the Job Analysis Kit (McIntyre, Bucklan & Scott, 2000).

Other factors that have to be taken into account are:

> Is the training mandatory in terms of health and safety or other legislation?
> Could a self-study package be used in place of training?
> Can people be hired who have already been trained?
> What would happen if we did not train the task?
> What will be the benefits if we do train the task?

The next step is to draw up a person specification. To do this entails eliciting from job holders, managers and senior managers information concerning the attitudes, skills and knowledge needed to undertake the task effectively (a KSA analysis: Goldstein, 1993). Board blasting by groups or individuals can accomplish this. For example, in a training programme designed to prepare negotiators for their role in hostage-taking incidents, the following nine competencies are thought desirable. These were divided into knowledge, skills and attitudes.

Knowledge:

1 know the strategy and tactics for managing a hostage-taking incident;
2 be able to describe the role, skills and tactics of the negotiator and others involved in an incident;
3 know how to use initiative without departing from instructions.

Skills:

1 demonstrate the application of negotiating skills in simulated incidents;
2 have basic empathy skills, verbal skills and tolerance of ambiguity;
3 be flexible, especially under pressure.

Attitudes:

1 must be determined, persuasive, intelligent, calm, discrete, patient, detached and confident;
2 must be sensitive to relationships and low in authoritarianism;
3 must be responsive to training.

A second method to draw up a person specification is to use Rodgers' (1952) seven-point plan, which is designed to identify the characteristics of the 'ideal candidate/job holder'. The seven points cover:

1 attainments;
2 intellectual abilities;
3 special aptitudes;
4 interests and motivations;
5 dispositions (personality);
6 practical considerations (working hours/willingness to travel);
7 relevant experience.

Another method of conducting a job analysis is to undertake a DIF analysis (Mills, 1974). In a DIF analysis job holders, and managers, are asked how Difficult a task is, how Important a task is, and how Frequently does the task occur. The results of a DIF analysis are important in terms of whether a training solution should be considered.

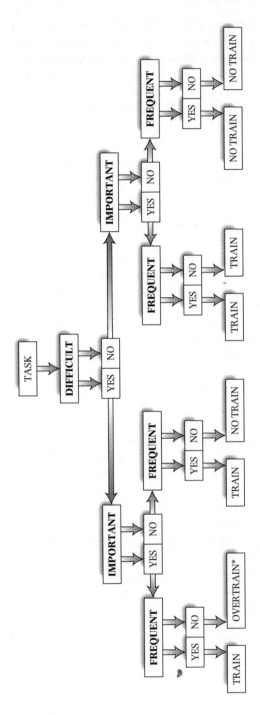

* practice beyond what is required for retention.

Figure 11.1 'DIF' (Difficulty, Importance and Frequency) Analysis

Consider figure 11.1: if a job was fairly routine, not critical to the operation of the organization and happened relatively infrequently, then we would consider that no training was required, in this case, for example, addenda to systems and procedures which may be notified to job holders in writing might be sufficient to improve performance. If, however, a task was difficult, and it was important that it was completed correctly, and happened frequently, then training would be considered, as in, for example the induction training of new staff. However, if a task was difficult, and it was important that no mistakes occurred during the task, and it happened relatively infrequently, then over-training would be required. An example of this is the case of hostage negotiators.

Identify training needs

Next we undertake a 'training needs analysis', which is often driven through a performance appraisal system or simply to prepare for a new job. Training needs are the skills and knowledge that people must acquire if they are to perform successfully (Robinson & Robinson, 1995). The training needs analysis identifies responsibilities, eliminates those staff that already perform satisfactorily, eliminates those tasks that can be learned easily, and prioritizes the training needs of individuals and the organization. It identifies the 'gaps' in performance between the ideal job holder and the current or aspiring job holder. The person specification identified in the job analysis holds the key to identifying theses 'gaps'. Another situation where identification of training needs takes place is when a supervisor or manager asks for help with a specific problem. A training need exists when a job holder lacks the attitudes, skills or knowledge to perform an assigned task satisfactorily. It arises when the training 'gap' has been identified between what the job holder is expected to do on a job, and what the job holder can actually do.

The point may be illustrated with reference to figure 11.2. The x axis measures the passage of time, and the y axis level of performance. Given no training/minimal training or inappropriate training input, for example, 'sitting by Nelly' (a discredited form of training where the learner observes an 'expert' perform a task), job holders may nevertheless improve in performance. However if we instigate effective training at an early stage, there should be a rapid increase in performance on a given task due to the training. The difference between no training and training is the training gap. The function of training is to improve performance and reduce the training gap.

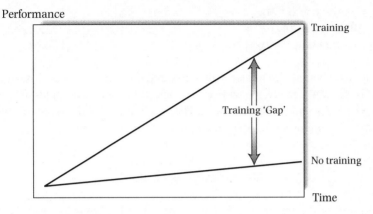

Figure 11.2 The training gap

Determine SMART objectives

SMART Objectives are written to determine what the trainee will be able to do following the training in terms of improved performance. The objectives should also state what is an acceptable level of performance, in other words the standard that is to be achieved. In order to do this we ask the following questions:

> What are we trying to achieve as a result of the training?
> What behaviours do we want participants to accomplish as a result of the training?
> What attitudes, skills and knowledge do we want participants to develop as a result of the training?

All of the objectives should be SMART: Specific, Measurable, Achievable, Realistic, and Time-bounded.

SMART objectives are written to focus attention on the specific requirements of the particular training. They should be written at this stage as all other actions in the development of the training depend on this. Objectives are precise statements, which clearly define the changes in attitudes, skills knowledge and behaviour expected by the training. Aims, on the other hand, are statements of what the trainer wishes to achieve. They are usually broadly based and may be stated in more general terms.

There are three learning domains associated with objectives (Cawthray, 1984):

Cognitive (thinking)
Affective (feeling)
Psychomotor (doing)

The cognitive domain includes recall, knowledge, and higher-order intellectual skills (for example, problem solving). The affective domain includes attitudes, interests, values and emotional states. The psychomotor domain includes body movements, manipulation of stimuli and overt physical activity.

Devise training content

The content of the training is derived from a detailed breakdown of the attitudes, skills and knowledge needed to achieve a given training objective, taking into account what the participants of the training programme already know before beginning the training. Knowledge is the information needed to do a particular job. Skills are the behaviour required to do the job competently and attitudes are the underlying values or beliefs needed to do the job.

Having determined the knowledge, skills and attitudes (KSAs) required, armed with their academic knowledge and usually following a literature review, the forensic psychologist is in a position to begin formulating lesson plans. The number of teaching points derived from the KSAs determines the length of the training programme. A typical lesson plan may look like figure 11.3.

The lesson plan should be on one page to be seen at a glance. It must incorporate descriptions of the following features.

1   the aim of the session;
2   the SMART objectives;
3   the activities involved to achieve the objectives;
4   the methods required to conduct the activity;
5   the materials required for the methods;
6   the time to be taken for each activity.

It is good practice to highlight the main teaching point somewhere prominent on the lesson plan. This has the effect of focusing the tutor on the purpose of the session. The necessary Tutor Guide Notes (TGN) should support the lesson plan. The TGN go into depth about the particular activity being trained, including the results of literature reviews and details of the topic. The TGN should be read and understood by the tutor prior to the session and should only be used as for reference during the session.

Any additional materials, for example exercises, role-play scenarios and hand-

Lesson 1 of 4 = 90 minutes

Introduction			
AIM: To introduce the training, the participants and the tutor to each other To break the ice To complete the initial assessment	OBJECTIVES: Participants will have : – • Outlined the aims and objectives of the programme • Established 'ground rules' • Identified the ten key areas that the training concerns		
ACTIVITY	METHOD	MATERIALS	TIME (minutes)
1. Introductions	Introduce tutor and training schedule	Tutor Guide Notes (TGN)	5
2. Aims and Objectives	'Show and tell'	Aims and Objectives OHT	5
3. Ice Breaker	Round Robin (Participants to introduce themselves – e.g. name, background, hopes and fears for training		15
4. Establish Ground Rules	Flip chart on the ground rules to hang on wall throughout the day	Flip chart/pen, blue tack	10
5. What are Interpersonal Skills?	Board blast and *introduce* the ten topics concerned: • Non-verbal behaviour • Knowing self • Perceptions • Communication skills • Listening skills • Negotiation skills • Interviewing skills • Assertiveness • Teamwork • Conflict Resolution	White board/pens, Tutor Guide Notes	55
			90

Figure 11.3 Interpersonal skills one-day workshop (example)

outs, should be prepared prior to the lesson. Handouts should be used sparingly, and issued at the end of a lesson, if at all. With the best will in the world, course participants often disregard the handout or, if they take it, the handout is filed in their office never to be looked at again. (As a young psychologist, who spent a great deal of time and effort preparing handouts, it was sometimes disheartening to find them left behind in the classroom, covered in coffee stains or, worse still, in the bin!)

Sometimes course materials can be purchased commercially, and the materials can be used as they stand. However, training in the CJS usually necessitates that most of the materials have to be modified in order to suit the context within which they are being used. Often it is necessary and more beneficial to design your own materials, so there can be a better fit between, for example, the objective to be met and an exercise.

Deliver training

One of the first questions to be considered is how the training will be delivered. There are several solutions to this issue, only one of which is expensive classroom delivery. Think of the cost of the participants' downtime, the cost of trainers' time, the cost of a training venue and materials. Depending very much on the training to be delivered one of the following alternatives may be applied: individual self-study, programme text, CD-ROMs, college courses – full- or part-time attendance, or distance learning, online learning, evening classes, and so on. If classroom training is to be considered, is it to be residential in a corporate training establishment, hotel, or some other facility, or is it to be 'in-house'? One of the benefits of residential courses is the team building that occurs outside of the classroom.

A further consideration for the classroom training option is the style of delivery and the type of person who is to deliver it. Some trainers are better suited to a lecturing/instructional style of delivery, whilst others are more at ease with a facilitative, Socratic style of teaching, that is, teaching by asking questions not by telling. Experience suggests that adult trainees learn better by doing rather than being lectured at.

In the presentation of training, trainers should check the classroom prior to the participants' arrival for aspects such as seating arrangements, ensuring also that they can operate the overhead projector, television, camcorder, video player, computer and any other technology that may be required for the session, that the correct pens are available for use on the whiteboard, and so forth. There are few things more embarrassing in life than to discover half-way through a session that you cannot work the TV/video or that you have used a permanent marker on a whiteboard, or worse still, OHT screen. (If you do use a permanent marker on a whiteboard one handy hint is to go over the text again immediately using a dry whiteboard marker. I know, I have been there!)

When working with offenders I often ask them to teach their peers the skills they have learned as homework between sessions. (For example, the application of Novaco's (1978) anger-management model.) With hostage negotiators, following training I ask them to become 'first on scene hostage incident' trainers.

In the delivery of training it is often the singer and not the song that gets the message across. A good trainer sells the message and not himself/herself. S/he can work with poor materials or deliver a message that they do not particularly agree with themselves. Conversely, a poor trainer, even with the best materials available, will fail to deliver the message.

A good trainer:

1 is able to establish an almost instant rapport with the group;
2 is able to create a positive learning environment;
3 knows more about the subject than they are actually training (unless facilitating a group of experts);
4 uses the group dynamics;
5 is flexible in approach;
6 is aware of the individual needs of group members;
7 constantly scans the group, making eye contact to ensure that all course members are participating fully in the session;
8 makes use of examples and anecdotes to highlight teaching points;
9 is punctual and properly prepared (Proper Preparation Prevents Poor Performance);
10 can motivate a group, brings to life the training materials and therefore make even a dull subject sound interesting.

Each session should have high IMPACT on participants (Jacobs, 1994). IMPACT interventions are based on an approach to working with people that takes into account the way in which they learn, change and develop. The approach emphasizes making interventions clear, concrete, and thought-provoking, rather than vague, abstract and emotional.

The IMPACT approach for training involves:

Purpose: clear aims and SMART objectives are essential.
Plan: good session planning is essential. Activities and methods must meet the aims and objectives of the training. Each session is mapped out before the session.

Focus: directing the group towards the topic. Knowing how to focus the group is one of the essential skills of the trainer.

Funnel: funnelling the group is using methods in such a way that a new level of understanding or insight is reached. The topic is introduced and gradually gone into in more depth.

Jacobs adumbrates a number of key principles:

1   People do not change easily.
2   People do not mind being led when they are led well.
3   The trainer is primarily responsible for achieving the objectives.
4   Sessions should be clear and concrete.
5   Sessions should never be boring.

Typical methods adopted by trainers are simulations, role-plays, games, 'chalk and talk', discussion groups, graduated practice with personal performance feedback and the Socratic (i.e. question and answer) method of delivery.

One of the details that a training manager should consider is whether to use internal trainers or training consultants. This depends very much on the training to be delivered and the KSAs of the internal trainers. In some cases it may be too expensive to train internal trainers and cheaper to employ outside consultants.

Validate training

Confusion sometimes exists concerning the terms 'evaluation' and 'validation'. There are in fact three processes to consider: internal validation, external validation and evaluation. The Prison Service Training Planning Unit, P6 Division (1990a) advises that:

> internal validation is the process of determining how successful training has been in achieving specific objectives;
> external validation is the process of determining whether the training objectives for an internally validated programme are realistically based on the current requirements of the job;
> evaluation is concerned with the wider relevance of training and asks questions about the need for training personnel, the need to perform the job at all, the numbers required to perform that job, the acceptability of methods, whether the training makes the best use of resources and cost/benefits to the organization; in other words evaluation is about the value of the training to the organization.

One of the most widely known methods of evaluation is Kirkpatrick's Four Level Evaluation Model (1998), reaction, learning, behaviour and evaluation. The first three levels encompass validation, and the fourth level is the only level that covers evaluation.

Level 1: *Reaction.* As the term implies, level 1 is concerned with participants' immediate reaction to the training event, and is often measured by what are disparagingly known as 'happiness sheets' or 'smile sheets' (the reason being that the training has come to an end and everyone is happy that they are going home). A typical 'Reactionnaire' might cover the degree to which the programme material was relevant to the participant's job, whether the material was presented in an interesting way, whether the tutor was an effective communicator and was well prepared, the effectiveness of audio-visual aids and handouts, the appropriateness of duration, and whether the participant enjoyed the training and the facilities were to a satisfactory standard.

An example of a 'Reactionnaire' administered at the end of a training programme is shown in figure 11.4.

In a review of the literature Foxon (1989) noted that whilst many organizations expressed a belief in the principles of evaluation few were assessing anything other than trainee reaction.

Level 2: *Learning.* Level 2 is concerned with the extent to which session objectives have been achieved. In other words, questions to be investigated at this level typically encompass patterns of change in relation to acquisition of knowledge, the development or enhancement of skills, and the modification of attitudes.

One, informal, technique I often employ to validate that participants have been listening and understanding the training is the 'Colombo technique': pretending to be vague and a bit lost in my flow of thought; if participants do understand what I have been saying they will fill in for me and help me to 'remember' my point.

More formal validation measurements, at this level, during and ideally after training can include achievement tests, aptitude tests, job-performance tests, knowledge tests, progress tests, games, simulations, role-plays, surveys, psychometrics, and so on. All of the devices or techniques used to measure the performance of individuals are directed at the KSAs of participants.

Level 3: *Behaviour.* Level 3 is very much concerned with the fundamentally important, though often neglected, issue of the transfer of training from the training event to the workplace (Baldwin and Ford, 1988). The transfer of training is the generalization of learning to performance in a new situation (typically, the work environment). The KSAs learned during training should be demonstrable in participants' job performance. Analysis can involve, for example, direct observation – as in 'show me a rub down search', interviews with partici-

CONFIDENTIAL
Training Feedback Reactionnaire

Training title: Date:

Congratulations on completing the Training. In our endeavour to improve training we would value your feedback. Complete the following confidential questionaire, and return it to your tutor.

1. What do you think have been the main aims of the Training?

2. How much have you enjoyed the Training? (circle one)

Not at all   **Not very much**   **A fair bit**   **Quite a lot**   **A great deal**

3. Overall the Training was:
For each pair of words below circle a dot. E.g. if you thought the Training was good but not very good you would circle: **Good** ● ◉ ● ● ● ● **Bad**

Good	●	●	●	●	●	●	**Bad**
Valuable	●	●	●	●	●	●	**Worthless**
Pleasant	●	●	●	●	●	●	**Unpleasant**
Weak	●	●	●	●	●	●	**Powerful**
Interesting	●	●	●	●	●	●	**Boring**
Relaxed	●	●	●	●	●	●	**Tense**
Rigid	●	●	●	●	●	●	**Flexible**
Full	●	●	●	●	●	●	**Empty**
Cold	●	●	●	●	●	●	**Warm**
Active	●	●	●	●	●	●	**Passive**

4. During the Training the tutor was (circle a dot on every pair of words as appropriate):

Skilful	●	●	●	●	●	●	**Unskilful**
Cold	●	●	●	●	●	●	**Warm**
Trustworthy	●	●	●	●	●	●	**Untrustworthy**
A good communicator	●	●	●	●	●	●	**A poor communicator**

Please turn over >>>

5. To what extent has the Training helped you with your training needs? (circle one)

    Not at all   **Not very much**   **A fair bit**   **Quite a lot**   **A great deal**

6. How confident are you of applying what you have been trained to do in this training programme? (circle one)

    0%   10%   20%   30%   40%   50%   60%   70%   80%   90%   100%

7. What are the five most important things you have learned as a result of the Training?

    1.

    2.

    3.

    4.

    5.

8. What features of the Training did you find most valuable and why?

9. What changes would you say have taken place in your attitude and behaviour as a result of attending this Training?

10. What features of the Training were of least value and why?

11. Any final comments regarding the Training?

Figure 11.4

pants and their line managers or surveys. Essentially, line managers are in an ideal position to state whether or not a change in behaviour has occurred because the participants attended the training programme.

Evaluate training

Kirkpatrick's Level 4: *Evaluation*. Evaluation is concerned with the impact the training has had on the organization. Did the changes in KSAs and behaviour positively affect the organization? Did the training have 'value' for the organization? For example, has the training in interpersonal skills reduced the number of staff assaults occurring? Has there been a reduction in staff sickness rates? Has the establishment now met its Key Performance Indicators? However, how do we know that it was the training that has caused the effect? Without an adequate control group we may never know. The observed changes might have occurred spontaneously or as a result of unforeseen factors such as improved staff morale. Also, as mentioned earlier, evaluation is concerned with issues of wider relevance to the organization, for example, the need to perform the job at all, the number of job holders required to do the job, the need for training personnel, and whether the training makes the best use of resources in terms of time, human resources, equipment, training areas and money, and the big question: does the cost of the training justify the investment?

It could be argued that the evaluation is in part the concern of others besides the trainer and in fact may involve consideration of factors beyond the competence of those immediately involved in training. For example, a cost/benefit analysis of the training event may be better placed in the hands of an accountant, although the accountant may not understand the training process, psychological analysis or the scientific method. Therefore evaluation is very much the concern of the trainer, not least for the reasons given in the next section.

Modify and update training

Training should be part of a continuous cycle of improvement. Following the validation and evaluation of training and sometimes due to changes in the job itself, in work conditions, or in response to new ideas, further modifications in the training should be made. Trainers should never be too proud to alter their content, approach and delivery.

Start again

At this point the whole systematic approach to training starts again.

Summary

In conclusion, training is one area in which a forensic psychologist can make a highly positive impact on the CJS. However, prior to considering a training solution, the astute forensic psychologist should apply a DOT analysis to the issue in question. In essence, can the problem be designed out, can it be organized out, or does it have to be trained out? Bear in mind that training is very costly, and may not be the best solution. If it has to be trained out, then the systematic approach to training should be followed.

Chapter Twelve

Facilitating Multi-disciplinary Teams

Adrian Needs and Jo Capelin

Introduction

Although many forensic psychologists work in multi-disciplinary organizations, there is no single pattern in their roles and responsibilities in relation to other professionals such as prison officers, nurses and the police. The traditional, and for some still the dominant role, is that of 'expert'. Within this capacity psychological skills and knowledge are used in the performance of specialized functions which complement the work of other staff. Examples of these functions include the provision of assessment or research reports and the direct delivery of interventions. Other psychologists, usually in addition to the expert role, support the contributions of other professionals more directly through activities such as the giving of advice or training. This role is essentially that of 'consultant'. More recently, sizeable numbers of forensic psychologists have been given responsibility for aspects of the work of other professionals. This 'manager' role includes the mobilization, supervision and coordination of multidisciplinary teams. It is seen most clearly in the large-scale implementation within the prison and probation services of offending behaviour groupwork, where the establishment of the role of 'treatment manager' has resulted in a massive expansion in the number of trainee forensic psychologists employed.

Accounts of the rationale, targets and methods of intervention of specific programmes have been published elsewhere (e.g. Blud, 1999; Mann & Riches, 1999). The central importance of procedures for maintaining a consistent quality of delivery in line with principles of evidence-based practice (or 'programme integrity') has been asserted (see Hollin, 1995). Far less attention has been given to the demands of facilitating the multi-disciplinary teams which deliver groupwork. The operation of work teams in other areas of the criminal justice system appears to have been similarly neglected.

Definitions of work teams place emphasis on features such as interdependence of tasks, shared responsibility for outcomes and an identification with concerns and interests of the team (e.g. Mueller, 1994). Models of team functioning commonly distinguish between inputs to the team (such as team composition), processes (such as communication) and outputs of the team (such as performance). Such models can be useful in research and theorizing concerning relationships between variables (Ilgen, 1999; Cordery, 2002). The present chapter, however, follows broadly the pragmatic or 'action-centred' approach proposed by Adair (1986). In this approach the involvement of the leader, manager or facilitator is directed towards three overlapping elements: the task, the team and the individual.

To date, discussion of offending behaviour programmes has been dominated by a concern with task-related aspects. This clear commitment to tasks has undoubtedly played a major part in establishing programmes, to national standards, on an unprecedented scale. It has been a central aspect of strategic management, which has integrated programme delivery with organizational objectives and helped secure a key position for psychologists in the organizational structure (McDougall, 1996). However, relative neglect of the 'team' element may be more than just a question of emphasis.

Firstly, although new 'treatment managers' now complete a one-week residential course which provides guidance and support in key areas such as tutor selection and supervision skills (and separate courses on supervision skills are now offered), the focus is on specific procedures rather than creating a comprehensive understanding of teams and their management. A practical emphasis is commendable, but it may also reflect the fact that a coherent and contextualized knowledge base concerning relevant aspects such as processes within teams has not been readily available. Also, whilst the assertion that MSc courses in forensic psychology 'offer little management training' (McDougall & Towl, 1999 p. 75) is an oversimplification, there is little doubt that most courses could usefully increase their provision in this area.

Secondly, there may in some quarters be a degree of scepticism concerning the relevance to organizations which are inclined to be formal, hierarchical and conservative in their styles of management (see Lambert, Hogan and Barton, 2002) of approaches which emphasize active participation and quality of relationships. Certainly, there is scope for more research on the influence of organizational context on forms and applicability of team working, and this is not helped by imprecision in concepts and analysis in much of the existing literature (Buchanan, 2000). Teams are not a unitary phenomenon (Dunphy & Bryant, 1996). They differ fundamentally according to the degree of autonomy or self-direction which is exercised (Marchington, 2000), and some of the features of high-performance teams such as self-regulation, peer selection and negotiation of targets (Buchanan & McCalman, 1989) may at first sight seem singularly inappropriate for many settings in the criminal justice system. Scepticism may be compounded by some publications and training courses aimed at the popular commercial market, in which sometimes simplistic arguments are presented in a rather evangelical fashion. Much of the area of working in teams can be seen as a 'bandwagon' or 'faddish', with techniques for promoting team functioning ranging 'from the ridiculous to the sublime' (Wheelan, 1999, p. 3).

This should not distract from the existence of a less hyperbolic body of literature based on more familiar standards of scientific rigour, critical appraisal and theory (e.g. Guirdham, 1995; Furnham, 1997; Brotherton, 1999; Procter & Mueller, 2000). Much of this more scientifically based literature will be familiar to practitioners with a background in occupational psychology. Furthermore, in applied psychology there are numerous instances of concepts and practice formulated in one context being adapted and used selectively in another. The distinction between counselling as a process undertaken in closely specified conditions and the use of counselling skills during the course of less circumscribed interactions and opportunities for helping comes to mind. There are also precedents within the prison services for forensic psychologists being concerned with the efficient functioning and well-being of multi-disciplinary work groups. At some distance from the top-down level of strategic management, forensic psychologists working in, for example, special units for prisoners who are persistently violent, disruptive or judged for other reasons to require conditions of exceptionally high security have come to appreciate the value of approaching their work with staff groups from a team working perspective (see Selvey, 2003). In such settings issues of staff direction, stress, morale and the attempted exploitation by manipulative prisoners of any weaknesses within the staff group have been pressing concerns and have awakened interest in the building and support of multi-disciplinary staff teams.

The present chapter introduces some of the broader literature relevant to the nature and functioning of teams, although in this it is by no means exhaustive. It also outlines the work of treatment managers and organizes issues and practices in programme delivery in terms of the framework based on that of Adair (1986). This account might also have implications for enhancing the service provided by forensic psychologists in other settings where there may be benefits, for performance and well-being, in approaching a work group as more than just a disparate collection of individuals engaged in a disparate collection of tasks. Whilst the second author of the present chapter has considerable experience as a treatment manager, the first author gained an awareness of importance of team functioning and processes in work within and in relation to special units for difficult prisoners.

Each of the elements (and major areas of interaction between elements) of the framework will be considered briefly in turn. Relevant points are mapped in Figure 12.1.

With the exception of the overlap between all three elements, a general description of each area of the diagram will be followed by a short section highlighting issues relevant to the delivery of offending behaviour programmes.

The Task

A team approach needs clear objectives. These specify goals and required outputs. A team approach is only relevant, however, when the achievement

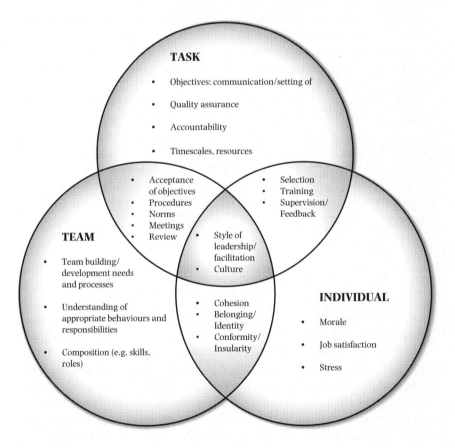

Figure 12.1

of objectives requires interdependent working. It is most appropriate when in addition tasks are complex, requiring flexibility and a range of skills, and meeting demands effectively involves learning as an ongoing process. In an example from manufacturing industry, Jackson, Sprigg and Parker (2000) reported that using a team-based approach with work activities involving high interdependence was associated with higher levels of commitment and satisfaction. When tasks are simple, routine, and do not need interaction between individuals for successful completion, a team-based approach is unlikely to be effective. Where the expectations for participation and the social processes engendered by a team approach cannot be channelled appropriately, it may even be counterproductive, increasing strain and dis-satisfaction (ibid).

Work teams can be characterized according to their primary purpose and responsibilities. Cohen and Bailey (1997) differentiated between: work teams with responsibility for performing core activities of the organization; parallel teams which work alongside formal structures to enhance participation and problem solving; project teams with a remit to develop and implement an initiative in a specific area; management teams with responsibility for overall performance of an organizational unit.

Even within the constraints of the prison services, examples of all four types might be discerned. For example, systematic use of parallel teams can be effective in encouraging ideas and a sense of ownership in major institutional change initiatives (Fisher & Staples, 1994; Clark, 1996). Project teams are used in the development of training or to address a specific issue such as bullying. Whilst the focus of the present chapter is on work teams responsible for the delivery of programmes, management teams responsible for the coordination and oversight of programmes will also be described briefly.

Groupwork programmes

Accredited offending behaviour groupwork adhere to set guidelines laid down by an independent panel in line with the research literature regarding what is believed to be effective in reducing offending behaviour (see, for example, McGuire, 1995). So far the Sex Offender Treatment Programme (SOPT), Cognitive Self-Change Programme (CSCP) and Controlling Anger and Learning to Manage It (CALM) programmes have been accredited, with others at varying stages of development. Programmes are monitored and evaluated to ensure that they adhere to accreditation criteria and produce positive outcomes for the participants. Not all prisons use these programmes, but those that do will use one or more programmes, and will require to have two teams set up for each programme: one for management of the programme, and one for delivering the group-based intervention to prisoners.

The management of an 'accredited' programme is carried out by three people. The 'programme manager' is usually an operational manager, and is responsible for ensuring that tutors are made available and given adequate time to run the programme, and that prisoners are able to attend sessions and are not transferred out of the prison, without good reason, for the duration of the course. The 'throughcare manager' is usually a senior probation officer and is responsible for liaising with participating prisoners' supervising probation officers, arranging a review meeting for each participant at the end of the course, and for following up prisoners after the course. The treatment manager is often a trainee forensic psychologist and is responsible for the management of the tutor team, the selection of prisoners for the course and ensuring programme integrity and quality of delivery. The smooth running of a programme is dependent on this tripartite team communicating well and working cohesively.

Treatment managers are, therefore, part of a multi-disciplinary management team as well as having responsibility for facilitating the work of the tutor team. The role of a treatment manager (as for those of the other two managers) is specified in an audit document, against which he or she is assessed on an annual basis by an auditor from the Offending Behaviour Programmes Unit (OBPU) at HM Prison Service headquarters. Even those at the highest levels are subject to auditing: operational managers and senior operational managers must achieve key performance targets, ensuring, for example, that an agreed number of prisoners complete accredited programmes each year. Treatment managers play an essential role in enabling such targets to be met, whilst additional duties in relation to OBPU include forwarding all documentation, videos and test results for each course as part of the process of monitoring and evaluation. They are at the hub of a wide variety of organizational demands.

Legitimate concerns for future research include the extent to which features of team working such as involvement in decisions and a sense of control over decision making (Whybrow & Parker, 2000) are possible when key aspects of delivery are not negotiable. However, a dimensional view of autonomy (Marchington, 2000) and recognition of 'directed' as well as 'self-directed' teams (Park & Harris, 2000) suggest that the application to programmes of a range of insights from the team-working literature could prove fruitful.

Task/Team

Even when tasks are non-routine and require the coordinated activity of several individuals, it is not enough that clear objectives should be formulated for collaborative, interdependent working to take place. Objectives must receive acceptance and commitment from the team members and be part of the 'shared mental models' of the team (Cordery, 2002). A sense of common purpose can be a powerful energizing and regulatory factor, tending to generate effort and persistence. Indeed, identification with objectives, commitment and trust are amongst the major benefits of a team approach postulated by Mueller (1994). A concern with such processes is not exclusive to a team approach. Most definitions of leadership emphasize the process of influencing others to contribute to group tasks so that organizational objectives can be met (Alimo-Metcalfe & Alban-Metcalfe, 2002). As the latter authors suggest, leadership (or facilitation) can be seen in terms of 'proactive' functions such as creating a vision and encouraging innovation. These contribute directly to a sense of common purpose and can be distinguished from 'static' managerial functions such as budgeting, creating systems and monitoring. In practice these broad classes of function tend to be or should be complementary, but it is still possible to pursue one at the expense of the other.

Facilitation of a team involves promoting a shared understanding of how objectives will be met as well as an understanding and acceptance of the objectives themselves. Behaviours and attitudes associated with effective participation in teams have been identified (McGregor, 1960; Wheelan, 1999). These can be encouraged through appropriate working practices and by the development of norms. Norms can be defined as 'collective value judgements about how members should behave and what should be done in a group' (Wheelan, 1999, p. 61). For example, within an effective team there should be a commitment to open communication. This can be promulgated by norms of listening and respect and can play a vital part in clarification of goals, roles and tasks as well as the generation of ideas and the management of potential difficulties. Open communication tends to promote active participation in areas such as decision making.

Decision making, problem solving and any conflict are best handled through explicit procedures which are accepted by the team (Guzzo & Salas, 1995). Avoiding conflict can result in an accumulation of problems or decisions flawed by false consensus. Becoming enmeshed in conflict, on the other hand, can cause the team to degenerate into blaming, power struggles, personal agendas and fragmentation. Diversity of experience, abilities and views within a team can increase the scope for conflict, although such diversity can be a valuable resource and conflict can be constructive (Alper, Tjosvold & Law, 1998). Overall, the team should feel confident about examining its own progress and functioning. The actions and style of the facilitator (for example, providing encouragement, clarification and guidance) are likely to be very influential in setting the tone. Indeed, attempting to foster team working without adopting an open and participative style of management is a quick route to disenchantment amongst team members (Buchanan & Preston, 1992).

Groupwork programmes

While a course is running the treatment manager will meet with the team on a weekly basis for supervision, to discuss how the group is progressing, to resolve any problems with individuals within their group, to help the tutors plan and to prepare them for future sessions, to assist them with the preparation of post-course reports, and to give feedback on how well the tutors are delivering the course material. It is important for this supervision to be done with all tutors involved in a particular course. This means that any problems are raised in the group setting and reduces the likelihood of tutors complaining about each other to the treatment manager. It also provides a useful opportunity to air any difficulties relating to individual commitment or attitudes to supervisors (see Brown & Blount, 1999). In between supervision sessions it is good practice for treatment managers to try to meet with the tutors as often as possible after sessions to debrief them and to ensure that any problems can be resolved as quickly as possible.

Although it is expected for tutor teams to meet with the treatment manager for supervision during the course of a programme, it is often not easy to find opportunities for the whole of the tutor team to meet together. Difficulties arise because of other work commitments. Officers work shifts, which means they will be out of the prison on rest days. They may have a period of working nights, be sent out on escort, or even to another prison for a period of detached duty. Other disciplines, similarly, are likely to have other work commitments in addition to their tutoring work, and there are, of course, periods of annual leave or illness, all of which can make it difficult for a whole team to meet. Despite this, it is important where possible to try to get the team together at regular intervals to reinforce the message that the group is a team, to allow the treatment manager to brief them on any new developments or other information, and to allow the team to raise any grievances or ideas.

It is important for tutors to model good interpersonal and problem-solving skills on a day-to-day basis. Problems can arise when this does not happen. For example, the treatment manager would have to act if a tutor was overheard telling racist or homophobic jokes. The diverse experience and backgrounds of members of teams which deliver programmes, and the different styles to which they are accustomed for handling difficulties and other matters, makes the need for appropriate norms and agreed procedures all the more important. It can also prevent undue personalizing of issues.

The Team

Working with others on tasks which require coordination and collaboration to achieve common goals can be stimulating and rewarding. It can promote effort and mutual assistance, and transcend self-interest (Furnham, 1997; Cordery, 2002). However, just as emergent social processes can energize and support team activity, they can also, if not properly handled, cause the team to lose its way. It should not be assumed that a team approach is automatically effective (Whybrow & Parker, 2000). Understanding a range of possibilities, and possible solutions, is especially important for the facilitator. More generally (and in line with the earlier point concerning the desirability of shared mental models), the examination by a team of its own functioning can be enhanced if members have a shared conceptual awareness in order to make sense of their experience.

It has been suggested, notably by Tuckman (e.g. Tuckman, 1965; Tuckman & Jensen, 1977) that teams tend to go through several stages before reaching a mature level of operation. Immediately after formation, team members tend to be passive, dependent on the facilitator for direction and initiative and concerned with issues such as embarrassment and rejection. In Tuckman's terminology this stage is referred to as 'forming'. This stage gives way to a more active negotiation of issues such as autonomy, roles, values and practices. As the term used to refer to this stage ('storming') suggests, there is particular scope for conflict. A working resolution of these matters enables a stage of productive discussion and formulation ('norming') to be reached. When (usually after a minimum of six months, according to Wheelan, 1999) a mature style of conflict resolution, decision making, planning and review is attained, the team can be said to be 'performing'.

Each of these stages present different challenges for the facilitator, and different styles are necessary to nurture progress and meet emerging group needs (Wheelan, 1999). Initially, for example, there is a need for confident direction and promoting an orientation towards tasks through clarification of goals, standards and expectations while reducing anxiety and encouraging discussion and participation. The second stage requires that the facilitator relinquishes a degree of control, instead acting variously as stimulus, sounding board or support, creating appropriate conditions for establishing a working agreement on roles, communication structures, conflict resolution, cooperation and participation. Domination and power struggles should be avoided. In the third stage, progress is consolidated and the team is encouraged to assume collective responsibility, with assistance from the facilitator directed especially towards planning and the identification and overseeing of obstacles. Trust and cohesion are fostered and the team develops a more stable sense of its own identity.

Concerns in the fourth stage include monitoring progress, especially in the light of changes in membership, task requirements or internal conditions. The facilitator will usually continue to contribute as appropriate in an expert role, and represent the team in dealings with other groups. Generally speaking, however, the facilitator can be seen as moving from a directive to a more consultative style, and key skills include the ability to appraise the needs of the team at any given time and the flexibility to respond accordingly (Wheelan, 1999). Failure to do this can result in a team beset by uncertainty, anxiety and conflict, in many respects lodged in the 'storming' stage.

The precise relevance to the delivery of such a model of team development to the delivery of groupwork programmea is uncertain. Indeed, not all studies of teams reported in the literature have found this kind of pattern. For example, a study by Gersick (1988) of project teams found a pattern of periods of inertia punctuated by bursts of activity. This was irrespective of the team's previous history or time allocated to complete the task. In the field as a whole, there are several areas where relationships between inputs, process and outputs are not entirely clear (Cordery, 2002). Nonetheless, as suggested above, there can be benefits in facilitators and team members alike having an awareness of possible processes and issues if only to guard against disillusionment and to provide alternative avenues of comprehension when difficulties are encountered. It can also highlight actions and responsibilities (such as supporting and listening to others, rather than blaming) which can help the team find ways forward.

It is in helping a team become aware of the variety and consequences of styles of interaction and problem solving that team-building interventions can be useful. As Wheelan (1999) points out, these have been variable in the quality of their design and implementation. At best, practical exercises can provide direct experience of possibilities and pitfalls of working together, promoting shared understanding and a sense of cohesion. Memories of support and success can echo through future activities. Attention can be drawn to relevant behaviours (Rackham & Morgan, 1977), skills and functions (Stevens & Campion, 1994) and roles (Belbin, 1981; Buchanan & Storey, 1997), providing a common base for subsequent reflection and feedback. It is, however, necessary to maintain a focus on implications for the workplace. As with any training, there should be a clear rationale and appropriate standards of delivery. The possible consequences of a training experience which is perceived as irrelevant or as provoking unresolved mutual antagonism need hardly be spelled out. Interventions should be based on solid research evidence (Wheelan, 1999). Noting that over half of team interventions tend to be ineffective (Sundstrom, De Meuse & Futrell, 1990), Wheelan (1999) concludes that the most promising interventions involve active goal setting by members combined with feedback on performance and group-development issues, tailored to meet the needs of the team at the time. She does not, on the other hand, recommend 'rock climbing, white water rafting, blind trust walks, or playing basketball on donkeys' (p. 16)!

Groupwork programmes

As indicated above, there is much research that needs to be done on processes within teams responsible for delivering offending behaviour programmes. Experiences within tripartite teams could also be usefully addressed. It could be that the same emphasis give to careful selection and adherence to ready-made procedures, standards and monitoring practices within a disciplined service which may give limited room for autonomy also allows little scope for gross departures from expected outputs or conduct. Then again, reports suggest that difficulties are not unknown and incidents such as deselection, resignation or problems in meeting targets may warrant further investigation. Furthermore, HM Prison Service has not been immune to problems in team functioning in settings as special units (see, for example, Woodcock, 1994).

Building up a tutor team from scratch is helped by the selection process, which requires that candidates need to be fully aware of what is expected of them before being sent for training. In addition to appropriate skills and attitudes, they need to understand and accept the objectives of the team and be prepared to work with other team members and the treatment manager. It is also worth sending two or more tutors from the same team together for their initial training, as they can support and get to know each other before becoming part of the tutor team back at their establishment.

At other times a treatment manager may not be building up a team from scratch but may be taking over the management of an already established team. This may be difficult if the team is closely knit, as its members may be wary of a newcomer. Similarly, the new treatment manager may wish to change some of the team's established methods of working. This can need careful handling. Some treatment managers use the team-building facilities at the Prison Service College to give the team and its managers an opportunity to allow the group to gel, to start to get to know each other, and to start working together as a team under the eyes of experienced facilitators. It is, however, important to recognize that this is merely the start of a process. All training requires opportunities to put relevant behaviours and understanding into practice. There should also be a congruence between expectations engendered by training and the reality of how a team is permitted to function.

Team/Individual

The potential benefits of working in a team for the individual member are social and emotional as well as practical and instrumental. As previously suggested, team membership can be stimulating and enjoyable and the source of a sense of worth and belonging. Whether a team is experienced in this way, or merely in terms of frustration and indifference, is largely dependent on the related dimensions of cohesion and morale. Manning (1991) offers a useful review of these concepts from the perspective of military psychology.

A cohesive team is characterized by shared commitment and mutual concerns. Participation in the team and its activities is valued, and in turn makes the individual feel valued. Members of the team are united by a sense of mutual obligation and a willingness to make an effort for the sake of the team. Manning argues that morale (considered in more detail under 'Individual') is linked to high performance, and that the relationship is likely to become reciprocal. A belief that others in the team (including the leader, manager or facilitator) can be relied upon to give help, support and recognition is central. In non-military settings, the related concept of trust has been linked to productivity (Dirks, 1999), a finding which may be explained in part by the role of trust in providing a safe environment for learning (Edmondson, 1999). Ultimately, too, a sense of pride, commitment and identification can extend beyond the primary group to the wider organization: Manning (1991) refers to this as 'esprit de corps'.

It is important to emphasize that cohesion of the team is not an aim to be pursued at the expense of the task and individuals. The preservation of unity at any cost can lead to conformity and inhibitions (Edmonson, 1999), failure to consider alternatives in problem solving (Janis, 1982), collusion with extreme decisions (Isenberg, 1986) or reduced effort (Karau & Williams, 1993). Tendencies such as poor decision making are especially likely when teams are insular, feel under pressure and lack structured procedures for making decisions (Esser, 1998). Insularity combined with cohesiveness in the absence of clear procedures to facilitate relevant interactions can also lead to problems in relation to groups external to the team (see Ancona & Caldwell, 1992). The excesses of 'groupthink' (Janis, 1982) can, however, be avoided by the development of appropriate norms and procedures for decision making, encouragement of participation and individual autonomy and increasing external contacts (Moorhead, Neck & West, 1998). Not that this is an easy task, and the pivotal role of the facilitator in balancing these aspects with a clear commitment to agreed objectives should be emphasized (Park & Harris, 2000).

Groupwork programmes

Again, little research on offending behaviour programmes has been done in this area. Working as a tutor is clearly demanding (Crighton, 1995), but camaraderie and social support are valued by prison staff and can be a sustaining factor in the face of potentially stressful demands of prison work (Boag, 1991). In addition, the maintenance of clear structures, explicit task requirements and close supervision may be expected to help prevent any drift from proper standards, although the findings of Brown and Blount (1999) suggested that, especially for new (and female) treatment managers, the reality may at times be a little more complex.

It is good practice for the responsibilities of tutors to be included in annual performance-appraisal reports, so that they become an integrated part of the individual's work. However, this does not always happen, as officer tutors are usually reported on by other, more senior officers, who may not view the work as tutor as important, or who may not feel qualified to comment on how well this part of their staff member's work is being fulfilled.

Treatment managers need to be aware that their tutors are also members of other groups, both in and out of the prison, and that the group membership may affect their approach to the tutor team. Anecdotal evidence suggests that differences in background can influence expectations, attitudes and preferred solutions to problems. Prison officers may also have pressure put on them by their other colleagues, who may feel that an officer's place is patrolling landings and searching prisoners rather than teaching prisoners new skills. Treatment managers can work towards overcoming this by raising the awareness of the non-programme staff through training. Similarly, it can help the treatment manager if the officer tutors, who are often better at answering other officers' questions and comments, carry out some of this training. It is tempting to speculate that there may also be benefits for personal commitment via the reduction of cognitive dissonance.

Individual

Several factors influence an individual's job performance (see, for example, Rummler, 1996). Some of these factors, such as the existence of clear goals, procedures and standards, have already been mentioned. Others, such as promoting the necessary skills and attitudes through selection and training, and the importance of feedback, will be discussed in the next section. The motivating factors of cohesion, trust and morale were introduced in the previous section, and it is here that discussion resumes.

To some managers, notions such as morale and job satisfaction may be seen as referring to a nebulous, optional 'feel good factor', desirable but probably not worthy of serious attention. This would be a mistake. Neglect of job satisfaction in the prison setting can limit performance. Job satisfaction has been defined by Lambert, Hogan and Barton (2002) as 'a subjective, individual-level feeling reflecting whether a person's needs are or are not being met by a particular job' (pp. 116–17). These authors contend that low job satisfaction can lead to poor work output, lack of creativity, resistance to innovation, high stress and absenteeism, wastefulness and poor relations with management. On the other hand, the benefits of high job satisfaction amongst prison staff include a 'human service orientation' and support for rehabilitation (ibid.).

The related concept of morale can be defined in terms of 'the enthusiasm and persistence with which a member of a group engages in the prescribed activities of the group' (Manning, 1991, p. 405). When appropriate and accepted procedures, roles and objectives are in place, cohesion can contribute to morale by instilling a sense of confidence in the group. Feeling that others in the team are both able and willing to help encourages commitment and increases expectations that one will succeed. Similarly, the willingness of others to make a sustained effort in pursuit of shared objectives increases confidence in the attainment of objectives and in the belief that these objectives are worthwhile. Confidence in one's own abilities is also bolstered when one feels that one's contributions are recognized and valued. The manager or facilitator has a key role in this, and style of communication is of paramount importance.

Indeed effective communication can only take place in a climate of respect and recognition of concerns (Reilly and Di Angelo, 1990). In prisons, failure to take the trouble to communicate effectively or to allow an appropriate degree of autonomy (due, for example, to use of a style which is domineering and authoritarian) can be associated with feelings of powerlessness (Lambert, Hogan & Barton, 2002). In other contexts such a style has been found to inhibit commitment and learning (Edmondson, 1999). In contrast, a style which is consultative and encouraging tends to reduce feelings of powerlessness, enhance job satisfaction and lead to a reduction in stress (Lancefield, Jennings & Thomson, 1997; Lambert, Hogan & Barton, 2002).

Low morale can be epitomized by Camp and Carney's (1989, cited in Manning, 1991) description of a graffiti code which arose amongst US troops in later stages of the war in Vietnam. This consisted of 'UUUU' – the unwilling, led by the unqualified, doing the unnecessary for the ungrateful. Readers with experience of prisons or others areas of the criminal justice system are invited to ponder whether such a state of affairs has any resonance with what they may on occasion have encountered.

Groupwork programmes

There is little research on morale and job satisfaction in teams delivering offending behaviour programmes. Of particular interest, however is the finding of Lambert, Hogan and Barton (2002) of an association between job satisfaction and favourable attitudes to rehabilitation. In a similar vein, Hogue (1995) argued that positive attitudes of staff in the Sex Offender Treatment Programme are linked to effectiveness of intervention. The importance of managerial communication style and opportunities for participation in decision making to promoting positive attitudes requires further exploration, but general principles would indicate that it is important to accord recognition and respect, and to listen. These actions promote self-confidence and a confidence that one's efforts are not misplaced. Confidence in fellow team members and the likelihood of success are also encouraged through ensuring the development in the team of the skills necessary to do the job. This will be discussed further in the next section, and the issue of facilitator style will be revisited in the section after that.

In addition, it is important for the facilitator to be aware of possible sources of stress, and to handle this area with sensitivity. This has been recognized particularly in work with sex offenders (Turner, 1993; Crighton, 1995). Whether one is driven by a concern for quality of performance, fear of litigation, or more humanitarian considerations, it is likely that the way a treatment manager addresses the issue of stress will itself will be perceived as signifying the regard in which staff are held. It is also likely to have a bearing on the treatment manager's credibility as a psychologist.

Task/Individual

Confidence in the abilities of team members rests most convincingly on actual abilities. Selection, training, supervision and feedback are of fundamental importance. Selection should be based on a clear identification of aptitudes and attitudes necessary both for task performance and for working in a team. Task performance is likely to require certain intellectual, practical, interpersonal and emotional skills; the latter include resilience and self-control. Effective performance within a team also involves, for example, being a good listener, being able to work cooperatively, flexibility of attitude and being able to give and receive trust (Wheelan, 1999). The level of skill and the nature of underlying attitudes should be sufficient to provide a foundation for training and development. Perfection is not sought, but neither is it possible (or justifiable in terms of resources) to attempt to 'make a silk purse out of a sow's ear'. Selecting appropriate individuals does of course raise the issue of constructing valid and reliable forms of assessment.

Training, too, should rest upon proper analysis and evaluation. It should go beyond a narrow emphasis on tasks (Buchanan, 1994, cited in Procter & Mueller, 2000). The experience of training should promote awareness of objectives, methods, personal development issues and shared experience which contribute to the development of cohesion, whilst opportunities for mastery of skills contribute to the development of confidence. Being able to use skills, once acquired, is another factor related to job satisfaction (Hepburn & Knepper, 1993).

Supervision and feedback are necessary for promoting continuous learning. Indeed, openness and consistency of supervision, with constructive feedback, play a vital role in setting a positive tone and enhancing job satisfaction (Lambert, Hogan & Barton, 2002), and a meta-analysis of team interventions by Guzzo, Jett and Katzell (1985) found that feedback and goal setting made an important contribution to group productivity. In the prison setting supervision and feedback are likely to be especially valuable in reconciling ambiguities and conflicts concerning role (for example, balancing the demands of security and custody with those of welfare and rehabilitation) which can otherwise be a major source of uncertainty and stress in what is an intrinsically complex area of work (Hay & Sparks, 1991; Lancefield, Jennings & Thomson, 1997). Such activities have also been found to enhance working relationships between facilitators and team members in healthcare settings (Quarry & Burbach, 1998). An emphasis on developing, encouraging and supporting can be seen as representing a shift in role for the facilitator from 'manager' to 'coach' (Wheelan, 1999). The drawback is that the precise nature of this role is in considerable need of further development (Park & Harris, 2000).

Groupwork programmes

Setting up a new programme entails informing staff about the programme and about expectations regarding tutors. It also involves advertising for volunteers and then undertaking a process of selection to decide which of the volunteers should be trained. There are guidelines from OBPU as to how this should be done. Candidates undertake interviews to assess their cognitive skills (clearly, tutors should not have cognitive deficits similar to those of prisoners who will be taking part in the programme) and are asked to make a presentation to the tripartite management team to demonstrate their delivery skills and problem-solving abilities. Although not an explicit intention of the selection process, it is very likely that such skills are also relevant to effective participation in the team outside the conduct of sessions in the programme. Prospective SOTP tutors are also required to undertake an interview with a member of staff playing the role of a sex offender, and there are additional interviews to ensure that the candidate is aware of and comfortable with the sexual aspects of the programme. Before being sent for training, candidates need to understand and accept the objectives of the team and what such work means in terms of working with the other team members and the treatment manager.

Initial training consists of a three-day presentation skills course followed by two weeks of training in how to deliver the programme material. Both aspects are assessed on a pass/fail basis. As well as providing support before and during training, treatment managers need to try to accommodate individuals' training needs beyond the initial training courses and to be sensitive to tutors' anxieties about different areas of their work. They also need to ensure that individuals' qualities and abilities are recognized and that any criticism is constructive. We understand that the possibility of providing certificated courses in cognitive-behavioural methods to motivated tutors, as an additional incentive and recognition of their contributions, is currently being explored by OBPU. Areas of training provided by the treatment manager at the establishment include the crucial function of providing comprehensive reports on each prisoner who has participated in the programme. It is important that final reports are detailed and based on clear evidence as they are distributed to a variety of parties both inside and outside of the prisons (including the Parole Board) and may have an effect on a prisoner's date of release.

The quality of reports that tutors write on prisoners' progress at the end of a course is one of the concerns of supervision. As part of the process of supervision, tutors are also observed whilst tutoring and are given feedback on what they are doing well and on how they could improve. Particular attention is paid to the development of style of delivery and to ensuring that material is delivered in the right order, at the right pace, using the right teaching aids and so on.

Throughout, treatment managers should be mindful that all members of the tutor team are individuals and that developing the individual is an essential part of facilitating teamwork and achieving the task. Individuals are likely to come to the team not only with different levels and types of experience but also with different motivations for undertaking this type of work. The treatment manager needs to be aware of individuals' needs, strengths, weaknesses and personal goals.

There is little systematic research on the success of these endeavours, although Hogue (1995) reported that six months after training the confidence in their own skills and knowledge of SOTP tutors had continued to increase. Rather more disquieting are the findings of Brown and Blount (1999) that about one-third of SOTP treatment managers reported problems of lack of commitment and resistance to supervision by some tutors to be a significant source of stress to themselves, although these problems appeared to diminish with increasing experience in the treatment manager role. It is not clear whether the ability to handle these problems as they arose improved with time or whether improvements in facilitation skills tended to prevent them from arising in the first place.

Task/Team/Individual

Characteristics of functioning and experiences centred upon the areas of task, team and individual become reflected in the emerging culture of the team. Culture can be defined in terms of 'the dominant pattern of shared beliefs and values' (Cole, 1996, p. 96). As the team develops, its history of challenges met and of interactions both within the team and with those external to the team leads to the generation of shared assumptions concerning ways of handling problems and interactions (Schein, 1992). Many of the interactions within a team through which shared meanings are negotiated are informal in nature (Middleton, 1996). Culture can be seen as a normative framework for the regulation of behaviour, the definition of events and the generation of solutions.

However, as noted by Schein (1992), there may be some disparity between the 'espoused values' of the organization and the actual assumptions, beliefs and values of its members. For example, individuals suffering from 'initiative fatigue' may be acutely aware of a mismatch between expectations of increased effort and the actual gains from increased effort (Buchanan, Claydon & Doyle, 1999). Like cohesion, culture can be a mixed blessing (see for example, Brown & Campbell, 1994), especially if new members are taught the 'correct' way to think by existing members who have become tinged with cynicism. Modifying an established culture can benefit from analysis and action by the facilitator in terms of the elements of the Adair model. For example, at times this can entail reaffirmation of standards of task performance, and on occasion a renewed emphasis on individual development through training or supervision may be necessary. A range of checks and actions both within and across elements may be required in addition to examination of assumptions and beliefs.

As noted by Wheelan (1999) with regard to team development, all this calls for sensitivity and flexibility on the part of the facilitator. Certainly facilitators should not be defensive, preoccupied with status or become engaged in power struggles. It is also to be hoped that they do not fall into the kind of inept practices described by Dixon (1976), identified in the military context but likely to have implications for managers more generally. These include ignoring evidence that does not fit with assumptions, withholding crucial information to maintain advantage and a pervasive rigidity of decision making and interactional style. These tendencies can have their roots in an autocratic organizational culture.

There may be an important lesson here. In the prison context, concerns with modern management techniques can lead to procedures for measuring performance becoming ends in themselves rather than means to ends. Bryans (2000b) has used the term 'managerialism' to refer to this tendency. He argues that serving very time-consuming demands from the centre for monitoring data has encouraged a focus on short-term thinking and neglect of a more integrated approach to quality of delivery. In a climate of key performance indicators, audits, strategic and business planning and policy frameworks, use of managerial rhetoric can sometimes be confused with managerial effectiveness. In terms of the present chapter, it could be argued that such thinking may be reflected in an almost exclusive emphasis on the task.

The need for quality assurance measures is not being denied. In the context of programmes these can be an important means of ensuring the programme integrity which is an essential ingredient of therapeutic effectiveness (Hollin, 1995). Yet it is interesting that as far back as 1987, Evans, writing of trends in HM Prison Service management, described 'the observation of some staff that performance indicators couched in quantified terms miss the point about the quality of the functions being delivered and that the approach is too narrowly conceived' (p. 11). This might be seen as moving in the direction of Weber's 'paradox of consequences', where 'the means chosen to meet any particular purpose in the social world tend to subvert the ends for which they were intended' (Watson & Rosborough, 2000, p. 166). Of course, several of the performance measures used in programme delivery (such as videotapes of sessions) are very much concerned with quality. Other measures, such as number of programmes delivered and numbers of prisoners involved, are less so. In the police context, Loveday (2000) described how the introduction of a 'performance culture' led to the rejection of consultation with more junior ranks and to a narrow focus in some forces on rather questionable reporting practices. Even in the military setting, Manning (1991) recommended that military psychologists oppose 'the ever more frequent attempts to replace old fashioned customs with more modern centralized and less expensive practices borrowed from contemporary business which mistakenly trade off peacetime economy for actual effectiveness' (p. 465). 'Old-fashioned customs' include those inputs that inspire a sense of allegiance and duty, of being supported and valued.

These tensions arise from differing systems of values (and not necessarily the values expressed in mission statements and the like). Indeed, it is in such terms that they are perceived and often articulated by those on the receiving end of changes in management style and policy, as Tollinton (1992) observed in the National Health Service. Such perceptions and mismatches (for example, between 'business' and 'service' values) should not be ignored by researchers or facilitators. Several authors have emphasized that the ability to apprehend perspectives which are different to one's own is a crucial managerial skill (e.g. Porter, 1985). Very necessary for treatment managers, this is a skill that rarely finds encouragement (other than lip service) when managerialism prevails. It is essential that currently fashionable managerial rhetoric which emphasizes outputs should not blind any facilitator or manager, at any level, to the importance of factors which promote the effective functioning and well-being of those on whom the outputs depend.

Conclusions

For many forensic psychologists in prisons working in a multi-disciplinary team is now an intrinsic part of the job, and for an increasing number responsibility for the team's effectiveness and psychological health is at the forefront of their work. An understanding of relevant processes and actions is crucial. It is argued here that Adair's (1986) framework can be helpful in drawing attention to areas for examination in both practice and research. Such a perspective appears to have some utility, not least in highlighting issues for future consideration, in the major growth area of offending behaviour programmes, which has in the past been dominated by task-related considerations. There is an urgent need for research on aspects such as the nature and development of these teams, the operation of variables such as cohesion and morale, and the impact of managerial inputs and styles. This research may result in a more detailed and precise specification of relationships between inputs, processes and outputs. It may also prompt a research agenda which addresses other types of teams or work groups in the criminal justice system and related settings. Possible targets include investigative teams, child protection teams, those responsible for mental healthcare services, project teams, senior management teams and workers in specialized units in custodial environments. It is likely that in the years to come, the role of forensic psychologists as consultants if not managers in relation to such teams will continue to be developed. Certainly, there is the potential for beneficial effects on their integration and influence within multidisciplinary contexts and for improving overall functioning within the organizations concerned.

Chapter Thirteen

Applied Psychological Services in HM Prison Service and the National Probation Service

Graham Towl

Introduction

There has been a relatively long history of psychologists working in prisons, since 1946 (McEwan & McGurk, 1981; McMurran & Shapland, 1989). The history of the work of psychologists in the probation service is less clear. However, what is clear is that there has been a marked and rapid pace of change in recent years in psychological services for both prisons and probation (Towl & McDougall, 1999; Towl, 1999a, 2000). The developments may be seen in the context of changes in public services and professional developments in the British Psychological Society. This chapter outlines, explores and examines these developments with a focus on current practice and future developments.

Changes in Public Services

Since the launch of the 'welfare' state, which broadly accords with when psychologists appear to have been introduced to prisons, there have been a great deal of changes in how public services have been structured, driven and delivered. There has been, with successive governments, significant stability in overall public social expenditure as a percentage of the Gross National Product (GDP). (For a fuller discussion on this see, for example, Flynn, 1997). However, there have been significant changes in where and how such funding is used. The Conservative manifesto for the 1951 election promised to make the civil service more efficient (Theakston, 1995). This is a theme which has echoed across post-war administrations during the last half of the twentieth century. Indeed, the Civil Service, the National Health Service and local government have been subject to this broadly (politically) shared governmental mantra. It is neither possible nor appropriate to attempt to do such a history anything like sufficient justice here. However, it does set some of the important historical context of what follows. In this section of the chapter I will focus primarily on the more recent manifestation of the policy developments touched upon above. Such recent developments have generally been captured under the modern rubric of 'New Public Management' (NPM).

The central feature of NPM is to assert that more sophisticated, 'customer-orientated' management techniques and methods will produce better services (Farnham & Horton, 1996). The ideology that underpins the approach tends to reflect a belief which essentially amounts to 'private sector efficient, public sector inefficient'. This has been a pervasive theme and concern in much of the literature (for example, Flynn, 1997). More recently, such generalizations have been called into question. However, it has been acknowledged that there will often be opportunities for joint learning across both the public and private sector in terms of appropriate management methods and techniques (Towl, 2000).

Traditionally, the term 'public administration' has been used to describe management activities in the public sector. This is changing, with the application of terms previously associated with the private sector but now part of the public-sector managerial lexicon. For example, public-sector organizations routinely now refer to business plans and business management. One of the many challenges that often arise in public-sector management is the need to address the needs of multiple stakeholders. We shall return to this when looking at ethical issues in psychological practice (see page 233). Goals are set by elected politicians and the public sector is judged in relation to the achievement (or failure to achieve) such goals (Farnham & Horton, 1996). It is important that applied psychologists working in the public sector have a good understanding of the context within which they work. This applies across the public sector; however, for our purposes I focus upon prisons and probation.

The current government is keen to drive reform in public-sector service delivery (Office of Public Services Reform, 2002). This applies to both prisons and probation. A number of themes pervade the change agenda. The first is the need to lay foundations for change. This involves the appropriate resourcing for changes. Resourcing is not simply a matter of appropriate levels of financial resources, but rather it is a broader application of the term that needs to be understood. Thus resources may include appropriate workforce planning. As we shall see later in the chapter, 'area psychologists' are uniquely well placed to drive appropriate workforce planning amongst the psychological grades of staff in their areas (see below).

The notion of 'putting the customer first' is a pervasive theme in public-sector reform. The term 'customer' in the context of the delivery of services on behalf of the public to offenders sounds somewhat inappropriate. The term 'stakeholders' is perhaps better is this context. Indeed, there are multiple stakeholders in criminal justice processes and structures. Psychologists have not always focused sufficiently in the past on the needs of stakeholders. This has sometimes been reflected in publications by psychologists in prisons, which appear to have primarily reflected the interests of psychologists rather than providing a primary focus on what the organization needed (for example, McGurk, Thornton & Williams, 1987). We will revisit this area again later. Too often, psychological services in prisons have developed on an *ad hoc* basis. Indeed, the development of psychological services often reflected the value or otherwise that individual operational managers saw in psychological services. Services were not linked, to use the modern nomenclature, to business need.

Standards and accountability constitute a third theme which is given emphasis in government documentation. This has a particular resonance with psychologists. It is essential that if applied psychological services are to offer ethical and professional services to stakeholders, then there must be high professional standards and clear lines of accountability. To be promoted to the 'senior psychologist' grade in HM Prison Service candidates must be either chartered psychologists or have full membership of a relevant Division of the British Psychological Society, depending upon the exact nature of the post. All training grade psychological staff should have a named supervisor and receive full and appropriate training in working towards chartership. There are, of course, a number of routes to chartership and what is important is that each individual has a clear plan for how they will achieve chartership; this is a joint responsibility with their coordinating supervisor. Chartered psychologists are accountable for the standards of their professional practice and that of their supervisees.

The devolution and delegation of budgets and performance management accountability have been key milestones in the managerial changes in HM Prison Service. Much of the devolution and delegation has taken place at the 'area' level as well as at the individual prison establishment. In keeping with these structural and cultural changes, area psychologists have been placed in each of the operational area offices. Increasingly, area psychologists are advising and coordinating the effective delivery of psychological services both within individual prisons and across HM Prison Service areas. They also play a pivotal role in professional links with the National Probation Service (NPS). Some area psychologist posts have been jointly funded by HM Prison Service and local probation services (for example, in Wales). Area psychologists are sometimes involved in devolving and delegating particular roles to psychologists in their areas in consultation with operational managers. Their location in the organization at an area level helps integrate them into other area-based developments. Area psychologists are one of a number of specialists who are increasingly being placed at this level of the organization. Such posts have the potential for major strategic influence across prisons, and ultimately nationally too, with direct professional linkages to the head of psychology for probation and prisons.

Government policy documents exhort public-service providers to ensure that there is flexibility in service delivery and that there are appropriate incentives in place particularly for frontline staff. In psychological services in prisons and probation this has a number of potential applications. Psychologists in the Probation Service have taken the lead in delivering services when they are needed outside the traditional nine-to-five day, running groupwork in the evenings to suit the needs of their clients. Such interventions may then be augmented by the offenders having the opportunity to have employment during the day. This is an example of flexible working. Similarly, in HM Prison Service many psychologists are on call for set periods of time to attend serious incidents in prisons as and when they occur, for example, hostage incidents. Traditionally, many have also risen to the occasion to meet the demands of detached duty assignments such as the delivery of staff training. Such flexible working patterns add enormously to the credibility of applied psychologists providing services where and when they are needed.

The other aspect to flexibility is the organizations' ability to provide opportunities for flexible working patterns that meet the needs of employees. In terms of the employment of psychologists, the organizations have perhaps significant room for improvement in the area of opportunities for part-time working. The workforce in psychological services has a relatively young average age and over 80 per cent of psychologists in prisons and probation are women. This profile contrasts markedly with that of staff in general in HM Prison Service, where the majority of staff are men with an older average age. However, increased flexibility is not just about opportunities for part-time working. Working patterns may also be looked at; this is a real opportunity for psychologists to examine the structuring of service provision, taking account of the business needs of the organization and individual needs.

As part of a process of ensuring that there are appropriate financial rewards for fully trained psychologists in whatever specialism, salaries have been significantly increased in recent years. Also, promotion opportunities have increased markedly with a continued growth in the number of senior positions, and a selection focus on evidence of effective delivery rather than 'time served' in the organization. The variety of roles undertaken by applied psychologists in prisons and probation are on the increase. It is perhaps note-worthy that the National Health Service is increasingly advertising for foren-sic psychologists to work in some of their mental health facilities. This is a double-edged sword for HM Prison Service and the National Probation Serv-ice. This is because, on the one hand it indicates how much value is placed upon the quality of the work of forensic psychologists who have trained and worked in prisons and probation. On the other hand, such 'marketability' of these skills could potentially result in a draining of experienced personnel from prisons and probation. However, the opportunities in prisons and probation are better than they have ever been and this will undoubtedly serve to keep good quality staff in the organizations.

In the past there has been a great deal of discussion and debate about how the supervision and training of trainee forensic psychologists may best be organized. The structures and systems for such supervision and training are in place. It is a matter for area psychologists to seek to ensure that such arrange-ments are appropriately implemented. An area that needs to be more firmly grasped is that of the Continuing Professional Development (CPD) of qualified and experienced applied psychologists. Although there has been some progress, there is clearly still much to be done. Improvements in the initial training and supervision of trainee forensic psychologists have been linked to significant improvements in retention levels. CPD which is of good quality may also serve to incentivize further improvements to retention levels amongst experienced applied psychologists.

The expansion of choice in the design of public services is another important governmental theme. This applies to the services delivered by applied psycholo-gists too. Too often, in the past, there has been an exclusive focus on the contri-butions of forensic psychologists in the delivery of services. Their customary versatility and the broad-based, applied nature of forensic psychology aside (see Series Editors' Preface, this volume), there is a need to look at the full range of applied psychology specialisms when considering the provision and design of psychological services in prisons and probation.

Applied psychologists need to be agents of change in prisons and probation. It is necessary to deliver good-quality applied psychological services. However, it is not sufficient to do so, if psychologists are to play the full role that they potentially can. There is a need proactively to take forward and integrate the four principles of reform outlined above: standards and accountability; devolu-tion and delegation; flexibility and incentives; and expanding choice in the con-text of improved public-service delivery.

Having outlined the broader public-sector context of the work of psycholo-gists in prisons and probation, in the next section of this chapter we will focus upon the narrower, but professionally very important, developments within the

British Psychological Society (BPS). This includes some developments across the BPS but also within the specialist Division of Forensic Psychology (DFP).

Developments in the British Psychological Society

Over the past decade or so there have been a number of changes within the British Psychological Society. From 1990 to 2000 the overall number of members nearly doubled. The number of members of the specialist Division of Forensic Psychology (formerly named the Division of Criminological and Legal Psychology) increased by over threefold in the same time-frame (British Psychological Society, 2000). The forensic field is booming (Towl, 2003).

With the advent of the introduction of chartership in the late 1980s, debate continued about the use of specialist titles to indicate which area of applied psychology the individual was chartered in. It was agreed to have specialist titles by a ballot of BPS members. Unfortunately, members struggled to agree on what the specialist title should be for those full members of the then named 'Division of Criminological and Legal Psychology' (DCLP). The debate in the correspondence pages of the *DCLP Newsletter* (May 1990) was colourful. The use of the term 'forensic' was finally agreed upon as the specialist title.

Despite this the specialist Division maintained its name as the Division of Criminological Psychology. The metamorphosized newsletter relaunched as *Forensic Update* (FU) in July 1994 captured this duality on the front cover: the upper half read, *Forensic Update; A Newsletter for Forensic Psychologists*; at the bottom of the page it said that it was published by the DCLP. Two issues later, the addendum was abandoned. But it was not until 1999 that members were given the opportunity to vote on whether or not they wanted the Division to change its name to the Division of Forensic Psychology. The editorial of the July issue of FU exhorted members to vote in favour of the change. They did just that with a thumping majority, agreeing to the change of the name of the Division. Thus the terms 'chartered forensic psychologist' and 'full member of the Division of Forensic Psychology' came into use.

One impact for psychologists working in prisons was that finally (some would say this was long overdue) the use of the term 'prison psychologist' began to fall out of usage. This was an important symbolic step in the professional development of applied psychologists working in prisons. The editorial of the FU of the day summed it up, 'The term "forensic" is increasingly being more widely used within the Division. For example, in the Prison Service growing numbers of psychologists are dispensing with the curious tradition of referring to themselves by their place of work in favour of a focus upon their function. The term "prison psychologist" is becoming an anachronism' (Division of Forensic Psychology, 1999). This was an important development in terms of the more appropriate recognition of the professional status of those working in prisons, which had perhaps not always previously been seen as on a par with, for example, that of clinical psychology.

Since that time, developments within the BPS have continued apace. Perhaps most pertinently for our purposes has been the development of the 'Occupational Standards in Applied Psychology' project (Needs, 1997). This sets out to provide a taxonomy of commonalities in terms of the required core competencies of the full range of applied psychology specialisms.

There has also been a significant tightening up of the requirements for trainee forensic psychologists working towards chartership. In contrast to the situation which preceded this, there is an emphasis on the provision of appropriate supervisors and a structured approach to training and development. The system drew heavily from the occupational standards mentioned above. Chartership also exists to provide professional regulation of those who are 'qualified' and those who are not, in principle a perfectly reasonable concept. As with any profession, the potential vulnerability from a public-interest perspective is that such professional bodies can end up being as much about professional self-interest as public interest. We need to be ever mindful of this.

The two preceding sections of this chapter have been intended to put the work of psychologists in prisons and probation in their public-sector and professional context. Clearly, full justice cannot be done to this area in such a chapter. However, in more fully understanding the work of psychologists in these challenging environments, it is important to have an awareness of some of the broader context. The next section focuses upon current psychological practice within prisons and probation.

Current Psychological Practice in Prisons and Probation Services

Introduction

In April 2001, the National Probation Service was formally launched. The structural and cultural change that this represented was probably one of the most significant in the history of probation services. The essence of the change marked a shift to a more centralized direction of the forty-two probation areas and a shift in emphasis to enforcement as a prominent service aim. It was at this point (April 2001) that there was the first joint recruitment of training-grade psychologists for both organizations. For psychological services in criminal justice this was a significant manifestation of closer partnership working.

HM Prison Service has a history of recruiting trainee psychologists. The respective recruitment histories of both organizations will inevitably have an impact on what, precisely, such psychologists actually do. A number of probation services had previously had links with National Health Service facilities and would sometimes receive clinical (and forensic) psychological services through this route. Other probation services had links with private-sector provision for a range of services. Some probation services will, no doubt, keep such links for the delivery of some of their psychological services. The partnership between psychological services in prisons and probation is by no means exclusive, nor should it be. However, the advent of joint recruitment and increased secondments of experienced staff has served to foster some mutually productive relationships between the two services which has the potential to contribute to improved service delivery.

Psychological services delivery

One of the primary drivers of the increase in the numbers of psychologists working in prisons and probation has been the development and implementation of 'accredited offending behaviour programmes'. These involve structured groupwork interventions based on cognitive behaviourally based approaches to working with a range of offenders. The implementation of these groupwork interventions have been underpinned by a growing area of evidence-based practice commonly referred to as the 'What Works?' literature. This literature has tended to draw heavily upon meta-analytic studies in assessing those methods which are most likely to have a positive impact on reducing the risk of reoffending. In relation to offending behaviour programmes a panel of professionals independent of HM Prison Service and the National Probation Service set standards for the 'accreditation' of such interventions for both prisons and probation services. They have recently been renamed the Correctional Services Accreditation Panel (CSAP). The efficacy of these approaches will ultimately be judged by the emerging empirical evidence of the impact of such current practices.

There are no roles across the family of accredited offending behaviour programmes that have to be performed by a psychologist. However, psychologists tend to have relevant competencies (or be able to assimilate them speedily) and are rightly valued by the organizations in delivering such services. HM Prison Service is far more heavily reliant upon the contributions of psychologists in this area than are probation services. Psychologists working for probation services have tended to get involved in psychometric testing and sometimes the interpretation of such tests. Such psychometric testing can have a number of functions including assessing suitability for particular interventions and measuring progress.

A great deal of the work of psychologists, particularly, perhaps, those under training, is involved in this area. The two most common roles across the interventions are a facilitator/tutor role and what is termed a 'treatment manager' role. (For a fuller discussion of the range of such programmes and roles see the edited collection of papers and chapters in Towl and McDougall, 1999 and Towl, 2003, and the chapter by Needs and Capelin, this volume.)

In training terms for psychologists such manualized approaches to working with offenders enjoy a number of advantages. The training is highly structured, as are the manuals outlining the sessions which require delivery. Such structure is of enormous potential benefit, especially to those new to doing direct work with offenders. Many of the skills, experiences and knowledge developed in undertaking such work are very important to have in working towards chartership as a forensic psychologist. Indeed, the range of skills picked up are perhaps sometimes underestimated. This is demanding work which contributes to some of the core business of the organizations.

In terms of the needs of psychologists under training, notwithstanding the point about the range of skills that can be developed in this area of key work, those under training to be forensic psychologists will need a broader range of experiences. It is important in terms of the professional development and standing of forensic psychology that we are not seen to 'dumb down' such training by relying exclusively on a manualized approach. There is plenty of potential for incorporating wider or different roles at various stages of those under training, so this is by means an insurmountable potential problem.

Still on the theme of working with offenders to assess and reduce the risk of reoffending, another significant area of work of forensic psychologists in prisons is in the area of groupwork and individual interventions with life-sentenced prisoners. Much work is undertaken in this important area. In terms of stakeholder needs, work aimed at reducing the risk of reoffending clearly meets the agenda of public protection. This is challenging work. There are a number of aspects to this work. Traditionally, three areas have been argued to characterize the types of groupwork: information-based groups, supportive groups and groups addressing offending behaviour (Morrissey, 1995). The balance of these functions in terms of service delivery may well have shifted in more recent years towards a primary focus on addressing offending behaviour. The territory is similar for individual intervention work. Increasingly, psychologists are being called upon to explain and justify their recommendations with lifers at formal hearings. This helpfully brings into sharp focus the need to draw upon high professional ethical standards in practice, but also to ensure that, as professionals, psychologists keep themselves up to date with best practice in terms of the relevant research base. Such work with lifers is less prevalent in the probation services for psychologists at the moment, but it may be an area of development for the future depending upon the business priorities of the probation services. Such experiences afford psychologists with significant skills development opportunities.

One of the underlying themes of much of forensic psychological practice is risk assessment. This theme underpins the two key areas of work outlined above; however, it may be less commonly, yet no less appropriately, applied to work in reducing the risk of suicides (Towl, 2000). Suicides in prison are on the increase and this has been the general pattern over at least the past decade (Towl, McHugh & Snow, 2000). This is an area where there is much room for improvement and development in terms of more involvement from psychological staff (Towl, 2003). This is not to diminish the sterling work that has taken place, it is merely to observe that more could, and should, be done in this area. However, rates of suicide are high in prisons, as indeed they are for those just released from prison. Offenders as a group share in common a range of factors associated with a marked increase in the risk of suicide. Unemployment and drug misusage would be two striking examples of such potential vulnerability (Crighton, 2001).

Suicide prevention may be used to illustrate how a range of the applied psychology specialisms may be used to address such difficulties. This is by no means exclusive to the work of psychologists with the suicidal. It applies to many other areas of work currently undertaken by predominantly forensic psychologists or those on a training route to chartership as a forensic psychologist. For example, counselling psychologists have already started to play a part in helping women prisoners who may suffer from suicidal ideation and self-injury. Clinical psychologists are potentially well placed to provide interventions, particularly given the recently introduced in-reach psychiatric services. Moreover, there is the potential for health psychologists to look at ways of helping offenders with drug dependency-related difficulties. Occupational psychologists may be able to assist offenders in improving their employment prospects as indeed might educational psychologists.

Undertaking direct work with suicidal offenders is a role that perhaps insufficient numbers of psychologists get involved in. There is an abundance of information available to psychologists wishing to undertake either assessment or intervention work with the suicidal (see for example, Towl & Crighton, 1996; Towl & Forbes, 2000; Towl & Crighton, 2000). Also for a concise review of germane UK research see Crighton, 2000. Direct work with suicidal offenders is not the only level at which psychologists can have a beneficial impact.

Area psychologists are well placed (as we have seen) organizationally to contribute at a strategic level in terms of suicide prevention and management. This may involve driving the delivery of preventative measures and interventions at an area level. This can take a number of forms. Training and supporting other staff in working effectively with suicidal offenders can be one potentially useful contribution. Active involvement in Suicide Prevention Teams (SPTs) in prisons can be a helpful role. Some psychologists have got involved in the quality control of administrative processes which are used as the basis of structuring such interventions in prisons.

Other perhaps less well-known areas of work that psychologists make contributions to are: incident management, research, management consultancy, project management, staff training, staff recruitment and managerial contributions as members of senior management teams in prisons. The potential of the role in probation services has perhaps (understandably) not been fully explored and examined at this very early stage of the development of such services.

Incident management is a key area of activity within prisons (Ashmore, 2003). The ability of the organization to manage a range of such incidents swiftly and effectively is important in maintaining public confidence in prisons and is also important in terms of the health and safety of prisoners and staff. Incidents can include hostage situations and a range of disturbances within prisons. Maintaining an orderly environment is critical to the smooth and effective running of prisons.

The research role, particularly at an area level, includes the coordination of appropriate research. Increasingly, area psychologists are taking a proactive approach to this area of work. This can in practice mean having a menu of areas of potential research work that is needed and linking with universities in trying to ensure that such work is cost-effectively undertaken. This can sometimes be with postgraduate students.

Management consultancy work has been undertaken by psychologists in prisons for a number of years, particularly by more experienced staff who tend to have a broader understanding of the organization and skills of working effectively with senior operational managers. On the other hand, it is by no means unknown for less experienced staff to be given special responsibility for supporting a particular functional unit or area.

Project management tasks, again, have long been undertaken by psychologists working in prisons and these have tended to cover a broad range of areas such as addressing specific issues within regimes in prisons. As an approach to undertaking some potentially key tasks there has recently been a renewed interest in this area. For example, at the Applied Psychology Group for prisons and probation a programme management-based approach is being taken to addressing a number of issues. Such programme management lends itself to a more strategic and structured approach to service delivery in the Group. Currently, three potential outputs of such an approach have been identified: professional policy and practice guidelines; scoping studies; and professional informational sources. The programme manager oversees, at a strategic level, the balance and timing of the project-management tasks being undertaken. This serves to give a greater logical coherence and strategic integration to such work. Recent outputs from such an approach have included professional policy and practice guidelines.

Staff training is another area where there has been much activity from psychologists working in prisons (Forbes, 2003). This cuts across a number of areas of work including training in groupwork, counselling skills, risk assessment, hostage negotiation, report writing, interpersonal skills, interviewing, staff selection and lifer work, to name but a few.

There has been a history of involvement by psychologists in staff recruitment and selection (e.g. see McGurk & Fludger, 1987). More recently, such methodologies have become more sophisticated, building upon previous approaches, with the development of Job Simulation Assessment Centres (Roden, 1999; see also Baxter et al., chapter 10 of this volume).

It was mentioned above that a number of psychologists perform roles on individual prison establishment senior management teams. Often such roles are by no means exclusively 'psychological' in their nature; generic managerial and analytical skills are often highly valued. The investment in such work can serve to make the undertaking of more strictly 'psychological' tasks more straightforward because of an increase in the receptivity of senior and middle managers in the organization supporting the work.

In this section an overview of some of the work undertaken in prisons and, albeit to a lesser extent, probation has been given. The discussion has been markedly skewed to prisons in recognition of the fact that such services are far more firmly established in the prison environment than in probation. It is simply too early in the implementation of the services in the NPS to cover such territory in meaningful detail because of the fledgling status of this service development. This warrants further comment in the next section.

Future Directions in Psychological Services in Probation and Prisons

Ethical issues in psychological practice

It took the DFP (formerly the DCLP) twenty years before it delivered on one of its core initial aims, which was to provide ethical guidelines for members. In 1997 the DFP produced a set of ethical guidelines for members (Division of Criminological and Legal Psychology, 1997). This set of guidelines augmented materials already produced by the BPS. In its structure it drew heavily upon the work of a sister organization, the American Psychological Association (APA). Those involved in forensic psychological practice in probation and prisons are expected to abide by such codes of practice.

Professional ethics are a collective matter which we all (as psychologists) need to address (Towl, 1994).

> The bases of ethical dilemmas in forensic psychology are not unique to the specialism, but such dilemmas are often brought into sharper focus for forensic psychologists. This sharper focus on ethical dilemmas is largely the product of working within a coercive context. Coercion is the antithesis of consent. This pervasive tension underpins a number of ethical dilemmas which are recurrent in the forensic field. (Towl, 1994, p. 23)

The above quotation still holds true. However, the author tended to focus his analysis and commentary on ethical issues around the then existing BPS code of ethics. This restricted his analysis and resulted in his missing a number of important ethical issues. For example, there has been a growing awareness within psychological services that we have been ineffective in the past in adequately addressing issues of diversity. Our ability to address diversity in terms beyond having a more diverse workforce (although that would be a very positive start) is one of the key ethical challenges for the professional forensic psychologist at the beginning of the twenty-first century. We need to embrace these challenges.

A critical awareness and understanding of ethical issues is crucial to the future of the discipline. The practical resolution of ethical issues should amount to doing the right thing. Sometimes this can mean being unpopular. Sometimes we learn by our mistakes, but learn we must. The long-term credibility of forensic psychology will be judged at least as much by its ethics as by its empiricism. Thus, whereas it is quite right that evidence-based practice should inform service delivery, this needs to be underpinned by sound ethical principles. To fail to consider these is to fail.

Future directions

This is an exciting time in the development of applied psychological services in general and forensic psychology in particular. There has been an unprecedented growth in the membership of the Division of Forensic Psychology, which quite possibly now totals over 1,000. As mentioned earlier, on closer inspection the pattern is quite striking. For the five-year period from 1985 to 1990, the Division increased in size by forty-three members. In the five-year period from 1995 to 2000, the membership increased by 358 members (British Psychological Society, 2000). The increases in the size of the membership of the specialist professional division were also reflected in the growth of posts, particularly in HM Prison Service. As we have seen, the increase in the number of posts has been largely driven by the growth of the application of that area of evidence-based practice known as the 'What Works?' literature. As indicated earlier, the future of that particular enterprise is likely to be determined on the basis of the emerging empirical evidence.

The partnership work between the National Probation Service and HM Prison Service will need to develop further if it is to fulfil its initial promise. Also there will need to be further work done on developing the linkages with the National Health Service and the Youth Justice Board (YJB).

If applied psychologists are to thrive, and there are good reasons to believe that they will, the work must meet the business needs of the organizations, taking account of multiple stakeholder perspectives. The context of public-service delivery is a changing one, as is that of the currently dominant professional association for psychologists, the British Psychological Society. Psychologists are well placed to take forward an agenda of improving public services; we must not lose sight of the need to achieve this. If there is such a broader understanding of the context, then professional, ethical and empirical practice is ripe to flourish. To be most fruitful for all concerned, the direction of that change needs to embrace a range of specialist applied disciplines in psychology so that the full range of applied psychological perspectives and skills can be drawn upon to improve the services we provide.

References

Titles with four or more authors, which are referred to in the text by the use of 'et al.', are listed in chronological order and can be found, for ease of access, at the end of the titles listed under the name of the first author.

Adair, J. (1986) *Effective teambuilding*. London: Pan.

Adams-Webber, J.R. (1979) *Personal Construct Theory: Concepts and Applications*. Chichester: Wiley.

Adelson, H.S. & Taylor L. (2000) Moving prevention from the fringes into the fabric of school improvement. *Journal of Educational and Psychological Consultation* 11(1), 7–36.

Ainsworth, P.B. (2000) *Psychology and Crime: Myths and Reality*. Harlow: Pearson Education.

Alexander, D.A. & Walker, L.G. (1994) A study of methods used by Scottish police officers to cope with work induced stress. *Stress Medicine* 10, 131–8.

Alimo-Metcalfe, B. & Alban-Metcalfe, R.J. (2002) Leadership. In Warr, P. (ed.), *Psychology at work* (5th edn). London: Penguin.

Allen, R., Lindsay, W.R., Macleod, F. & Smith, A.H.W. (2001) Treatment of women with intellectual disabilities who have been involved with the criminal justice system for reasons of aggression. *Journal of Applied Research in Intellectual Disabilities* 14(4), 340–7.

Alper, S., Tjosvold, D. & Law, K. (1998) Interdependence and controversy in group decision making: Antecedents to effective self-managing teams. *Organisational Behaviour and Human Decision Processes* 74, 33–52.

American Federation of State, County and Municipal Employees (1982) A study of occupational stress amongst state correctional officers. Unpublished paper: AFSCME.

American Psychiatric Association (1994) *Diagnostic and Statistical Manual of Mental Disorders* (4th edn). Washington, DC: APA.

Ancona, D.G. & Caldwell, D.F. (1992) Bridging the boundary: External activity and performance in organisational teams. *Administrative Science Quarterly* 37, 634–65.

Anderson, R. C. & Pichert, J.W. (1978) Recall of previously unrecallable information following a shift in perspective. *Journal of Verbal Learning and Verbal Behaviour* 17, 1–12.

Andrews, D.A. & Bonta, J.L. (1998) *The Psychology of Criminal Conduct* (2nd edn). Cincinnati: Anderson.

Armenakis, A.A. & Bedeian, A. (1999) Organisational change: A review of theory and research in the 1990s. *Journal of Management* 25, 293–315.

Ashmore, Z. (2003) Incident management. In Towl, G.J. (ed.), 2003.

Asquith, S. (1996) *Children, Young People in Conflict with the Law*. London: Jessica Kingsley.

Asquith, S., & Samuel, E., (1994*) Criminal Justice and Related Services for Young Adult Offenders*. London: Stationery Office.

Audit Commission (1990) *Police Paper 9: Reviewing the Organisation of Provincial Police Forces*. London: HMSO.

Audit Commission (2001) *A Change of Direction: Managing Changes in Local Probation Areas*. London: Stationery Office.

Bagshaw, M. & Baxter, K. (1987) Interpersonal skills training for prison officers. In McGurk, Thornton & Williams (eds), 1987.

Baldwin, T.T. & Ford K. (1988) Transfer of training: A review and directions for future research. *Personnel Psychology* 41, 63–105.

Bamberger-Schorr, L. (1991) Effective programs for children growing up in concentrated poverty. In Huston, A.C. (ed.), *Children in Poverty: Child Development and Public Policy*. Cambridge: Cambridge University Press.

Bannister, D. (1970) Comment on explanation and the concept of personality by H.J.Eysenck. In Borger, R. & Cioffi, F. (eds), *Explanation in the Behavioural Sciences*. Cambridge: Cambridge University Press.

Barnardo's Matrix (2000) *Barnardo's Matrix Project Annual Report*. Edinburgh: Barnardo's Scotland.

Baroff, G.S. (1996) The mentally retarded offender. In Jacobsen, J. & Mulick, J. (eds), *Manual of Diagnosis and Professional Practice in Mental Retardation*. Washington, DC: American Psychological Association.

Bar On, R., Brown, J.M., Kirkcaldly, B.D. & Thome, E.P. (2000) Emotional expression and implications for occupational stress: An application of the emotional quotient inventory (EQ-I). *Personality and Individual Differences* 28, 1,107–18.

Barton, J. (2000) Psychological factors on the trigger: Police use of lethal force in Britain. Unpublished Ph.D. thesis, University of Portsmouth Psychology Department.

Barton, J., Vrij, A. & Bull, R. (1998) New paradigms in researching police use of firearms. *Journal of Police and Criminal Psychology* 13, 36–42.

Barton, J., Vrij, A. & Bull, R. (2000a) High speed driving: Police use of lethal force during simulated incidents. *Legal and Criminological Psychology* 5, 107–21.

Barton, J., Vrij, A. & Bull, R. (2000b) The influence of field experience on excitation transfer by police officers during armed confrontations. In Czerederecka, A., Jaskiewicz-Obydzinskam, T. & Wojcikiewicz, J. (eds), *Forensic Psychology and Law: Traditional Questions and New Ideas*. Krakow: Institute of Forensic Research Publishers.

Bateman, A.W. & Fonagy, P. (2000) Effectiveness of psychotherapeutic treatment of personality disorder. *British Journal of Psychiatry* 177, 138–43.

Battistich, V. & Hom, A. (1997) The relationship between students' sense of their school as a community and their involvement in problem behaviors. *American Journal of Public Health* 87(12) (December), 1,997–2,001.

Baxter, K., & Bonito, A.M. (1984) A report on the application of the Systems Approach to the training of prison officers. Unpublished report, Prison Service College, HM Prison Service.

Beck, A.T., Kovacs, M. & Weissman, A.S. (1979) Assessment of suicidal intention: The scale for suicidal ideation. *Journal of Consulting and Clinical Psychology* 47, 343–50.

Beck, A.T. & Steer, R.A. (1989) Alcohol abuse and eventual suicide: A 5- to 10-year prospective study of alcohol-abusing suicide attempters. *Journal of Studies on Alcohol* 50 (3), 202–3.

Bekerian, D.A. & Dennett, J.L. (1993) The cognitive interview: Reviving the issues. *Applied Cognitive Psychology* 7(4), 275–98.

Belbin, R.M. (1981) *Management Teams: Why They Succeed or Fail.* London: Heinemann.

Bell, R.C. (1999) *GRIDSCAL: A Program for Analyzing the Data of Multiple Repertory Grids Version 1.0.* Department of Psychology, University of Melbourne. http://www.psyctc.org/grids/grids.htm.

Bell, R.E. (1991) Staff inmate relations: The Personal Officer Scheme. In Bottomley, A. K. & Hay, W. (eds), *Special Units for Difficult Prisoners.* Hull: Centre for Criminology and Criminal Justice, University of Hull.

Bell, R.E. (1992) C Wing Special Unit – Does it work? In Clar, N.K.& Stephenson, G.M. (eds), *Children, Evidence and Procedure, Issues in Criminological and Legal Psychology.* Leicester: BPS.

Bell, R.E. (1993) HMP Parkhurst C Wing Special Unit 1989–1990: Fourth and fifth years. Unpublished Report to the Home Office.

Bellack, A.S. & Hersen, M. (1988) *Behavioural Assessment: A Practical Handbook* (3rd edn). New York: Pergamon.

Bellezza, F.S. & Bower, G. H. (1982) Remembering script-based text. *Poetics*, 11(1), 1–23.

Belli, R.F., Shay, W.L. & Stafford, F.P. (2000) *Event History Calendar and Question List Surveys: A Direct Comparison of Interviewing Methods.* Survey Methodology Programme Working Paper Series, Survey Research Center, University of Michigan.

Benjamin, L. S. (1996) *Interpersonal Diagnosis and Treatment of Personality Disorders.* New York: Guilford.

Benjamin, L.S. (1997) Personality disorders: Models for treatment and strategies for treatment development. *Journal of Personality Disorders*, 11, 307–24.

Bennett, P., Pike, G., Brace, N. & Kemp, R. (2000) Accuracy and confidence in E-FIT construction. Paper presented at the 10th European Conference on Psychology and Law, Cyprus, April.

Bennett, P., Pike, G., Brace, N. & Kemp, R. (2001) Presenting facial composites: 3D images and composites of composites. Paper presented at The 11th European Conference on Psychology and Law, Lisbon, June.

Bennett, T. & Wright, R. (1984) *Burglars on Burglary.* Aldershot: Gower.

Biggam, F., Power, K.G., Macdonald, R., Carcary, W. & Moodie E. (1997) Self perceived occupational stress and distress in a Scottish police force. *Work and Stress* 11, 118–33.

Birchwood, M. (1994) Cognitive early intervention. In Haddock, G. & Slade, P. (eds),

Cognitive Behavioural Approaches to Schizophrenia. London: Routledge.

Black, L., Cullen, C. & Novaco, R.W. (1997) Anger assessment for people with mild learning disabilities in secure settings. In Kroese et al. (eds), 1997.

Blackburn, R. (1990) Treatment of the psychopathic offender. In Howells, K. & Hollin, C. (eds), Clinical approaches to working with mentally disordered and sexual offenders. *Issues in Criminological and Legal Psychology* 16, 54–66. Leicester: BPS.

Blackburn, R. (1996) What *is* forensic psychology? *Legal and Criminological Psychology* 1(1), 3–16.

Blackburn, R. (2000) Treatment or incapacitation? Implications of research on personality disorders for the management of dangerous offenders. *Legal and Criminological Psychology* 5, 1–21.

Blackburn, R., Crellin, M.C., Morgan, E.M. & Tulloch, R.M.B. (1990) Prevalence of personality disorders in a special hospital population. *Journal of Forensic Psychiatry* 1, 43–52.

Blanchard, R., Watson, M., Choy, A., Dickey, R., Klassen, P., Kuban, N. & Feren, D.J. (1999) Paedophiles: Mental retardation, maternal age and sexual orientation. *Archives of Sexual Behaviour* 28, 111–27.

Bland, R. C., Newman, S. C., Dyck, R. J. & Orn, H. (1990) Prevalence of psychiatric disorders and suicide attempts in a prison population. *Canadian Journal of Psychiatry* 35, 407–13.

Bligh, D. (1994) *Assessing Professional People by OSPRE.* London: Police Review Publishing.

Blom-Cooper, L., Hally, H. & Murphy, E. (1995) *The Falling Shadow: One Patient's Mental Health Care – 1978–1993.* London: Duckworth.

Blom-Cooper, L., Grounds, A., Guinan, P., Parker, A. & Taylor, M. (1996) *The Care of Jason Mitchell: Report of the Panel of Inquiry.* London: Duckworth.

Blud, L. (1999) Cognitive skills programmes. In Towl & McDougall (eds), 1999.

Boag, D. (1991) Lincoln Special Unit. In Bottomley, A.K. & Hay, W. (eds), *Special Units for Difficult Prisoners.* Hull: Centre for Criminology and Criminal Justice, University of Hull.

Boag, D. (1992) Validating training effectiveness. Unpublished report, Prison Service College.

Bodna, B. (1987) *Finding the Way: The Criminal Justice System and the Person with Intellectual Disabilities.* Melbourne: Office of the Public Advocate.

Body, J. (2001) Review of JSAC for selection of prison officers. Pearn Kandola Occupational Psychologists. Unpublished report.

Boehm, V.R. (1985) Using assessment centres for management development: Five applications. *Journal of Management Development* 4, 40–51.

Bond, C.F. & Titus, L.J. (1983) Social facilitation: A meta-analysis of 241 studies. *Psychological Bulletin* 94, 265–92.

Bordin, E. S. (1979) The generalisability of the psychoanalytic concept of the working alliance. *Psychotherapy: Theory, Research and Practice* 16, 252–60.

Bottoms, A.E. (1977) Reflections on the renaissance of dangerousness. *Howard Journal of Penology and Crime Prevention* 16, 70–96.

Bowden, P. (1996) Violence and mental disorder. In Walker, N. (ed.), *Dangerous People.*

London: Blackstone.

Bower, G. (1967) A multicomponent theory of the memory trace. In Spence, K.W. & Spence, J.T. (eds), *The Psychology of Learning and Motivation*, vol. 1. New York: Academic Press.

Bradburn, N.M., Rips, L.J. & Shevell, S.K. (1987) Answering autobiographic questions: The impact of memory and inference on surveys. *Science* 236, 157–61.

Bradford, J. & Dimock, J. (1986) A comparative study of adolescents and adults who wilfully set fires. *Psychiatric Journal of the University of Ottawa* 11, 228–34.

Brantingham, P.J. & Faust F.L. (1976) A conceptual model of crime prevention crime and delinquency. *Crime and Delinquency* 22, 130–46.

Brewer, J. & Hunter, A. (1989) *Multimethod Research: A Synthesis of Styles.* Newbury Park: Sage.

Brier, N. (1994) Targeted treatment of adjudicated youths with learning disabilities: Effects on recidivism. *Journal of Learning Disabilities* 27, 215–22.

Briggs, F. & Hawkins, R.M.F. (1996) A comparison of the childhood experiences of convicted male child molesters and men who were sexually abused in childhood and claimed to be nonoffenders. *Child Abuse and Neglect* 20(3), 221–33.

Briner, R. (1997) Improving stress assessment: toward an evidence based approach to organisational stress interventions. *Journal of Psychosomatic Research* 43, 61–71.

British Psychological Society (BPS) (1999) *Dangerous People with Severe Personality Disorder: A British Psychological Society Response* (final version, 9 December). Leicester: BPS.

British Psychological Society (2000) *The 2000 Annual Report.* Leicester: BPS.

Britton, D. (1997) Gendered organisational logic; policy and practice in men's and women's prison. *Gender and Society* 11, 796–818.

Broadbent, D. (1979) Human performance and noise. In Harris, C. (ed.), *Handbook of Noise Control.* New York: McGraw-Hill.

Bromley, M.L. & Blount, W. (1997) Criminal justice practitioners. In Hutchison, W.S. and Emenor, W.G. (eds), *Employee Assistance programs* (2nd edn). Springfield, IL: Charles C. Thomas.

Bronfenbrenner, Urie (1977) Toward an experimental ecology of human development. *American Psychologist* (July), 513–29.

Bronfenbrenner, Urie (1979) *The Ecology of Human Development.* Cambridge, MA: Harvard University Press.

Brooks, K.L., Mulaik, J.S., Gilead, M.P. & Daniels, B.S. (1994) Patient overcrowding in psychiatric hospital units: Effects on seclusion and restraint. *Administration and Policy in Mental Health* 22 (2), 133–44.

Brotherton, C. (1999) *Social Psychology and Management: Issues for a Changing Society.* Buckingham: Open University.

Brown, B.S. & Courtless, T.F. (1971) The Mentally Retarded Offender. Department of Health Education and Welfare Publication Number (HSM) 72, 90–39, Washington, DC: US Government Printing Office.

Brown, J. (1998) Aspects of discriminatory treatment of women police officers serving in England and Wales. *British Journal of Criminology* 38, 265–82.

Brown, J., Campbell, E. & Fife-Schaw, C. (1995) Adverse impacts experienced by police officers following exposure to sex discrimination and sexual harassment. *Stress Medi-cine* 11, 221–8.

Brown, J., Cooper, C., & Kirkcaldy, B. (1996) Occupational stress among senior police officers. *British Journal of Psychology* 87, 31–41.

Brown, J.M. & Blount, C. (1999) Occupational stress among sex offender treatment managers. *Journal of Managerial Psychology* 14, 108–20.

Brown, J.M. & Campbell, E.A. (1990) Sources of occupational stress in police. *Work and Stress* 4, 305–18.

Brown, J.M. & Campbell, E.A. (1994) *Stress and Policing: Sources and Strategies.* Chichester: Wiley.

Brown, J.M., Cooper, C. & Kirkcaldy, B.D. (1999) Stressor exposure and methods of coping among senior police managers at time of organisational and managerial change. *International Journal of Police Science and Management* 2, 217–28.

Brown. J.M. & Fielding, J. (1993) Qualitative differences in men and women police officers' experience of occupational stress. *Work and Stress* 7, 327–40.

Brown, J.M., Fielding, J. & Grover, J. (1999) Distinguishing traumatic, vicarious and routine operational stressor exposure and attendant adverse consequences in a sample of police officers. *Work and Stress* 13, 312–25.

Brown, J.M. & Grover, J. (1998) The role of moderating variables between stressor exposure and being distressed in a sample of serving police officers. *Personality and Individual Differences* 24, 181–5.

Browne, K. (1999) Breaking the cycle of violence. Presentation at Royal Society of Medicine Conference, The Roots of Violence in Children and Young People, London 26 March.

Bryans, S. (2000a) Governing prisons: An analysis of who is governing prisons and the competencies which they require to govern effectively. *Howard Journal* 39, 14–29.

Bryans, S. (2000b) The managerialisation of prisons – efficiency without a purpose? *Criminal Justice Matters* 40, 7–8.

Buchanan, Ann (1999) *What works for Troubled Children?* Barkingside: Barnardo's.

Buchanan, D.A. (2000) An eager and enduring embrace: the ongoing rediscovery of teamworking as a management idea. In Procter, S. & Mueller, F. (eds), 2000.

Buchanan, D.A., Claydon, T. & Doyle, M. (1999) Organisation development and change: the legacy of the nineties. *Human Resource Management Journal* 9(2), 20–37.

Buchanan, D.A. & McCalman, J. (1989) *High Performance Work Systems: The Digital Experience.* London: Routledge.

Buchanan, D.A. & Preston, D. (1992) Life in the cell: Supervision and teamwork in a 'manufacturing systems engineering' environment. *Human Resource Management Journal* 2(4), 55–76.

Buchanan, D.A. & Storey, J. (1997) Role-taking and role-switching in organisational change: The four pluralities. In McLoughlin, I. & Harris, M. (eds), *Innovation, Organizational Change and Technology.* London: International Thompson.

Bucke, T. & Brown, D. (1997) *In Police Custody: Police Powers and Suspects' Rights under the Revised P.A.C.E. Codes Of Practice.* Home Office Research Study No. 174, London: Home Office.

Bull, R. & Clifford, B. (1979) Eyewitness memory. In Gruneberg, M.M. and Morris, P.E. (eds), *Applied Problems in Memory*. London: Academic Press.

Bush, J. (1995) Cognitive self change program. In McGuire (ed.), 1995.

Cadbury, Paul (1998) NCH Intensive Probation Project, Inverclyde. Presentation at Children, Young People and Crime in Britain and Ireland Conference, University of Stirling, 17 June.

Cairns, R.B. & Cairns, D. (1994) *Lifelines and Risks: Pathways of Youth in Our Time*. Cambridge: Cambridge University Press.

Caldwell, M. (1994) Applying social constructionism in the treatment of clients who are intractably aggressive. *Hospital and Community Psychiatry* 45(6), 597–600.

Canter, D. & Fritzon, K. (1998) Differentiating arsonists: A model of firesetting actions and characteristics. *Legal and Criminological Psychology* 3, 73–96.

Canter, D. & Hodge, S. (1998) Victims of male sexual assault. *Journal of Interpersonal Violence* 13(2), 222–39.

Canter, D., Hughes, D. & Kirby, S. (1998) Paedophilia: pathology, criminality, or both? The development of a multivariate model of offence behaviour in child sexual abuse. *Journal of Forensic Psychiatry* 9(3), 532–55.

Caparulo, F. (1991) Identifying the developmentally disabled sex offender. Sexuality and Disability 9, 311–22.

Carroll, F. & Weaver, J. (1986) Shoplifters' perceptions of crime opportunities: A process-tracing study. In Cornish & Clarke (eds), 1986.

Carver, C.S. & Scheier, M.F. (1998) *On the Self-Regulation of Behaviour*. Cambridge: Cambridge University Press.

Caspi, A., Moffitt, T.E., Thornton, A., Freedman, D.J.W., Amell, J.W., Harrington, H., Smijers, J. & Silva, P.A. (1996) The life history calendar: A research and clinical assessment measure for collecting retrospective event-history data. *International Journal of Methods in Psychiatric Research* 6, 101–14.

Cawthray, B. (1984) *Outlines for Developing Managers*. Marshfield Publications.

Chaiken, J.M. & Chaiken, N. (1982) *Varieties of Criminal Behaviour*. Santa Monica: Rand Corporation.

Charlton, J., Kelly, S., Dunnell, K., Evans, B. & Jenkins, R. (1992) Suicide deaths in UK and Wales: Trends in factors associated with suicide deaths. Reprinted in Jenkins., R., Griffiths, S. & Wylie, I. (eds), *The Prevention of Suicide*. London: Department of Health.

Christie, D.F.M. & Ellis, H.D. (1981) Photo-fit constructions versus verbal descriptions of faces. *Journal of Applied Psychology* 66, 358–63.

Chrzanowski, C.M. (1980) Problem clients or troublemakers? Dynamic and therapeutic considerations. *American Journal of Psychotherapy* 34, 17–29.

Clare, I.C.H. (1993) Issues in the assessment and treatment of male sex offenders with mild learning disabilities. Sexual and Marital Therapy, 8, 167–80.

Clare, I.C.H. & Murphy, G.H. (1998) Working with offenders or alleged offenders with intellectual disabilities. In Emerson, E., Hatton, C., Bromley, J. & Caine, E. (eds), *Clinical Psychology in People with Intellectual Disabilities*. Chichester: Wiley.

Clare, I.C.H., Murphy, G.H., Cox, D. & Chaplain, E.H. (1992) Assessment and treatment of fire setting: a single case investigation using a cognitive behavioural model. Criminal Behaviour and Mental Health 2, 253–68.

Clark, B. (1996) The question of change. *Prison Service Journal* 106, 30–4.

Clarke, C. (2000) *Interviewing for Facial Identification*. Police Research Award Scheme report, Policing and Reducing Crime Unit, Home Office Research, Development and Statistics Directorate.

Clarke, C. & Milne, R. (2000) Interview supervision: the development of a behaviourally anchored rating scale. Paper presented at the 10th European Conference on Psychology and Law, Cyprus, April.

Clarke, D.D. & Crossland, J. (1985) *Action Systems: An Introduction to the Analysis of Complex Behaviour*. London and New York: Methuen.

Clayton, T. (1979) Residential observation and assessment under attack. *Association of Educational Psychologists Journal*, Summer.

Clifford, B.R. & Davies, G.M. (1989) Procedures for obtaining identification evidence. In Raskin, D.C. (ed.), *Psychological Methods in Criminal Investigation and Evidence*. New York: Springer-Verlag.

Clifford, B.R. & George, R.A. (1996) A field investigation of training in three methods of witness/victim investigative interviewing. *Psychology, Crime and Law* 2, 231–48.

Clifford, B.R. & Gwyer, P. (1999) The effects of the cognitive interview and other methods of context reinstatement on identification. *Psychology, Crime and Law* 5, 61–80.

Cohen, G. (1989) *Memory in the Real World*. Hillsdale, NJ: Lawrence Erlbaum.

Cohen, G. & Faulkner, D. (1989) Age differences in source forgetting – effects on reality monitoring and on eyewitness testimony. *Psychology and Ageing* 4(1), 10–17.

Cohen, S.G. & Bailey, D.E. (1997) What makes teams work: Group effectiveness research from the shop floor to the executive suite. *Journal of Management* 23, 239–90.

Cole, G.A. (1996) *Management: Theory and Practice* (5th edn). London: Letts Educatonal.

Concise Oxford Dictionary of Current English (1995) Oxford: Clarendon Press.

Conlin, B. (1986) Stress and the manager in the prison service. Paper presented to Southwest Regional Conference, September/October.

Connolly, T., Arkes, H.R. & Hammond, K.R. (eds) (2000) *Judgement and Decision Making: An Interdisciplinary Reader* (2nd edn). New York: Cambridge University Press.

Cooke, D.J. & Michie, C. (1998) *Predicting Recidivism in a Scottish Prison Sample*. Edinburgh: Scottish Office Central Research Unit.

Cooke, J. (1995) *Law of Tort* (2nd edn). London: Pitman Publishing.

Cooper, C. (1986) Job distress: recent research and emerging role of the clinical occupational psychologist. *Bulletin of the British Psychological Society* 39, 325–31.

Cooper, C. & Cartwright, S. (1997) An intervention strategy for workplace stress. *Journal of Psychosomatic Research* 43, 7–16.

Cooper, C.L., Cooper, R.D, & Eaker, L.H. (1988) *Living with Stress*. Harmondsworth: Penguin.

Copas, J.B. (1982) Statistical analysis for the redevelopment of the reconviction prediction score. Unpublished paper, University of Warwick.

Coppenhall, K. (1995) The stresses of working with clients who have been sexually abused. In Dryden, W. (ed.), *Stresses in Counselling in Action*. London: Sage.

Corbett, R.P. & Harris, M.K. (eds) (2000) Up to speed: A review of research for practitioners. *Probation* 64, 56–9.

Cordery, J. (2002) Team working. In Warr, P. (ed.), *Psychology at Work* (5th edn).

London: Penguin.

Cornish, D. & Clarke, R.V.G. (eds) (1986) *The Reasoning Criminal.* New York: Springer-Verlag.

Correctional Service of Canada (online, n.d.) Hostage taking of CSC staff: Psychological and institutional Management. Online at: www.csc-scc.gc.ca/test/pblct/sexoffender/hostage/toc_e.shtml.

Corrigan, P, Holmes, E.P., Luchins, D. & Basit, A. (1995) The effects of interactive staff training on staff programming and patient aggression in a psychiatric inpatient ward. *Behavioral Interventions* 10(1), 17–32.

Cox, T. & Smith, T. (1990) Organisational health; prison service. Unpublished report, HM Prison Service.

Craft, A. & Craft, M. (1983) *Sex Education and Counselling for Mentally Handicapped People.* Bath: Pitman Press.

Crighton, D.A. (1995) Sex offender groupwork. In G. Towl (ed.), *Groupwork in Prisons.* Issues in Criminological and Legal Psychology, 23. Leicester: BPS.

Crighton, D.A. (1997) Risk assessment in prisons. *Prison Service Journal_113*, September.

Crighton, D.A. (1999) Risk assessment in forensic mental health. *British Journal of Forensic Practice* 1(1), 18–16.

Crighton, D.A. (2000) Suicide in prisons: A critique of UK research. In Towl, G.J., McHugh, M.J. and Snow, L. (eds), 2000.

Crighton, D.A. (2001) Suicide in Prisons. Unpublished Ph.D. thesis, Anglia Polytechnic University, Cambridge.

Cromwell, P., Olson, J. & Avary, D. (1991) *Breaking and Entering: An Ethnographic Analysis of Burglary.* Newbury Park: Sage.

Crowe, G. & Stradling, S. (1993) Dimensions of perceived stress in a British police force. *Policing and Society* 3, 137–50.

Cutler, B.L., Penrod, S.D. & Martens, T.K. (1987) The reliability of eyewitness identification: The role of system and estimator variables. *Law and Human Behavior* 11(3), 233–58.

Cutler, B.L., Penrod, S.D., O'Rourke, T.E. & Martens, T.K. (1986) Unconfounding the effects of contextual cues on eyewitness identification accuracy. *Social Behaviour* 1, 113–34.

Davidson, K.M. & Tyrer, P. (1996) Cognitive therapy for antisocial and borderline personality disorders: single case study series. *British Journal of Clinical Psychology* 35, 413–29.

Davies, G., Ellis, H. & Shepherd, J. (1978) Face identification: The influence of delay upon accuracy of Photo-fit construction. *Journal of Police Science and Administration* 6, 35–42.

Davies, G., Milne, A. & Shepherd, J. (1983) Searching for operator skills in face composite production. *Journal of Police Science and Administration* 11, 405–9.

Davies, G.M. & Milne, A. (1985) Eyewitness composite production: A function of mental or physical reinstatement of context. *Criminal Justice and Behaviour* 12, 209–20.

Davies, W. (1983) When porridge is stirred. *New Society* (14 April), 62.

Day, K. (1988) A hospital-based treatment programme for male mentally handicapped offenders. *British Journal of Psychiatry* 153, 635–44.

Day, K. (1993) Crime and mental retardation: a review. In Howells, K. & Hollin, C.R. (eds), *Clinical Approaches to the Mentally Disordered Offender.* Chichester: Wiley.

Day, K. (1994) Male mentally handicapped sex offenders. British Journal of Psychiatry, 165, 630–9.

Department of Health (DoH) 2000 *Framework for the Assessment of Children in Need and their Families.* London: Department of Health.

Detterman, D.K. & Sternberg, R.J. (1993) *Transfer on Trial: Intelligence, Cognition, and Instruction.* Norwood: Ablex.

Diamond, R. &Carey, S. (1977) Developmental changes in the representation of faces. *Journal of Experimental Child Psychology* 23, 1–22.

Dirks, K.T. (1999) The effects of interpersonal trust on work group performance. *Journal of Applied Psychology* 84, 445–55.

Division of Criminological and Legal Psychology (1997) *Ethical Guidelines on Forensic Psychology.* Leicester: BPS.

Division of Forensic Psychology (1999) *Report from the Chair.* Leicester: BPS (Forensic Updates)

Dixon, N.F. (1976) *On the Psychology of Military Incompetence.* London: Jonathan Cape.

Dolan, B. (1998) Therapeutic community treatment for severe personality disorders. In Millon, T., Simonsen, E., Birket-Smith, M. & Davis, R.D. (eds), *Psychopathy: Antisocial, Criminal and Violent Behaviour.* New York: Guilford.

Doren, D.M., Miller, R. & Maier, G. J. (1993) Predicting threatening psychopathic patient behavior in an inpatient milieu. *International Journal of Offender Therapy and Comparative Criminology* 37(3), 221–9.

Douglas, K.S., Cox, D.N. & Webster, C.D. (1999) Violence risk assesment: science and practice. *Legal and Criminological Psychology* 4(2) 149–84.

Dowson, J. H., Butler, J. & Williams, O. (1999) Management of psychiatric in-patient violence in the Anglia region. *Psychiatric Bulletin* 23(8), 486–9.

Driscoll, R. (1984) *Pragmatic Psychotherapy.* New York: Van Nostrand Reinhold.

Dubin, W. and Lion, J. (eds) (1992) *Clinician Safety: Report of the American Psychiatric Association Task Force.* Washington, DC: American Psychiatric Press.

Duncan, B. (1995) Prisoner of politics and a 12 hour day. *Independent on Sunday* (8 January), 13.

Dunford, F.W. & Elliot, D.S. (1984) Identifying career offenders using self-reported data. *Journal of Research in Crime and Delinquency* 21, 57–86.

Dunphy, D. & Bryant, B. (1996) Teams: Panaceas or prescriptions for improved performance? *Human Relations* 49(5), 677–99.

Durlak, Joseph A. & Wells, Anne M. (1997) Primary prevention mental health programs for children and adolescents: A meta-analytic review. *American Journal of Community Psychology* 25(2), 111–244.

Easterbrook, J.A. (1959) The effect of emotion on cue utilisation and the organisation of behaviour. *Psychological Review* 66, 183–201.

Edelwich, J. & Brodsky, A. (1980) *Burnout: States of Disillusionment in the Helping Professions.* New York: Human Resources Press.

Edmondson, A. (1999) Psychological safety and learning behaviour in work teams. *Administrative Science Quarterly* 44, 350–83.

Egan, G. (2002) *The Skilled Helper* (7th edn). Pacific Grove, CA: Brooks/Cole.

Elam, K. (1988) *The Semiotics of Theatre and Drama*. London: Routledge.

Ellis, H., Shepherd, J. & Davies, G. (1975) An investigation of the use of Photo-fit technique for recalling faces. *British Journal of Psychology* 66, 29–37.

Ellis, H.D. (1984) Practical aspects of face memory. In Wells, G.L. & Loftus, E.F. (eds), *Eyewitness Testimony: Psychological Perspectives*. Cambridge: Cambridge University Press.

Ellis, H.D. (1986) Face recall: A psychological perspective. *Human Learning* 5, 189–96.

Emmett, D., Clifford, B. & Gwyer, P. (2001) Field dependency as a mediator of eyewitness identification accuracy. Paper presented at the 11th European Conference on Psychology and Law, Lisbon, June.

Emmett, D., Gwyer, P. & Clifford, B.R. (2000) An investigation of the interaction between the cognitive style of eyewitnesses, their memorial performance at event recall, and their sensitivity to context reinstatement. Paper presented at the 10th European Conference on Psychology and Law, Cyprus, April.

Esser, J.K. (1998) Alive and well after 25 years: A review of groupthink research. *Organisational Behaviour and Human Decision Processes* 73, 116–41.

Evans, R. (1987) Managerial performance and innovation. *Prison Service Journal* (April), 9–12.

Everington, C. & Fulero, S.M. (1999) Competence to confess: measuring understanding and suggestibility of defendants with mental retardation. *Mental Retardation* 37, 212–20.

Everington, C.T. & Luckasson, R. (1992) *Competence Assessment for Standing Trial for Defendants with Mental Retardation*. Worthington: International Diagnostic Systems.

Evershed, S. (1987) Special Unit C Wing, HMP Parkhurst. In Bottoms, A.E. and Light, R. (eds), *Patterns of Long Term Imprisonment*. Aldershot: Gower.

Evershed, S. (1989) Parkhurst Special Unit: The first two years. Paper presented to Cropwood Fellowship, Cambridge.

Evershed, S. (1991) Special Unit, C Wing, HMP Parkhurst. In Herbst, K. and Gunn, J. (eds), *The Mentally Disordered Offender*. London: Butterworth/Heinemann.

Evershed, S. & Fry, C. (1992) C Wing Special Unit: Does it work? Unpublished report to the Home Office.

Evershed, S., Tennant, A., Boomer, D., Rees, A., Barkham, M. & Watson, A. (under review) *Practice-Based Outcomes of Dialectical Behaviour Therapy (DBT) Targeting Violence and Aggression, with Male Forensic Patients: A Pragmatic and Non-Contemporaneous Comparison*.

Fahlberg, V. (1994) *A Child's Journey Through Placement*. London: British Agencies for Adoption and Fostering.

Fallon, E. (1983) Helping direct care workers manage self-injurious behaviour. *Milieu Therapy* 3(2).

Farnham, D. and Horton, S. (eds) (1996) *Managing the New Public Services*, Basingstoke: Macmillan Press.

Farrington, D.P. (1986) Age and crime. In Tonry, M. & Morris, N. (eds), *Crime and Justice* 7, 189–250. Chicago: University of Chicago Press

Farrington, D.P. (1994) Early Developmental Prevention of Juvenile Delinquency. *Criminal Behaviour and Mental Health* 4, 209–27.

Farrington, D.P. (1996) *Understanding and Preventing Youth Crime*. York: Joseph Rowntree Foundation.

Farrington, D.P. (1999) Delinquency prevention using family-based interventions. *Children and Society* 13, 287–303.

Farrington, D.P. & Tarling, R. (1985) Criminological prediction: An introduction. In Farrington, D.P. & Tarling, R. (eds), *Prediction in Criminology*. Albany: State University of New York Press.

Farrington, D.P. & Wilkström, P.-O. H. (1994) Criminal careers in London and Stockholm: A cross-national comparative study. In Weitekamp, E.G.M. & Kerner, H.-J. (eds), *Cross-National Longitudinal Research of Human Development and Criminal Behaviour*. Amsterdam: Kluwer Academic.

Faugier, J. (1996) Clinical supervision and mental health nursing. In Sandford, T. & Gournay, K. (eds), *Perspectives in Mental Health Nursing*. London: Balliere Tindall.

Feij, J.A. (1976) Field independence, impulsiveness, high school training, and academic achievement. *Journal of Education Psychology* 68, 793–9.

Felson, M. (1993) *Crime and Everyday Life*. London: Pine Forge.

Felson, R.B. & H.J. Steadman. (1983) Situational factors in disputes leading to criminal violence. *Criminology* 21, 59–74.

Feltham, R.T. (1989) Assessment centres. In Herriot, P. (ed.), *Assessment and Selection in Organisations: Methods and Practice for Recruitment and Appraisal*. Chichester: Wiley.

Fielding, N. (1994) Cop canteen culture. In Newborn, T. & Stanko, E. (eds), *Just the Boys Doing the Business: Men, Masculinities and Crime*. London: Routledge.

Figley, C. (1995) Compassion fatigue as secondary traumatic stress: An overview. In Figley, C. (ed.), *Compassion Fatigue: Coping with Secondary Traumatic Stress Disorder in Those Who Treat the Traumatized*. New York: Brunner Mazel.

Finger, K. & Pezdek, K. (1999) The effect of the cognitive interview on face identification accuracy: Release from verbal overshadowing. *Journal of Applied Psychology* 84(3), 340–8.

Fischoff, B., Bostrom, A. & Quadrel, M.J. (1993) Risk perception and communication. *Annual Review of Public Health* 14, 183–203.

Fisher, J. & Staples, J. (1994) Involvement and commitment: The staff consultation process at HMP Full Sutton. *Prison Service Journal* 92, 10–12.

Fisher, R.P. & Geiselman, R.E. (1988) *Evaluation and Field Implementation of the Cognitive Interview*. Final Report for National Institute of Justice (Grant U.S.D.J.-85-IJ-CX-0053).

Fisher R.P. & Geiselman R.E. (1992) *Memory-Enhancing Techniques for Investigative Interviewing: The Cognitive Interview*. Chicago: Charles Thomas.

Fisher, R.P., Geiselman, R.E. & Raymond, D.S. (1987) Critical analysis of police interview technique. *Journal of Police Science and Administration* 15(3), 177–85.

Fisher, R.P., McCauley, M.R. & Geiselman, R.E. (1994) Improving eyewitness testimony with the cognitive interview. In Ross, D.F., Read, J.D. & Toglia, M.P. (eds), *Adult Eyewitness Testimony: Current Trends and Developments*. Cambridge: Cambridge University Press.

Fisher, R.P., Geiselman, R.E., Raymond, D.S., Jurkevich, L. M. & Warhaftig, M.L. (1987) Enhancing enhanced eyewitness memory: Refining the cognitive interview. *Journal of Police Science and Administration* 15 (4), 291–7.

Flanagan J.C. (1954) The Critical Incident technique. *Psychological Bulletin* 51, 327–58.

Flannery, R.B., Hanson, M.A. & Penk, W. (1995) Clients' threats: expanded definition of assault. *General Hospital Psychiatry* 17(6), 451–3.

Flannery, R B., Hanson, M.A., Penk, W.E. & Flannery, G.J. (1996) Violence and the lax milieu? Preliminary data. *Psychiatric Quarterly* 67(1), 47–50.

Flannery, R.B., Hanson, M.A., Penk, W.E., Goldfinger, S., Pastava, G.J. & Navon, M.A. (1998) Replicated declines in assault rates after implementation of the Assaulted Staff Action Program. *Psychiatric Services* 49(2), 241–3.

Flynn, N. (1997) *Public Sector Management*. London: Prentice Hall.

Forbes, D. (2003) Staff training. In Towl, G.J. (ed.) 2003.

Forensic Update (1994) A newsletter for forensic psychologists. Leicester: Division of Criminological and Legal Psychology, BPS.

Foxon, M. (1989) Evaluation of training and development programs: A review of the literature. *Australian Journal of Educational Technology* 5(2), 89–104.

Freedman, D., Thornton, A., Camburn, D., Alwin, D. & Young-DeMarco, L. (1988) The life history calendar: a technique for collecting retrospective data. *Sociological Methodology*, 18, 37–68.

Friendship, C. & Thornton, D. (2001) Sexual reconviction for sexual offenders discharged from prison in UK and Wales: Implications for evaluating treatment. *British Journal of Criminology* 41, 285–92.

Frith, C.D. (1993) *The Cognitive Neuropsychology of Schizophrenia*. Hillsdale, NJ: Lawrence Erlbaum.

Fromm, E. (1981) *On Disobedience and Other Essays*. New York: Seabury Press.

Furnham, A. (1997) *The Psychology of Behaviour at Work: The Individual in the Organisation*. Hove: Psychology Press.

Galbraith, S. (2000) *Scottish Executive Response to the Advisory Group Report on Youth Crime Review*. Edinburgh: Scottish Executive.

Garbarino, J. (1999) *Lost Boys: Why Our Sons Turn Violent and How We Can Save Them*. New York: Free Press.

Garbarino, J. (2000) Lost boys. Presentation to South Lanarkshire Council, Hamilton, Scotland, 22 March.

Garbarino, J., Kostelny, K. & Dubrow, N. (1991) What children can tell us about living in danger. *American Psychologist* 46(4), 376–83.

Garbarino, J. & Stocking, S.H. (1980) *Protecting Children from Abuse and Neglect*. San Francisco: Jossey-Bass.

Gatewood, R.D. & Field, H.S. (1987) *Human Resource Selection* (4th edn). Dryden.

Gaugler B.B., Rosenthal D.B., Thornton, G.C. & Bentson, C. (1987) Meta-analysis of assessment centre validity. *Journal of Applied Psychology* 72, 493–511.

Geiselman, R.E. (1992) Cognitive interviewing techniques for use with child victim/witnesses. Paper presented at NATO ASI, Il Ciocco, May.

Geiselman, R.E. & Callot, R. (1990) Reverse and forward recall of script-based texts. *Applied Cognitive Psychology* 4(2), 141–4.

Geiselman, R.E., Fisher, R.P., Firstenberg, I., Hutton, L.A., Sullivan, S.J., Avetissian, I.V. & Prosk, A.L. (1984) Enhancement of eyewitness memory: An empirical evaluation of the cognitive interview. *Journal of Police Science and Administration* 12, 74–80.

Gendreau, P. (1996) Offender rehabilitation: what we know and what needs to be done. *Criminal Justice and Behaviour* 23, 144–61.

Gerald, M., Jones, D.M. & Chamberlain, A.G. (1990) Refining the measurement of mood: The UWIST mood adjective checklist. *British Journal of Psychology* 81, 17–42.

Gersick, C.J.E. (1988) Time and transition in work teams: toward a model of group development. *Academy of Management Journal* 31, 9–41.

Getty, D.J., Pickett, R.M., D'Orsi, C.J. & Swets, J.A. (1988) Enhanced interpretation of diagnostic images. *Investigative Radiology* 23, 240–52.

Gibbens, T.C. & Robertson, G. (1983) A survey of the criminal careers of restriction order patients. British Journal of Psychiatry 143, 370–5.

Gibbons, J. (1995) Family support in child protection. In Hill, M., Kirk, R.H. & Part, D. (eds), *Supporting Families*. Edinburgh: HMSO.

Gibling, F. & Bennett, P. (1994) Artistic enhancement in the production of Photo-fit likenesses: An examination of its effectiveness in leading to suspect identification. Psychology. *Crime and Law* 1, 93–100.

Glaser, B. & Strauss, A. L. (1967) *The Discovery of Grounded Theory*. Chicago: Adine.

Glaser, W. & Deane, K. (1999) Normalisation in an abnormal world: a study of prisoners with intellectual disability. *Journal of Offender Therapy and Comparative Criminology* 43, 338–50.

Godden, D.R. & Baddeley, A.D. (1975) Context dependent memory in two natural environments: On land and underwater. *British Journal of Psychology* 66, 325–32.

Goldstein, I.L. (1993) *Training in Organisations* (3rd edn). Pacific Grove, CA: Brooks/Cole.

Goldstein, R.B., Powers, S.I., McCusker, J., Lewis, B.F., Bigelow, C. & Mundt, K.A. (1998) Antisocial behavioral syndromes among residential drug abuse treatment clients. *Drug and Alcohol Dependence* 49(3), 202–16.

Goleman, D. (1995) *Working with Emotional Intelligence*. London: Bloomsbury.

Gollwitzer, P.M. & Bargh, J.A. (eds) (1996) *The Psychology of Action: Linking Cognition and Motivation to Behaviour*. New York: Guilford.

Golynkina, K. & Ryle, A. (1999) The identification and characteristics of partially dissociated states of patients with borderline personality disorder. *British Journal of Medical Psychology* 72, 429–45.

Goodman, J.H. (1997) How therapists cope with client suicidal behavior. *Dissertation Abstracts International: Section B: the Sciences and Engineering* 57, 9–13.

Graham J. & Bowling, B. (1995a) *Young People and Crime*. Home Office Research Study No. 145. London: Home Office.

Graham, J. & Bowling, B. (1995b) *Young People and Crime*. Research Findings No. 24, London: Home Office.

Gregory, J. & Lees, S. (1999) *Policing Sexual Assault*. London: Routledge.

Greimas, A.J. (1966) *Semantique structurale*. Paris: Larousse.

Greimas, A.J. (1970) *Du sens*. Paris: Seuil.

Gresswell, D.M. & Hollin, C.R. (1992) Towards a new methodology for making sense of case material: An illustrative case involving attempted multiple murder. *Criminal Behaviour and Mental Heath* 2, 329–41.

Griffiths, S.D.M., Quinsey, V.L. & Hingsburger, D. (1989) *Changing Inappropriate Sexual Behaviour: A Community Based Approach for Persons with Developmental Disabilities*. Baltimore: Paul Brooks.

Gritter, G.W., Love, C., Hunter, M. & Hixon, D. (1995) Containing patient violence. *Psychiatric Services* 46(4) (April), 409.

Gross, G. (1985) *Activities of a Development Disabilities Adult Offender Project*. Olympia, WA: Washington State Developmental Disabilities Planning Council.

Grubb-Blubaugh, V., Shire, B.J. & Leebaulser, M. (1994) Behaviour management and offenders with mental retardation: the jury system. *Mental Retardation* 32, 213–17.

Grubin, D. (1997) Inferring predictors of risk: sex offenders. *International Review of Psychiatry* 9, 225–31.

Grubin, D. (1999) Actuarial and clinical assessment of risk in serious sex offenders. *Journal of Interpersonal Violence* 14(3), 331–43.

Gudjonsson, G.H. (1992) *The Psychology of Interrogations, Confessions and Testimony*. Chichester: Wiley.

Gudjonsson, G.H. & MacKeith, J. (1994) Learning disability and the Police and Criminal Evidence Act 1984. Protection during investigative interviewing: A video recorded false confession to double murder. *Journal of Forensic Psychiatry* 5, 35–49.

Gudjonsson, G.H., Clare, I.C.H., Rutter, S. & Pearse, J. (1993) *Persons at Risk During Interviews in Police Custody: The Identification of Vulnerabilities*. Research Study No. 12, Royal Commission on Criminal Justice. London: HMSO.

Guerra, N.G., Tolan, P.H. & Hammond, R. (1994) Prevention and treatment of adolescent violence. In Eron, L.D., Gentry, J. & P. Schlegel (eds), *Reason to Hope: A Psychological Perspective on Violence and Youth*. Washington, DC: American Psychological Association.

Guirdham, M. (1995), *Interpersonal Skills at Work* (2nd edn). London: Prentice Hall.

Gunn, D. & Wilson, M. (1999) Youth crime: Changing the lifelines of repeat offenders. Presentation at Living at the Edge Conference, University of Strathclyde, 11 September.

Gunn, J. (1996) The management and discharge of violent patients. In Walker, N. (ed.) *Dangerous People*. London: Blackstone Press.

Gutheil, T.G. (1984) Clinical issues in psychiatry. In Michaels, R. (ed.) *Psychiatry: Volume 3*. Philadelphia: Lippinscott-Raven.

Guzzo, R.A., Jett, R.D. & Katzell, R.A. (1985) The effects of psychologically-based intervention programs on worker productivity: A meta-analysis. *Personnel Psychology* 38, 275–91.

Guzzo, R.A. & Salas, E. (eds) (1995) *Team Effectiveness and Decision Making in Organisations*. San Francisco: Jossey-Bass.

Haaven, J., Little, R. & Petre-Miller, D. (1990) *Treating Intellectually Disabled Sex Offenders: A Model Residential Programme*. Orwell, VT: Safer Society Press.

Hagell, A. & Newburn T. (1994) *The Persistent Offender.* London: Policy Studies Institute.

Hallam, R.S. (1987) Prospects for theoretical progress in behaviour therapy. In Eysenck, H.J. & Martin, I. (eds), *Theoretical Foundations of Behaviour Therapy.* New York: Plenum Press.

Hansen, J. & Berman, S. (1991) The relationship of family and staff expressed emotion to residents' functioning of community residences. *Psychosocial Rehabilitation Journal* 4, 85–90.

Hanson, R.K. & Harris, A.J.R. (2000) Where should we intervene? *Criminal Justice and Behaviour* 27(1), 6–35.

Hardy, G.E., Barkham, M., Shapiro, D.A., Stiles, W.B., Rees, A. & Reynolds, S. (1995) Impact of Cluster C personality disorders on outcomes of brief psychotherapies for depression. *Journal of Consulting and Clinical Psychology* 63(6), 997–1,004.

Hare, R.D. (1983) Diagnosis of antisocial personality disorder in two prison populations. *American Journal of Psychiatry* 140, 887–90.

Hare, R.D. (1991) *The Revised Psychopathy Checklist.* Toronto: Multi-Health Systems.

Harpur, T.J. & Hare, R.D. (1994) Assessment of psychopathy as a function of age. *Journal of Abnormal Psychology* 103(4), 604–9.

Harris, J. & Grace, C. (1999) *A Question of Evidence? Investigating and Prosecuting Rape in the 1990s.* Home Office Research Study No. 196. London: Home Office.

Hart, P., Wearing, A. & Headey, B. (1994) Work experience: construct validation of the policy daily hassles & uplift scales. *Criminal Justice and Behaviour* 21, 283–311.

Hart, P.M., Wearing, A.J. & Headey, B. (1995) Police stress and well-being: integrating personality, copying and daily work experience. *Journal of Occupational and Organizational Psychology* 68, 133–56.

Hart, S.D. (1998) The role of psychopathy in assessing risk for violence: Conceptual and methodological issues. *Legal and Criminological Psychology* 3(1), 121–38.

Hartley, J.F. (1992) The psychology of industrial relations. In Cooper, C.L. & Robertson, I.T. (eds), *International Review of Industrial and Organisational Psychology,* 201–43. Chichester: Wiley.

Hawton, K. (1994) Causes and opportunities for prevention. In Jenkins, R., Griffiths, S. & Wylie, I. (eds), *The Prevention of Suicide.* London: HMSO.

Hawton, K. & Kirk, J. (1989) Problem solving. In Hawton, K., Salkovskis, P.M., Kirk, J. & Clark, D.M. (eds), *Cognitive Behaviour Therapy for Psychiatric Problems: A Practical Guide,* 406–26. Oxford: Oxford University Press.

Hay, W. & Sparks, R. (1991) What is a prison officer? *Prison Service Journal* 83, 2–7.

Hayes, S. (1991) Sex offenders. *Australia and New Zealand Journal of Developmental Disabilities (Journal of Intellectual and Development Disabilities)* 17, 220–7.

Hayes, S. (1996) Recent research on offenders with learning disabilities. *Tizard Learning Disability Review* 1, 7–15.

Head, G. & O'Neil, W. (1999) Introducing Feuerstein's Instrumental Enrichment in a school for children with social, emotional, and behavioural difficulties. *Support For Learning* 14(3), 122–8.

Heady, R.B. (2002) PERMAP manual. Online at http://www.ucs.louisiana.edu/rbh8900/permap.html

Health and Safety Executive (n.d.) *Five Steps to Risk Assessment*. London: HSE.

Heidensohn, F. (1986) Models of justice: Portia or Persephone? Some thoughts on equality, fairness and gender in the field of criminal justice. *International Journal of the Sociology of Law* 14, 287–98.

Hellosøy, O., Gronhaug, K. & Kvitastein, O. (2000) Burnout: Some conceptual issues and empirical findings from a new research setting. *Scandinavian Journal of Management* 16, 233–47.

Helsel, W.J. & Matson, J.L. (1988) The relationship of depression to social skills and intellectual functioning in mentally retarded adults. *Journal of Mental Deficiency Research* 32(5), 411–18.

Hemphill, J.F., Hare, R.D. & Wong, S. (1998) Psychopathy and recidivism: A review. *Legal and Criminological Psychology* 3, 139–70.

Henggler, S.W., Cunningham, P.B., Pickrel, S.G., Schoenwald, S.K. & Brondino, M.J. (1996) Multisystemic therapy: An effective violence prevention approach for serious juvenile offenders. *Journal of Adolescence* 19, 47–61.

Hepburn, J. & Knepper, P. (1993) Correctional officers as human service workers: The effect of job satisfaction. *Justice Quarterly* 10, 315–35.

Hermans, J.M. (1995) From assessment to change: the personal meaning of clinical problems in the context of the self-narrative. In Neimeyer, A. & Mahoney, M.J. (eds), *Constructivism in Psychotherapy*. Washington, DC: American Psychological Association.

Higgs, M. & Dulewicz, V. (1997) *Making Sense of Emotional Intelligence*. Windsor: NFER-Nelson.

HM Prison Service (1994) *Advice to Governors* 26. London: HM Prison Service.

Hockey, G.R.J. (1979) Stress and the cognitive components of skilled performance. In Hamilton, V. (ed.), *Human Stress and Cognition*. New York: Wiley.

Hodge, J. (1997) Addiction to violence. In Hodge, J.E., McMurran, M. & Hollin, C. (eds) *Addicted to Crime*. Chichester: Wiley.

Hogue, T. (1995) Training multidisciplinary teams to work with sex offenders: effects on staff attitudes. *Psychology, Crime and Law* 1, 227–35.

Holland, A.J. (1991) Challenging and offending behaviour by adults with developmental disorders. *Australia and New Zealand Journal of Developmental Disabilities (Journal of Intellectual and Developmental Disabilities)* 17, 119–26.

Hollin, C.R. (1995) The meaning and implications of 'programme integrity'. In McGuire, J. (ed.), 1995.

Holmes, J. (1993) *John Bowlby and Attachment Theory*. New York: Routledge.

Holmes, J. (1996) *Attachment, Intimacy, Autonomy: Using Attachment in Adult Psychotherapy*. Northvale, NJ: Jason Aronson.

Home Office (1913) Mental Deficiency Act. Reported in Walker, N. & McCabe, S. (1973) *Crime and Insanity in UK*. Edinburgh: Edinburgh University Press.

Home Office (1983) Memorandum 114, *On Efficiency, Economy and Effectiveness in the Police Service*. London: Home Office.

Home Office (1984) *Managing the Long-Term Prison System: Report of the Control Review Committee*. London: HMSO.

Hope, L., Gabbert, F. & Memon, A. (in press) Psychology in progress: From identification parade to court appearance. *International Journal of Police Science and Management.*

Horney, J. (in press) Criminal events and criminal careers. In Meier, R., Kennedy, L. & Sacco V. (eds), *The Process and Structure of Crime: Criminal Events and Crime Analysis.* New Brunswick, NJ: Transaction Publishers.

Horney, J., Osgood, D.W. & Marshall, I.H. (1995) Criminal careers in the short terms: intra-individual variability in crime and its relation to local life circumstances. *American Sociological Review* 60, 655–73.

Horowitz, M. (1986) *Stress Response Syndromes.* London: Aronson.

Horwarth, Jan (ed.) (2001) *The Child's World: Assessing Children in Need.* London: Jessica Kingsley.

House of Representatives (1996) *Cycle of Abuse.* Report to the Sub-Committee on Crime, Committee on the Judiciary, House of Representatives. Washington, DC: United States General Accounting Office.

Howard J.M. & Howard P.J. (2000) Human resource optimisation: Creating training and development that sticks. *Selection Development Review* 16(6), 8–13.

Hubble M.A., Duncan B.L. & Miller S.D. (eds) (1999) *The Heart and Soul of Change: What Works in Therapy.* Washington, DC: American Psychological Association.

Hunter, J.E. & Hunter, R.F. (1984) Validity and utility of alternative predictors of job performance. *Psychological Bulletin* 96, 72–98.

Hurst, T.E. & Hurst, M.M. (1997) Gender differences in mediation of severe occupational stress in correctional officers. *American Journal of Criminal Justice* 22, 121–37.

Ilgen, D.R. (1999) Teams embedded in organizations: some implications. *American Psychologist* 54, 129–39.

Isenberg, D.J. (1986) Group polarization: a critical review and meta-analysis. *Journal of Personality and Social Psychology* 50, 1,141-51.

Jackson. P.R., Spriggs, C.A, & Parker, S.K. (2000) Interdependence as a key requirement for the successful introduction of teamworking: A case study. In Procter, S. & Mueller, F. (eds), 2000.

Jacobs E. (1994) *Impact therapy.* Psychological Assessment Resources Inc.

Jamieson, J., McIvor, G. & Murray, C. (1999) *Understanding Offending Among Young People.* London: Stationery Office.

Janis, I. L. (1982) *Groupthink: A Study of Foreign Policy Decisions and Fiascos.* Boston, MA: Houghton Mifflin.

Jenkins, F. & Davies, G. (1985) Contamination of facial memory through exposure to misleading composite pictures. *Journal of Applied Psychology* 70(1), 164–76.

Jones, E.E. & Nisbett, R.E. (1971) The actor and the observer: divergent perceptions of the causes of behaviour. In Jones, E.E., Kanouse, D.E., Kelley, H.H., Nisbett, R.E., Valins, S. & Weiner, B. (eds), *Attribution: Perceiving the Causes of Behaviour.* Morristown, NJ: General Learning Press.

Jones, L. & Brown, V. (1998) Motivation and motivational assessment of personality disordered offenders. Paper presented at Division of Forensic Psychology conference, Durham.

Jones, L. F. (1997) Developing models for managing treatment integrity and efficacy in a prison based TC: The Max Glatt Centre. In Cullen, E., Jones, L. & Woodward, R. (eds) *Therapeutic Communities for Offenders.* Chichester: Wiley.

Jones, L. F. (2000) Identifying and working with clinically relevant offence paralleling behaviour. Paper presented at Division of Clinical Psychology, forensic special interest group, Nottinghamshire 2000.

Jones, L. F. (2001) Anticipating offence paralleling behaviour. Paper presented at Division of Forensic Psychology conference, Birmingham.

Jones. L. F. (2002a) An individual case formulation approach to the assessment of motivation. In McMurran, M. (ed.), *Motivating Offenders to Change*. Chichester: Wiley.

Jones, L. F. (2002b) Iatrogenic interventions with 'personality disordered' offenders. Paper presented at the Division of Forensic Psychology conference, Manchester.

Junger-Tas, J. & Marshall, I.H. (1999) The self-report methodology in crime research. In Tonry, M. (ed.), *Crime and Justice, vol. 25: An Annual Review of Research*. Chicago: University of Chicago Press.

Kahneman, D., Slovic, P. & Tversky, A. (1982) *Judgement under Uncertainty: Heuristics and Biases*. Cambridge: Cambridge University Press.

Kane, J.S., Bernardin, H.J., Villanova, P. & Peyrefitte, J. (1995) Stability of rater leniency: Three studies. *Academy of Management Journal* 38, 1,036–51.

Karau, S.J. & Williams, K.D. (1993) Social loafing: A meta-analytic review and theoretical integration. *Journal of Personality and Social Psychology* 65, 681–706.

Karpman, S.B. (1968) Fairy tales and script drama analysis. *Transactional Analysis Bulletin* 7, 39–43.

Kazdin, A.E., Matson, J.L. & Senatore, V. (1983) Assessment of depression in mentally retarded adults. *American Journal of Psychiatry* 140, 1,040–3.

Kebbell, M.R. & Milne, R. (1998) Police officers' perceptions of eyewitness performance in forensic investigations. *Journal of Social Psychology* 138, 323–30.

Kelly, D. (1992) A personal construct psychology perspective on deviance. In P. Maitland (ed.) *Personal Construct Theory, Deviancy and Social Work*. London: Inner London Probation Service/Centre for Personal Construct Psychology.

Kelly, D. & Taylor, H. (1981) Take and escape: a personal construct study of car 'theft'. In Bonarius, H., Holland, R. & Rosenberg, S. (eds), *Personal Construct Psychology: Recent Advances in Theory and Practice*. London: Macmillan.

Kelly, G.A. (1955) *The Psychology of Personal Constructs*. Vols 1 and 2. New York: W.W. Norton.

Kemp, R., Pike, G. & Brace, N. (1999) Eyewitness identification: are we asking the right questions? Paper presented at the 9th European Conference on Psychology and Law, Dublin, July.

Kilbrandon, Lord (1964) *Children and Young Persons, Scotland*. Edinburgh: Scottish Home and Health Department.

Kirkcaldy, B., Brown, J. & Cooper, C.L. (1998) The demographics of occupational stress among police superintendents. *Journal of Managerial Psychology* 13, 90–101.

Kirkpatrick, D.L. (1998) *Evaluating Training Programs: The Four Levels* (2nd edn). San Francisco: Berrett-Koehler.

Klimecki, M.R., Jenkinson, J. & Wilson, L. (1994) A study of recidivism among offenders with intellectual disability. *Australia and New Zealand Journal of Developmental Disabilities (Journal of Intellectual and Developmental Disabilities)* 19, 209–19.

Kohlenberg, R. J. & Tsai, M. (1994) Functional analytic psychotherapy: A radical behavioral approach to treatment and integration. *Journal of Psychotherapy Integration* 4, 175–201.

Köhnken, G., Milne, R., Memon, A. & Bull, R. (1999) The cognitive interview: A meta-analysis. *Psychology, Crime and Law* 5, 3–27.

Kolvin, I., Miller, F.J.W., Fleeting, M. & Kolvin, P.A. (1988) Social and parenting factors affecting criminal-offence rates: findings from the Newcastle Thousand-Family Study (1947–1980). *British Journal of Psychiatry* 152, 80–90.

Krafka, C. & Penrod, S. (1985) Reinstatement of context in a field experiment on eyewitness identification. *Journal of Personality and Social Psychology* 49, 58–69.

Kreitman, N. (1977) *Parasuicide.* Chichester: Wiley.

Kroese, B.S., Dagnan, D. & Loumidis, K. (1997) *Cognitive Behaviour Therapy for People with Learning Disabilities.* London: Routledge.

Krua, I., Hickey, N. & Hubbard, C. (1995) The prevalence of post traumatic stress disorder in a special hospital population of legal psychopaths. *Psychology, Crime and Law* 2, 131–41.

Lambert, E.G., Hogan, N.L. & Barton, S.M. (2002) Satisfied correctional staff. A review of the literature on the correlates of correctional staff job satisfaction. *Criminal Justice and Behaviour* 29, 115–43.

Lancefield, K., Jennings, C.J. & Thomson, D. (1997) Managerial style and its effect on prison officers' stress. *International Journal of Stress Management* 4, 205–19.

Langevin, R. & Pope, S. (1993) Working with learning disabled sex offenders. *Annals of Sex Research* 6, 149–60.

Lanza, M.L. (1995) Nursing staff as victims of patient assault. In Eichelman, B.S. & Hartwig, A.C. (eds), *Patient Violence and the Clinician.* Clinical Practice 30, 105–23. Washington, DC: American Psychiatric Press Inc.

Lanza, M.L., Kayne, H.L., Hicks, C. & Milner, J. (1994) Environmental characteristics related to patient assault. *Issues in Mental Health Nursing* 15(3), 319–35.

LaPiere, R.T. (1934) Attitude and actions. *Social Forces* 13, 230–7.

Launay, G. & Fielding, P.J. (1989) Stress among prison officers: some empirical evidence based on self report. *Howard Journal* 28, 138–48.

Law, J., Lindsay, W.R. & Smith, A.H.W. (1999) *Outcome Evaluation of 161 People with Mild Learning Disabilities Who Have Offending or Challenging Behaviour.* Proceedings of 27th Annual Conference of BABCP.

Lawrenson, H. & Lindsay, W.R. (1998) The treatment of anger in individuals with learning disabilities. In Fraser, W., Sines, D. & Kerr, M. (eds), *'Hallas': The Care of People with Intellectual Disabilities.* Oxford: Butterworth Heinemann.

Lea, S., Auburn, T. & Kibblewhite, K. (1999) Working with sex offenders; the preceptions and experiences of professionals and paraprofessionals. *International Journal of Offender Therapy and Comparative Criminology* 43, 103–19.

Lee-Evans, M. (1994) Background to behaviour analysis. In McMurran, M. & Hodge, J. (eds), *The Assessment of Criminal Behaviours of Clients in Secure Settings.* London: Jessica Kingsley.

Leong, G.B. & Silva, J.A. (1999) Revisiting arson from an out-patient forensic perspective. *Journal of Forensic Science* 44, 558–63.

Lewis, D. & Mhlanga, B. (2001) A life of crime: the hidden truth behind criminal activity. *International Journal of Market Research* 43(2), 217–40.

Lichtenstein, S., Slovic, P., Fischoff, B., Layman, M. & Combs, B. (1978) Judged frequency of lethal events. *Journal of Experimental Psychology, Human Learning and Memory* 4, 551–78.

Light, R., Nee, C. & Ingham, H. (1992) *Car Theft: The Offender's Perspective.* Home Office Research Study 130. London: HMSO.

Lindsay, R.C.L. (1999) Applying applied research: Selling the sequential line-up. *Applied Cognitive Psychology* 14, 105–20.

Lindsay, R.C.L. & Bellinger, K. (1999) Alternatives to the sequential line-up: The importance of controlling the pictures. *Journal of Applied Psychology* 84(3), 315–21.

Lindsay, R.C.L., Lea, J., Nosworthy, G. J., Fulford, J., Hector, J., LeVan, V. & Seabrook, C. (1991) Biased line-ups: Sequential presentation reduces the problem. *Journal of Applied Psychology,* 76(6), 796–802.

Lindsay, W.R. (1999) Cognitive therapy. *The Psychologist,* 12, 238–41.

Lindsay, W.R., Carson, D. & Whitefield, E. (2000) Development of a questionnaire on attitudes consistent with sex offending for men with intellectual disabilities. *Journal of Intellectual Disability Research* 44, 368.

Lindsay, W.R. & Lees, M. (2002) *Sex offenders with intellectual disability show lower rates of anxiety and depression in comparison to control subjects.*

Lindsay, W.R. & Michie, A.M. (1988) Adaptation of the Zung Anxiety Inventory for people with a mental handicap. *Journal of Mental Deficiency Research* 32, 485–90.

Lindsay, W.R. & Smith, A.H.W. (1998) Responses to treatment for sex offenders with intellectual disability: a comparison of men with one and two year probation sentences. *Journal of Intellectual Disability Research* 42, 346–53.

Lindsay, W.R., Michie, A.M., Baty, F.J., Smith, A.H.W. & Miller, S. (1994) The consistency of reports about feelings and emotions from people with intellectual disability. *Journal of Intellectual Disability Research* 38, 61–6.

Lindsay, W.R., Marshall, I., Neilson, C.Q. Quinn, K. & Smith, A.H.W. (1998a) The treatment of men with learning disability convicted of exhibitionism. *Research on Developmental Disabilities* 19(4), 295–316.

Lindsay, W.R., Neilson, C.Q., Morrison, F. & Smith, A.H.W. (1998b) The treatment of six men with a learning disability convicted of sex offences with children. *British Journal of Clinical Psychology* 37, 83–98.

Lindsay, W.R., Olley, S., Jack, C., Morrison, F. & Smith, A.H.W. (1998c) The treatment of two stalkers with intellectual disabilities using a cognitive approach. *Journal of Applied Research in Intellectual Disabilities* 11, 333–44.

Lindsay, W.R., Olley, S., Baillie, N. & Smith, A.H.W. (1999) The treatment of adolescent sex offenders with intellectual disability. *Mental Retardation* 37(3), 201–11.

Lindsay, W.R., Law, J. Quinn, K., Smart, N. & Smith, A.H.W. (2001) A comparison of physical and sexual abuse histories: sexual and non-sexual offenders with intellectual disability. *Child Abuse and Neglect* 25(7), 989–95.

Lindsay, W.R., Smith, A.H.W., Law, J., Quinn, K., Anderson, A., Smith, A., Overend, T. & Allen, R. (2002) A treatment service for sex offenders and abusers with intellectual disability: characteristics of referrals and evaluation. *Journal of Applied Research in Intellectual Disabilities* 15(2), 166–75.

Linehan, M.M. (1993) *Cognitive Behavioural Treatment of Borderline Personality Disorder.* New York: Guilford.

Lion, J. & Reid, W. (eds) (1983) *Assaults within Psychiatric Facilities.* New York: Grune and Stratton.

Liotti, G. (1999) Disorganization of attachment as a model for understanding dissociative psychopathology. In Solomon, J.& George, C. (eds), *Attachment Disorganization.* New York: Guilford.

Lipsey, M.W. (1992) Juvenile delinquency treatment: A meta-analytic inquiry into the variability of effects. In Cook, T.D., Cooper, H., Cordray, D.S., Hartman, H., Hedges, L.V., Light, R.J., Louis, T.A. & Mosteller, F. (eds), *Meta-analysis for Explanation: A Casebook.* New York: Russell Sage Foundation.

Lipsey, M. W. (1995) What do we learn from 400 research studies on the effectiveness of treatment with juvenile delinquents? In McGuire, J. (ed.), 1995.

Littlechild, B. (1997) I needed to be told that I hadn't failed: experiences of violence against probation staff and of agency support. *British Journal of Social Work 27,* 219–40.

Livesey, W. J. (2001) A framework for an integrated approach to treatment. In Livesey, W. J. (ed.), *Handbook of Personality Disorders: Theory, Research, and Treatment.* New York: Guilford.

Lloyd, C., Mair, G. & Hough, J.M. (1994) *Explaining Reconviction Rates: A Critical Analysis.* Home Office Research Study No. 36. London: HMSO.

Lockyer, A. & Stone, F. (eds) (1998) *Juvenile Justice in Scotland: Twenty-five Years of the Welfare Approach.* Edinburgh: T & T Clark.

Loewen, L.J. & Sudfeld, P. (1992) Cognition and arousal effects of masking office noise. *Environment and Behaviour 11,* 55–63.

Loftus, E.F. (1996) *Eyewitness Testimony.* Cambridge, MA: Harvard University Press.

Loftus, E.F., Loftus, G.R. & Messo, J. (1987) Some facts about 'weapon focus'. *Law and Human Behavior 11,* 55–62.

Loftus, E.F., Manber, M. & Keating, J.F. (1983) Recollection of naturalistic events: Context enhancement versus negative cueing. *Human Learning 2,* 83–92.

Loftus E.F. & Marburger, W. (1983) Since the eruption of Mt. St. Helens has anyone beaten you up? Improving the accuracy of retrospective reports with landmark events. *Memory and Cognition 11,* 114–20.

Losel, F., Bender D., & Bliesener, T. (1998) Biosocial Risk and Protective Factors for Antisocial Behaviour in Juveniles. Paper quoted in Garbarino (1999).

Loucks, N. (1996) The effect of changes in regime on assaults and the fear of assaults at a local prison. *Prison Service Journal 104,* 10–21.

Loughran, N. (1998) Review of literature on children, young people and offending. In Asquith, S., Buist, M., Macaulay, C. & Montgomery, M. (eds), *Children, Young People and Offending in Scotland: A Research Review.* Edinburgh: Scottish Office Central Research Unit.

Loveday, B. (2000) Policing performance. *Criminal Justice Matters 40,* 23–4.

Lovibond, S, Mithiran H. & Adams, W.G. (1979) The effects of three experimental prison environments on the behaviour of non-convict volunteer subjects. *Australian Psychologist 14*(3), 273–87.

Lowry, R.D. (2000) United States probation/pretrial officer's concerns about victimisa-
tion and officer safety training. *Federal Probation* 64, 51–5.

Luborsky, L. (1984) *Principles of Psychoanalytical Psychotherapy*. New York: Basic Books.

Lund, J. (1990) Mentally retarded criminal offenders in Denmark. *British Journal of Psychiatry* 156, 726–31.

Lyall, I., Holland, A.J. & Collins, S. (1995a) Offending by adults with learning disabilities
and the attitudes of staff to offending behaviour: implications of service development.
Journal of Intellectual Disabilities Research 39, 501–8.

Lyall, I., Holland, A.J., Collins, S. & Styles, P. (1995b) Incidence of persons with a learning disability detained in police custody. *Medicine, Science and the Law* 35, 61–71.

Lynam, D., Moffitt, T.E. & Stouthamer-Loeber, M. (1993) Explaining the relationship
between IQ and delinquency: class, race, test motivation, school failure, or self control? *Journal of Abnormal Psychology* 102, 187–96.

Macan, T.H., Avedon, M.J., Paese, M. & Smith, D.E. (1994) The effects of applicants'
reactions to cognitive ability tests and an assessment centre. *Personnel Psychology* 47,
715–38.

MacEachron, A.E. (1979) Mentally retarded offenders: Prevalence and characteristics.
American Journal of Mental Deficiency 84, 165–76.

Maguire, E. M. W., & Bennett, T. (1982) *Burglary in a Dwelling: The Offence, the Offender
and the Victim*. London: Heinemann Educational Books.

Maier, G. J. & Fulton, L. (1998) Inpatient treatment of offenders with mental disorders.
In Wettstein, R.M. (ed.), *Treatment of Offenders with Mental Disorders*. New York:
Guilford.

Maier, G., Stava, L., Morrow, B., van Rybroek, G. & Bauman, K. (1987) A model for
understanding and managing cycles of aggressive psychiatric inclients. *Hospital and
Community Psychiatry* 38, 520–4.

Malpass, R.S. (1996) Enhancing eyewitness memory. In Sporer, S.L., Malpass, R.S. &
Köhnken, G. (eds), *Psychological Issues in Eyewitness Identification*. Hillsdale, NJ: Lawrence Erlbaum.

Malpass, R.S. & Devine, P.G. (1981) Guided memory in eyewitness identification. *Journal of Applied Psychology* 66, 343–50.

Mande, M. J. & English, K. (1988) *Individual Crime Rates of Colorado Prisoners*. Denver,
CO: Colorado Department of Public Safety.

Mann, R.E. & Riches, E. (1999) HM Prison Service sex offender programme. In Towl &
McDougall (eds), 1999.

Manning, F.J. (1991) Morale, cohesion and esprit de corps. In Gal, R. & Mangelsdorff,
A.D. (eds), *Handbook of Military Psychology*. New York: Wiley.

Manolias, M. (1983) *A Preliminary Study of Stress in the Police Service*. London: Home
Office.

Mapstone, E. & Buist, M. (1980) *Interim Report of the Research Project – The Skills and
Processes of Assessment and Their Impact upon Children*. Dundee: University of Dundee.

Marchington, M. (2000) Teamworking and employee involvement: Terminology, evaluation and context. In Procter, S. & Mueller F. (eds), 2000.

Martin, C. (ed.) (1998) *The ISTD Handbook of Community Programmes*. Winchester:
Waterside Press.

Martin, C.A., McKean, H.E. & Veltkamp, L.J. (1986) Post traumatic stress disorder in police and working with victims; a pilot study. *Journal of Police Science and Administration* 14, 98–101.

Martin, S.E. & Jurik, N. (1996) *Doing Justice, Doing Gender: Women in Law Enforcement and Criminal Justice Occupations.* Thousand Oaks, CA: Sage.

Maslach, C. & Leiter, M.P. (1997) *The Truth About Burnout. How Organisations Cause Personnel Stress and What to Do About It.* San Francisco: Jossey-Bass.

Matza, D. (1970) *Delinquency and Drift.* Chichester: Wiley.

Maughan, B. & Rutter, M. (2000) Antisocial children grown up. In Hill, J. and Maughan, B. (eds) *Conduct Disorder in Childhood and Adolescence.* Cambridge: Cambridge University Press.

May, D. (1971) Delinquency control and the treatment model: some implications of recent legislation. *British Journal of Criminology* 11, 359–70.

May, J. (1979) *Committee of Inquiry into the United Kingdom Prison Services Report.* London: HMSO.

Mayhew, P., Clarke, R., Sturman, A. & Hough, M. (1976) *Crime as Opportunity.* Home Office Research Study No. 34. London: HMSO.

McCann, I.L. & Pearlman, L.A. (1990) Vicarious traumatization; A framework for understanding the psychological effects of working with victims. *Journal of Traumatic Stress* 3, 131–49.

McClelland, D.C. (1973) Testing for competence rather than intelligence. *American Psychologist* 28, 1–14.

McCorkle, R.C., Miethe, T.D. & Drass, K.A. (1995) The roots of prison violence: A test of the deprivation, management, and 'not-so-total' institution models. *Crime and Delinquency* 41(3), 317–31.

McCormack, C. (1995) *War without Bullets.* Video, Channel 4 Television.

McCormick E.J., Jeanneret, R.R, & Mecham, R.C. (1972) A study of job characteristics and job dimensions as based on the Position Analysis Questionnaire. *Journal of Applied Psychology,* Monograph, 56(4), 347–68.

McDougall, C. (1996) Working in secure institutions. In Hollin, C.R. (ed.) *Working with Offenders: Psychological Practice in Offender Rehabilitation.* Chichester: Wiley.

McDougall, C. & Clark, D.A. (1991), A risk assessment model. In Boddis, S. (ed), *Proceedings of the Prison Psychology Conference.* London: HMSO.

McDougall, C., Clark, D.A. & Fisher, M. (1994) Assessment of violent offenders. In McMuran, M. and Hodge, J. (eds) *The Assessment of Criminal Behaviour of Clients in Secure Settings.* London: Jessica Kingsley.

McDougall, C. & Towl, G. (1999) Future directions. In Towl & McDougall (eds), 1999.

McEwan, A. & McGurk, B.J. (1981) The professionalism of prison psychologists, *Bulletin of the British Psychological Society* 34, 415–17.

McGallagly, J. (1998) *Evaluation of the Hamilton Child Safety Initiative.* Edinburgh: Scottish Office Central Research Unit.

McGregor, D. (1960) *The Human Side of the Enterprise.* London: McGraw-Hill.

McGuire, J. (ed.) (1995) *What Works? Reducing Reoffending: Guidelines from Research and Practice.* Chichester: Wiley.

McGuire, J. & Priestley, P. (1995) Reviewing 'What Works': past, present and future. In McGuire, J. (ed.), 1995.

McGurk, B.J. & Fludger, N. (1987) The selection of prison officers. In McGurk, Thornton and Williams, 1987.

McGurk, B.J., Thornton, D.M. & Williams, M. (1987) *Applying Psychology to Imprisonment*. London: HMSO.

McIntyre S.A., Bucklan M.S. & Scott M.S. (2000). *The Job Analysis Kit (JAK)*. Psychological Assessment Resources, Inc.

McKenzie, I. (1993) Equal opportunities in policing; A comparative examination of anti-discriminatory policy and practice in British policing. *International Journal of the Sociology of Law* 21, 159–74.

McKerracher, D.W., Street, D.R.K. & Segal, L.J. (1996) A comparison of the behaviour problems presented by male and female subnormal offenders. *British Journal of Psychiatry* 112, 891–7.

McMurran, M. & Shapland, P. (1989) What do prison psychologists do? *The Psychologist* 12(7), July, 287–9.

McPhee, H. (1992) Assessment – what is the problem? In Lloyd, G. (ed.), *Chosen with Care? Responses to Disturbing and Disruptive Behaviour.* Edinburgh: Moray House Publications.

Mednick, S.A. & Kandel, E. (1998) Genetic and perinatal factors in violence. In Mednick, S.A. & Moffitt, T. (eds), *Biological Contributions to Crime Causation.* Dordrecht, the Netherlands: Martins Nijhoff.

Meissner, C.A. & Brigham, J.C. (2001) A meta-analysis of the verbal overshadowing effect in face identification. *Applied Cognitive Psychology* 15(6), 603–16.

Memon, A. & Bull, R. (1991) The cognitive interview: its origins, empirical support, evaluation and practical implications. *Journal of Community and Applied Social Psychology* 1, 291–307.

Merz, J.F. (1991) Towards a standard of disclosure for medical informed consent: development and demonstration of a decision – analytic methodology. Unpublished Ph.D. dissertation, Carnegie Mellon University.

Messinger, E. & Apfelberg, B. (1961) A quarter century of court psychiatry. *Crime and Delinquency* 7, 343–62.

Middleton, D. (1996) Talking work: argument, common knowledge, and improvisation in teamwork. In Engestrom, Y. & Middleton , D. (eds), *Cognition and Communication at Work.* Cambridge: Cambridge University Press.

Miller, R.D., Maier, G.J., Blancke, F.W. & Doren, D.M. (1986) Litigiousness as a resistance to therapy. *Journal of Law and Psychiatry* 61, 109–23.

Miller, W.R. & Rollnick, S. (1991) *Motivational Interviewing: Preparing People to Change Addictive Behaviour.* New York: Guilford Press.

Mills, M. (1974) *Management of Training Course: Information for Training Design.* Unpublished report. Prison Service College.

Milne, R. & Bull, R. (1999) *Investigative Interviewing: Psychology and Practice.* Chichester: Wiley.

Mingay, D., Dennett, J. L. & Bekerian, D. A. (1984) Memory for a staged incident. *Forum* 17, 58–60.

Mingay, D.J., Shevell, S.K., Bradburn, N.M. & Ramirez, C. (1994) Self and proxy reports of everyday events. In N. Schwarz & S. Sudman (eds), *Autobiographical Memory and the*

Validity of Retrospective Reports. New York: Springer-Verlag.

Mintz, R.S. (1968) Psychotherapy of the suicidal patient. In Resnick, H.L.P. (ed.), *Suicidal Behaviors: Diagnosis and Management.* Boston: Little Brown.

Mischel, W. (1999) Personality coherence and dispositions in a cognitive-affective personality system (CAPS) Approach. In Cervone, D. & Shoda, Y. (eds), *The Coherence of Personality: Social-Cognitive Bases of Consistency, Variability, and Organisation.* New York: Guilford Press.

Mitchell, J. & Bray, B. (1990) *Emergency Services Stress: Guidelines for Preserving the Health and Careers of Emergency Services Personnel.* Englewood Cliffs: Prentice Hall.

Mitchell, M. (2000) *Managing Post Incident Reactions in the Police Service. End of Contract Report.* Glasgow: Police Research Unit, Glasgow Caledonian University.

Moen, P., Elder, G.H. & Luscher, K. (1995) *Examining Lives in Context: Perspectives on the Ecology of Human Development.* Washington, DC: American Psychological Association.

Monahan, J. (1981) *Predicting Violent Behaviour: An Assessment of Clinical Techniques.* Beverley Hills: Sage.

Monahan, J. (1997) Actuarial support for the clinical assessment of violence risk. *International Review of Psychiatry* 9(2/3), 167–9.

Monahan, J. & Steadman, H.J. (1994) *Violence and Mental Disorder: Developments in Risk Assessment.* Chicago: Chicago University Press.

Monahan, J. & Steadman, H.J. (1996) Violent storms and violent people: How meteorology can inform risk communication in mental health law. *American Psychologist* 51, 931–8.

Money, J. (1986) *Lovemaps: Clinical Concepts of Sexual/Erotic Health and Pathology, Paraphilia, and Gender Transposition in Childhood, Adolescence, and Maturity.* New York: Irvington.

Moorhead, G., Neck, C.P. & West, M.S. (1998) The tendency toward defective decision making within self-managing teams: The relevance of groupthink for the 21st century. *Organisational Behaviour and Human Decision Processes* 73, 327–51.

Morley, R. (1998) Respect: A schools-based approach to challenging violence and abuse in relationships. *Clinical Psychology Forum* 122, 18–19.

Morowitz, H.J. (1981) Jurisgenic disease. *Hospital Practice* 16 (June), 170–1.

Morris, R.J. & Magrath, K.H. (1983) The therapeutic relationship in behavior therapy. In Lambert, M. J. (ed.), *Psychotherapy and Patient Relationships.* Homewood, IL: Dorsey Press.

Morrissey, C.M. (1995) Groupwork with life sentenced prisoners. In Towl, G.J. (ed.), *Groupwork in Prisons, Issues in Criminological and Legal Psychology.* Leicester: BPS.

Mrazek, P.J. & Haggerty, R.J. (1994) *Reducing Risks for Mental Disorders: Frontiers for Preventive Intervention Research.* Institute of Medicine. Washington, DC: National Academy Press.

Mueller, F. (1994) Teams between hierarchy and commitment: change strategies and the 'internal environment'. *Journal of Management Studies* 31(3), 383–403.

Munn, Pamela (2000) Alternatives to exclusion: supporting schools, supporting teachers. *Scottish Educational Journal* 85(6), 20–1.

Munsterburg, H. (1908) *On the Witness Stand. Essays on Psychology and Crime.* New York: Doubleday, Page.

Murphy,G. & Clare, I. (1991) MIETS: A service option for people with mild mental handicaps or challenging behaviour or psychiatric problems: 2. Assessment, treatment, and outcome for service users and service effectiveness. *Mental Handicap Research* 4(2), 180–206.

Murphy, G., Harnett, H. & Holland, A.J. (1995) A survey of intellectual disabilities amongst men on remand in prison. *Mental Handicap Research* 8, 81–98.

Murphy, G., Holland, A., Fowler, P., & Reep, J. (1991) MIETS: A service option for people with mild mental handicaps and challenging behaviour or psychiatric problems: 1. Philosophy, service and service users. *Mental Handicap Research* 4(1), 41–66.

Murray, J. (2001) Situational factors in sexual offending. In Farrington D.P., Hollin C.R., & McMurran, M. (eds), *Sex and Violence*. London: Routledge.

Myhill, A. & Allen, J. (2002) *Rape and Sexual Assault of Women: The Extent and Nature of the Problem. Findings from the British Crime Survey*. Home Office Research Study No. 237. London: Home Office.

Narby, D.J., Cutler, B.L. & Penrod, S.D. (1996) The effects of witness, target and situational factors in eyewitness identifications. In Sporer, S.L., Malpass, R.S. & Köhnken, G. (eds), *Psychological Issues in Eyewitness Identification*. Hillsdale, NJ: Lawrence Erlbaum.

National Institute for Clinical Excellence (2000) *Guidance on Methylphenidate (Ritalin/ Equasym) for Attention Deficit/Hyperactivity Disorder (ADHD)*. London: National Institute for Clinical Excellence.

National Statistics Website (UK) (2002) http://www.statistics.gov.ukinfigs/crime.asp.

Nee, C. & Taylor, M. (1987) Residential burglary in the Republic of Ireland: some support for the situational approach. In Tomlinson, M., Varley, T. & McCullagh, C. (eds), *Whose Law and Order*. Galway: The Sociological Association of Ireland.

Nee, C. & Taylor, M. (1988) Residential burglary in the Republic of Ireland: A situational perspective. *The Howard Journal* 27(2), 105–16.

Nee, C. & Taylor, M. (2000) Examining burglars' target selection: interview, experiment, or ethnomethodology? *Psychology, Crime and Law* 6(1), 45–59.

Needs, A. (1988) Psychological investigation of offending behaviour. In Fransella, F. & Thomas, L. (eds), *Experimenting with Personal Construct Psychology*. London: Routledge and Kegan Paul.

Needs A. (1997) Occupational standards in applied psychology. *Forensic Update* 48, 18–23.

Needs, A. & Towl, G.J. (1997) Reflections on clinical risk assessment with lifers. *Prison Service Journal* 113, 14–17.

Neighbors, H. (1987) The prevalence of mental disorder in Michigan prisons. *DIS Newsletter* 4, 8–11.

Ness, H., Hancock, P., Bowie, L.& Bruce, V. (2001) Are two views better than one? A study examining recognition of three-quarter and full face composites using PRO-FIT. Paper presented at The 11th European Conference on Psychology and Law, Lisbon, June 2001.

Newlands, P. J. (1997) *Eyewitness Interviewing: Does the Cognitive Interview Fit the Bill?* Unpublished Ph.D. thesis, University of Westminster.

Noble, J.H. & Conley, R.W. (1992) Toward an epidemiology of relevant attributes. In

Conley, R.W., Luckasson, R. & Bouthilet, G. (eds), *The Criminal Justice System and Mental Retardation*. Baltimore: Paul Brookes.

Norman, D. & Bobrow, D. (1978) Descriptions: An intermediate stage in memory retrieval. *Cognitive Psychology* 11, 107–123.

Norton, K. & McGauley, G. (1998) *Counselling Difficult Clients*. London: Sage.

Novaco, R.W. (1978) Anger and coping with stress. In Foeyt, J.P. & Rathjen, D.P. (eds), *Cognitive Behaviour Therapy*. New York: Plenum Press.

Novaco, R.W. (1986) Anger as a clinical and social problem. In Blanchard, R. & Blanchard, C. (eds), *Advances in the Study of Aggression*, vol. 2. New York: Academic Press.

Novaco, R.W. (1994) Anger as a risk factor for violence among the mentally disordered. In Monahan, J. & Steadman, H.J. (eds), 1994.

O'Conner, W. (1996) A problem solving intervention for sex offenders with intellectual disability. *Journal of Intellectual and Developmental Disability* 21, 219–35.

Office of Public Services Reform (2002) *Reforming our Public Services*. London: Cabinet Office.

O'Leary, K.D. & Wilson, G.T. (1975) *Behavior Therapy: Application and Outcome*. New Jersey: Prentice Hall.

Orford, J. (1992) *Community Psychology: Theory and Practice*. Chichester: Wiley.

Owen, C., Tarantello, C., Jones, M. & Tennant, C. (1998) Violence and aggression in psychiatric units. *Psychiatric Services* 49(11), 1,452–7.

Palmer, E.J. (2001) Risk assessment: review of psychometric measures. In Farrington, D.P., Hollin, C.R. & McMurran, M. (eds), *Sex and Violence: The Psychology of Crime and Risk Assessment*. London: Routledge.

Park, B. & Harris, R., (2000) Roles and responsibilities of team leaders and members: A case study of the Australian automotive industry. In Procter, S. & Mueller, F. (eds), 2000.

Parrott, L. (1987) Rule-governed behaviour: an implicit analysis of reference. In Modgil S., & Modgil C. (eds), *B. F. Skinner: Consensus and Controversy*. New York: Falmer Press.

Patrick, J. (1997) *Training: Research and Practice*. New York: Academic Press.

Patterson, B.L. (1992) Job experience and perceived job stress among police, correctional, and probation/parole officers. *Criminal Justice and Behaviour* 19, 260–85.

Pease, K. (1997) Crime prevention. In Maguire, M., Morgan, R. & Reiner, R. (eds), *The Oxford Handbook of Criminology* (2nd edn). Oxford: Oxford University Press.

Peters, T.J. & Waterman, R.H. (1987) *In Search of Excellence*. New York: Harper Row.

Petrella, R.C. (1992) Defendants with mental retardation in the forensic services system. In Conley, R.W., Luckasson, R. & Bouthilet, G. (eds), *The Criminal Justice System and Mental Retardation*. Baltimore: Paul Brookes.

Phillips, R. J. (1978) Recognition, recall and imagery of faces. In Gruneberg, M.M., Morris, P.E. & Sykes, R.N. (eds), *Practical Aspects of Memory*. London: Routledge.

Pickett, M., Brennan, A.M.W., Greenberg, H.S., Licht, L. & Worrell, J.D. (1994) Using debriefing techniques to prevent compassion fatigue in research teams. *Nursing Research* 43, 250–2.

Pilgrim, D. (2000) Psychiatric diagnosis: More questions than answers. *Psychologist* 13(6) (June), 302–3.

Plant, B. (2001) Psychological trauma in the police service. *International Journal of Police Management and Science* 3, 327–49.

Plaud, J.J., Plaud, D.M., Colstoe, P.D. & Orvedal, L. (2000) Behavioural treatment of sexually offending behaviour. *Mental Health Aspects of Developmental Disabilities* 3, 54–61.

Plous, S. (1993) *The Psychology of Judgement and Decision Making.* New York: McGraw Hill.

Plutchik, R. (1997) Suicide and violence: The two stage model of countervailing forces. In Botsis, A.J., Soldatos, C.R. & Stefanis, C.N. (eds), *Suicide: Biopsychosocial Approaches.* Amsterdam: Elsevier.

Plutchik, R. & Van Praag, H.M. (1990) A self-report measure of violence risk, II. *Comprehensive Psychiatry* 31, 450–6.

Podsakoff, P.M., MacKenzie, S.B. & Ahearne, M. (1997) Moderating effects of goal acceptance on the relationship between group cohesiveness and productivity. *Journal of Applied Psychology* 82, 974–83.

Porter, J. (1985) A construct approach to management and motivation. *Constructs: The Newsletter of the Centre for Personal Construct Psychology* 3(2), 1–2.

Power, K.G., Dyson, G.P. & Wozniak, E. (1997) Bullying among Scottish young offenders: Inmates' self-reported attitudes and behaviour. *Journal of Community and Applied Social Psychology* 7(3), 209–18.

Prins, H. (1995) *Offenders, Deviants or Patients?* (2nd edn). London: Routledge.

Prins, H. (1996) Risk assessment and management in criminal justice and psychiatry. *Journal of Forensic Psychiatry* 7(1), 42–62.

Prins, H. (2002) Risk assessment – still a risky business. *British Journal of Forensic Practice* 4(1), 3–8.

Prison Service Training Planning Unit, P6 Division (1990a) The systematic approach to training. Unpublished report.

Prison Service Training Planning Unit, P6 Division (1990b) Training needs analysis: a managers' guide. Unpublished report.

Probation Officers' Association of Ontario (2001a) Presentation to Ministry of Finance. Online at: http://www.poao.org/positionpapers_m.htm.

Probation Officers' Association of Ontario (2001b) Discussion paper on the safety of probation and patrol officers. Online at: http://www.poao.org/positionpapers_m.htm.

Prochaska, J.O., Norcross, J.C. & Di Clemente, C.C. (1994) *Changing For Good.* New York: Morrow.

Procter, S. & Mueller, F. (eds) (2000) *Teamworking.* Basingstoke: Palgrave Macmillan.

Propp, V. (1968) *The Morphology of the Folktale,* trans. Laurence Scott. Austin: University of Texas Press.

Puri, B.K., Baxter, R.& Cordess, C.C. (1995) Characteristics of fire setters: A study and proposed multi-axial psychiatric classification. *British Journal of Psychiatry* 166, 393–6.

Quadrel, M.J. (1990) Elicitation of adolescents' perceptions: Qualitative and quantitative dimensions. Unpublished Ph.D. thesis, Carnegie Mellon University.

Quarry, A. & Burbach, F.R. (1998) Clinical consultancy in adult mental health: integrating whole team training and supervision. *Clinical Psychology Forum* 120, 14–17.

Quinsey, V.L., Harris, G.T., Rice, M.E. & Cormier, C.A. (1998) *Violent Offenders: Appraising and Managing Risk.* Washington, DC: American Psychological Association.

Rackham, N & Morgan, T. (1977) *Behaviour Analysis in Training.* London: McGraw-Hill.

Raesaenen, P., Hirvenoj, A., Hakko, H. & Vaeisaenen, E. (1994) Cognitive functioning ability of arsonists. *Journal of Forensic Psychiatry* 5, 615–20.

Rand Corporation (1975) *The Criminal Investigative Process,* vols. 1–3. Rand Corporation Technical Report R-1777-DOJ. Santa Monica, CA.

Reich, J.H. & Vasile R.G. (1993) Effect of personality disorder on the treatment outcome of Axis 1 conditions: an update. *Journal of Nervous and Mental Disease* 181, 475–84.

Reilly, B.J. & Di Angelo, J.A. (1990) Communication: a cultural system of meaning and value. *Human Relations* 43, 129–40.

Reiner, R. (1985) *The Politics of the Police* (3rd edn). Oxford: Oxford University Press.

Reppetto, T.A. (1974) *Residential Crime.* Massachusetts: Ballinger.

Ressler, R.K., Douglas, J.E. Burgess, A.W. & Burgess, A.G. (1992) *Crime Classification Manual: The Standard System for Investigating and Classifying Violent Crimes.* London: Simon and Schuster.

Rice, M.E., Harris, G.T. & Quinsey, V.L. (1994) Control in the psychiatric setting. In Hersen, M. and Ammerman, R.T. (eds), *Handbook of Aggressive and Destructive Behavior in Psychiatric Clients.* New York: Plenum Press.

Rix, K.J.B. (1994) A psychiatric study of adult arsonists. *Medicine, Science and the Law* 34, 21–34.

Robins, L.N., Tipp, J. & Przybeck, T. (1991) Antisocial personality. In Robins, L.N. & Regier, D. (eds), *Psychiatric Disorders in America: The Epidemiologic Catchment Area Study.* New York: Free Press.

Robinson, D. (1992) Commitment, attitudes, career aspirations and work stress; The experiences of correctional staff. *Canadian Correction Service Forum* 4(1).

Robinson D.G. & Robinson J.C. (1995). *Performance Consulting: Moving Beyond Training.* San Francisco: Berrett-Koehler.

Robson, C. (1997) *Real World Research.* Oxford: Blackwell

Rockoff, E. (1978) The retarded offender: missing in action. *Corrective and Social Psychiatry (Journal of Behaviour Technology Methods and Therapy)* 24, 130–2.

Roden, C. (1999) Culture and change: Linking business focus to operational competence in the prison service, *British Journal of Forensic Practice* 1(3), 3–8.

Rodgers, A. (1952) *The Seven Point Plan.* London: National Institute of Industrial Psychology.

Roediger, H. L. & Payne, D. G. (1982) Hypermnesia: The role of repeated testing. *Journal of Experimental Psychology: Learning, Memory and Cognition* 8, 66–72.

Rogers, C. (1957) The necessary and sufficient conditions of therapeutic personality change. *Journal of Consulting Psychology* 21, 95–103.

Rose, J. (1996) Anger management: a group treatment programme for people with mental retardation. *Journal of Physical and Development Disabilities* 8, 133–50.

Rose, J. & West, C. (1999) Assessment of anger in people with intellectual disabilities. *Journal of Applied Research in Intellectual Disabilities* 12, 211–24.

Rose, J., West, C. & Clifford, D. (2000) Group interventions for anger and people with intellectual disabilities. *Research in Developmental Disabilities* 21, 171–81.

Rummler, G. (1996) Linking training and performance. Paper presented at the Conference of the American Society for Training and Development, Orlando, Florida.

Rutter, M. (1997) Nature-Nurture Integration. *American Psychologist* (April), 390–8.

Rutter, M., Giller, H. & Hagell, A. (1998) *Antisocial Behaviour by Young People.* Cambridge: Cambridge University Press.

Ryan, R. S. & Schooler, J. W. (1998) Whom do words hurt? Individual differences in susceptibility to verbal overshadowing. *Applied Cognitive Psychology* 12, 105–25.

Ryle, A. (1997) *Cognitive Analytic Therapy and Borderline Personality Disorder: The Model and the Method.* Chichester: Wiley.

Ryle, A. & Golynkina, K. (2000) Effectiveness of time limited cognitive analytic therapy of borderline personality disorder: Factors associated with outcome. *British Journal of Medical Psychology* 73(2), 197–210.

Safran, J.D. & Muran, J.C. (1996) The resolution of ruptures in the therapeutic alliance. *Journal of Consulting and Clinical Psychology* 29, 552–7.

Sanders, G. S. (1986) *The usefulness of eyewitness research from the perspective of police investigators.* Unpublished manuscript. State University of New York at Albany, Albany.

Scarr, H.A. (1973) *Patterns of burglary.* Washington, DC: Government Printing Office.

Schaufeli, W.B. & Peeters, M.C. (2000) Job stress and burnout among correctional officers; a literature review. *International Journal of Stress Management* 7, 19–47.

Schein, E. (1992) *Organisational Culture and Leadership* (2nd edn). San Francisco: Jossey-Bass.

Schneider, B. (1987) The people make the place. *Personnel Psychology* 40, 437–53.

Schooler, J. W. & Engstler-Schooler, T. Y. (1990) Verbal overshadowing of visual memories: some things are better left unsaid. *Cognitive Psychology* 22, 36–71.

Schwarz, N. & Sudman, S. (eds) (1994) *Autobiographical Memory and the Validity of Retrospective Reports.* New York: Springer-Verlag.

Scorzelli, J.F. & Reinke-Scorzelli, M. (1979) Mentally retarded offender: a follow-up study. *Rehabilitation Counselling Bulletin* (September), 70–3.

Scott, P.D. (1977) Assessing dangerousness in criminals. *British Journal of Psychiatry* 131, 127–42.

Scottish Prison Service (2000) *Intervention and Integration for a Safer Society.* Edinburgh: Scottish Prison Service.

Searcy, J. H., Bartlett, J. C. & Memon, A. (1999) Age differences in accuracy and choosing in eyewitness identification and face recognition. *Memory and Cognition* 27(3), 538–52.

Searcy, J. H., Bartlett, J. C., Memon, A. & Swanson, K. (2001) Ageing and lineup performance at long retention intervals: Effects of metamemory and context reinstatement. *Journal of Applied Psychology* 86(2), 207–14.

Seghorn, T.K. & Ball, C.J. (2000) Assessment of sexual deviance in adults with developmental disabilities. *Mental Health Aspects of Developmental Disabilities* 3, 47–53.

Selvey, S. (2003) Managing of disruptive prisoners. In Towl, G.J. (ed.), 2003.

Shackleton, V. J. & Newell, S. (1991) A comparative survey of methods used in top British and French companies. *Journal of Occupational Psychology* 64, 23–36.

Shamir, B. & Drory, A. (1982) Occupational tedium among prison officers. *Criminal Justice and Behaviour* 9(1), 79–99.

Shapiro, P. N. & Penrod, S. D. (1986) Meta-analysis of facial identification studies. *Psychological Bulletin* 100, 139–56.

Sharron, H. (1997) *Changing Children's Minds*. Birmingham: Interactive Minds.

Sharron, H. & Coulter, M. (1996) *Changing Children's Minds: Feuerstein's Revolution in the Teaching of Intelligence* (3rd edn). Birmingham: Imaginative Minds.

Sheldrick,C. (1999) Practitioner review: the assessment and management of risk in adolescents. *Journal of Child Psychology and Psychiatry* 40(4), 507–18.

Shepherd, E. (1993) Ethical interviewing. *Policing* 7, 42–60.

Shepherd, J.W. (1975) *The Aberdeen Supplement Facial Database*. Aberdeen: Aberdeen University Press.

Shepherd, J.W. (1986) An interactive computer system for retrieving faces. In Ellis, H.D., Jeeves, M.A., Newcombe F. & Young A.W. (eds), *Aspects of Face Processing*. Dordrecht: Martinus Nijhoff.

Shepherd, J.W., Davies, G.M. & Ellis, H.D. (1978) How best shall a face be described? In Gruneberg, M.M., Morris, P.E. & Sykes, R.N. (eds), *Practical Aspects of Memory*. London: Academic Press.

Shepherd, J.W. & Ellis, H.D. (1996) Face recall – methods and problems. In Sporer, S.L., Malpass, R.S. & Köhnken G. (eds), *Psychological Issues in Eyewitness Identification*. Hillsdale, NJ: Lawrence Erlbaum.

Shoda, Y. (1999) Behavioural expressions of a personality system: generation and perception of behavioural signatures. In Cervone, D. & Shoda, Y. (eds), *The Coherence of Personality: Social-Cognitive Bases of Consistency, Variability, and Organization*. New York: Guilford Press.

Shover, N. (1973) The social organisation of burglary. *Social Problems* 20, 499–514.

Shover, N. (1996) *Great Pretenders: Pursuits and Careers of Persistent Thieves*. London: HarperCollins.

Silverman, S. (1987) Silence as a resistance to medical intervention. *General Hospital Psychiatry* 9(4), 259–66.

Simmons, C., Cochran, J.K. & Blount, W.R. (1997) The effects of job related stress and job satisfaction on probation officers' inclinations to quit. *American Journal of Criminal Justice* 21, 213–29.

Singleton, N., Meltzer, H. & Gatwood, R. (1998) Psychiatric morbidity among Prisoners in England and Wales. The Office for National Statistics. London: Stationery Office.

Slate, R.N., Johnson, W.W. & Wells, T.L. (2000) Probation officer stress. Is there an organisational issue? *Federal Probation* 64, 56–9.

Smith, A., Brice, C., Collins, A., Matthews, V. & McNamara, R. (2000) *The Scale of Occupational Stress; A Further Analysis of the Impact of Demographic Factors and Type of Job*. Contract Research Report 311/2000, Cardiff: Centre for Occupational and Health Psychology, Cardiff University.

Smith, D. (2000) Learning from the Scottish juvenile justice system. *Probation Journal* 47(1), 12–17.

Smith, S. (1979) Remembering in and out of context. *Journal of Experimental Psychology: Human Learning and Memory* 5, 460–71.

Smith, S.M. (1988) Environmental context-dependent memory. In Davies, G.M. & Thomson, D.M. (eds), *Memory in Context: Context in Memory*. Chichester: Wiley.

Souriau, E. (1950) *Les deux cent mille situations dramatiques*. Paris: Flammarion.

Sporer, S.L. (1989) Verbal & visual processes in person identification. In Wegener, H., Losel, F. & Haisch, J. (eds), *Criminal Behavior and the Justice System: Psychological Perspectives*. New York: Springer-Verlag.

Sporer, S.L. (1992) An archival analysis of person descriptions. Paper presented at the Biennial Meeting of the American-Law Society in San Diego, CA (March).

Sporer, S.L. (1996) Person descriptions in criminal investigations. In Sporer, S.L., Malpass, R.S. & Köhnken G. (eds), *Psychological Issues in Eyewitness Identification*. Hillsdale, NJ: Lawrence Erlbaum.

Sprague, J.R. & Horner, R.H. (1999) Low-frequency high-intensity problem behaviour: towards an allied technology of functional assessment and intervention. In Re, A.C. & Horner, R.H. *Functional Analysis of Problem Behaviour: From Effective Assessment to Effective Support*. Belmont: Wadsworth.

Spruill, J. & May, J. (1998) The mentally retarded offender: Prevalence rates based on individual versus group intelligence tests. *Criminal Justice and Behaviour* 15, 484–91.

Spychalski, A.C., Quiñones, M., Gaugler, B.B. & Pohley, K. (1997) A survey of assessment centre practices in organisations in the United States. *Personnel Psychology* 50, 71–90.

Steadman, H.J., Monahan, J., Robbins, P., Appelbaum, P., Grisso, T., Klassen, D., Mulvey, E.P. & Roth, L. (1993) From dangerousness to risk assessment: Implications for appropriate research strategies. In Hodgins, S. (ed.), *Mental Disorder and Crime*. Newbury Park: Sage.

Stephens, C., Long, N. & Miller, I. (1997) The impact of trauma and social support on posttraumatic stress disorder: A study of New Zealand police officers. *Journal of Criminal Justice* 25, 303–14.

Stevens, M.J. & Campion, M.A. (1994) The knowledge, skill and ability requirements for teamwork: Implications for human resource management. *Journal of Management* 20, 503–30.

Stone, M.H., Stone, D.K. & Hurt, S.W. (1987) Natural history of borderline clients treated by intensive hospitalization. *Psychiatric Clinics of North America* 10, 185–206.

Strathclyde Regional Council (1988) *Young People in Trouble*. Glasgow: Strathclyde Regional Council.

Sudman, S., Bradburn, N.M. & Schwarz, N. (eds) (1996) *Thinking about Answers: The Application of Cognitive Processes to Survey Methodology*. San Francisco: Jossey-Bass.

Sundstrom, E., De Meuse, K.P. & Futrell, D. (1990) Work teams: applications and effectiveness. *American Psychologist* 45, 54–63.

Swanson, C.K. & Garwick, G.B. (1990) Treatment for low functioning sex offenders: group therapy and interagency co-ordination. *Mental Retardation* 28, 155–61.

Swanson, J. (1994) Mental disorder, substance abuse, and community violence: an epidemiological approach. In Monahan, J. & Steadman, H.J. (eds), 1994.

Swets, J.A. (2000) Enhancing diagnostic decisions. In Connolly, T., Arkes, H.R. & Hammond, K.R. (eds), 2000.

Swets, J.A., Getty, D.J. & Pickett, R.M. (1991) Enhancing and evaluating diagnostic accuracy. *Medical Decision Making* 11, 9–18.

Symonds, M. (1970) Emotional hazards of police work. *American Journal of Psychoanalysis* 30, 155–60.

Tarling, R. (1993) *Analysing Offending: Data, Models and Interpretations*. London: Sage.

Taylor, J.L., Novaco, R.W., Gillmer, B. & Thorne, I. (2002) Cognitive behavioural treatment of anger intensity among offenders with intellectual disabilities. *Journal of Applied Research in Intellectual Disabilities* 15(2), 151–65.

Taylor, M. & Nee, C. (1988) The role of cues in simulated residential burglary. *British Journal of Criminology* 28(3), 396–401.

Tennant, A., Davies, C. & Tennant, I. (2000) Working with the personality disordered offender. In Chaloner, C. & Coffey, M. (eds), *Forensic Mental Health Nursing: Current Approaches*. Oxford: Blackwell.

Terman, L. (1916) *The Measurement of Intelligence*. Boston: Houghton Mifflin.

Theakston, K. (1995) *The Civil Service since 1945*. Oxford: Blackwell.

Thomas, D.H. & Singh, T. (1995) Offenders referred to a learning disabilities service: A retrospective study from one country. *British Journal of Learning Disabilities* 23, 24–7.

Thomas, R.L. (1988) Stress perceptions among select federal probation and pretrial services officers and their supervisors. *Federal Probation* 52, 48–58.

Thompson, D. & Brown, H. (1997) Men with intellectual disabilities who sexually abuse: a review of the literature. *Journal of Applied Research in Intellectual Disabilities* 10, 140–58.

Thornton, D. (1987) Correctional evaluation of custodial regimes. In McGurk, B.J., Thornton, D.M. & Williams, M. (eds), 1987.

Times Educational Supplement (TES) (2000) Jury still out on thinking skills. *Times Education Supplement* (Scotland), 19 May, 4.

Timmerman, I.G.H. & Emmelkamp, P.M.G. (2001) The prevalence and comorbidity of Axis I and Axis II pathology in a group of forensic clients. *International Journal of Offender Therapy and Comparative Criminology* 45(2), 198–213.

Tin, E. (1999) The four justice models: Organisation creativity in judicial administration. *Singapore Academy of Law Journal* 157, 377–92.

Tollinton, G. (1992) Some reflections on the organizational changes in the N.H.S. *Clinical Psychology Forum* 46, 24–6.

Towl, G.J. (1994) Ethical issues in forensic psychology. *Forensic Update* 39, 23–6.

Towl, G.J. (1999a) What do forensic psychologists in prisons do? *The British Journal of Forensic Practice* 1(3), 9–11.

Towl, G.J. (1999b) Report from the chair. *Forensic Update* 58 (July), 3.

Towl, G.J. (1999c) Notes from the chair, *Forensic Update* 59 (October), 4.

Towl, G.J. (2000) Forensic psychology in the prison and probation services: working towards an effective partnership. *Prison Service Journal* 131, 32–3.

Towl, G.J. (ed.) (2003) *Psychology in Prisons*, Oxford: BPS/Blackwell.

Towl, G.J. & Crighton, D.A. (1995) Risk assessment in prisons: a psychological critique. *Forensic Update* 40, 6–14.

Towl, G.J. & Crighton, D.A. (1996) *The Handbook of Psychology for Forensic Practitioners*. London: Routledge.

Towl, G.J. & Crighton, D.A. (1997) Risk assessment with offenders. *International Review of Psychiatry* 9, 187–93.

Towl, G.J. & Crighton, D.A. (2000) Risk assessment and management. In Towl et al. (eds), 2000.

Towl, G.J. & Forbes, D.I. (2000) Working with suicidal prisoners. In Towl, G.J., McHugh, M.J. and Snow, L. (eds), 2000.

Towl, G.J. & McDougall, C. (eds) (1999) *What Do Forensic Psychologists Do? Current and Future Directions in the Prison and Probation Services.* Issues in Forensic Psychology. Leicester: Division of Criminological and Legal Psychology, BPS.

Towl, G.J., McHugh, M.J. & Snow, L. (eds) (2000) *Suicide in Prisons.* Leicester: BPS Books.

Tuckman, B.W. (1965) Developmental sequences in small groups. *Psychological Bulletin* 63, 384–99.

Tuckman, B.W. & Jensen, M.A.C. (1977) Stages in small group development revisited. *Group and Organisational Studies* 2, 419–27.

Tulving, E. (1974) Cue-dependent forgetting. *American Scientist* 62, 74–82.

Tulving, E. (1983) *Elements of Episodic Memory.* Oxford: Oxford University Press.

Tulving, E. & Thompson, D.M. (1973) Encoding specificity and retrieval processes in episodic memory. *Psychological Review* 80, 352–79.

Turner, C. (1993) The experience of staff conducting the core programme. Unpublished M.Sc. dissertation, Birkbeck College, London University.

Turner, J., Pike, G., Brace, N. & Kemp, R. (2001) The eyes have it: Feature saliency and facial composite construction. Paper presented at the 11th European Conference of Psychology and Law, Lisbon, June 2001.

Underwood, B. J. (1969) Attributes of memory. *Psychological Review* 76, 559–73.

Valentine, E.R. (1992) *Conceptual Issues in Psychology.* London and New York: Routledge.

Van der Kolk, B.A. (1989) The compulsion to repeat the trauma: re-enactment, re-victimisation and masochism. *Psychiatric Clinics of North America* 12(2), 389–411.

Van Rybroek, G. (2000) Chronically dangerous clients: Balancing staff issues with treatment approaches. In Mercer, D., Mason, T., McKeown, M. & McCann, G. (eds), *Forensic Mental Health Care: A Case Study Approach.* London: Churchill, Livingstone.

Vrij, A. (1996) Police officers' aggression in confrontations with offenders as a result of physical effort. In Clark, N.K. & Stephenson, G.M. (eds), *Issues in Criminological and Legal Psychology, Volume 25: Psychological Perspectives on Police and Custodial Culture and Organisation,* 59–65. Leicester: BPS.

Vrij, A. (1997) Wearing black clothes: The impact of offenders' and suspects' clothing on impression formation. *Applied Cognitive Psychology* 11, 47–53.

Vrij, A. (1998) Police officers' inadequate impression formation in confrontations with offenders as a result of physical effort. In Boros, J., Munnich, I. & Szegedi, M. (eds), *Psychology and Criminal Justice: International Review of Theory and Practice.* New York: Walter de Gruyter.

Vrij, A. (2000) *Detecting Lies and Deceit: The Psychology of Lying and the Implications for Professional Practice.* Chichester: John Wiley.

Vrij, A. & Dingemans, L. (1996) Physical effort of police officers as a determinant of their behaviour toward offenders. *Journal of Social Psychology* 136, 461–9.

Vrij, A. & Morris, P. (1998) Caffeine as a source of misattribution in police–offender confrontations: An experiment with the Fire Arms Training System. *International Journal of Police Science and Management* 1, 39–49.

Vrij, A., van der Steen, J.C. & Koppelaar, L. (1994) Aggression of police officers as a function of temperature: An experiment with the Fire Arms Training System. *Journal of Community and Applied Social Psychology* 4(5), 365–71.

Vrij, A., van der Steen, J.C. & Koppelaar, L. (1995a) The effects of physical effort on police officers' perception and aggression in simulated shooting incidents. *Psychology, Crime, and Law* 1, 301–8.

Vrij, A., van der Steen, J.C. & Koppelaar, L. (1995b) The effects of street noise and field independency on police officer shooting behaviour. *Journal of Applied Social Psychology* 15, 1,714–25.

Vrij, A., van der Steen, J.C., Koppelaar, L. & Vermaas, D. (1994) Afljeiding en persoonskenmerken als gedragspredictoren in potentiele schietsituaties: Een experiment rond het Fire Arms Training Systems. *Gedrag en Organisatie* 7, 261–72.

Wagenaar, W.A. (1986) My memory: A study of autobiographical memory over six years. *Cognitive Psychology* 18, 225–52.

Walker, N. & McCabe, S. (1973) *Crime and Insanity in UK*. Edinburgh: Edinburgh University Press.

Waller, I. & Okihiro, N. (1978) *Burglary: The Victim and the Public*. Toronto: University of Toronto Press.

Walsh, E. & Murray, R.M. (1998) Does case management influence the rate of violence and self-destructive behaviours in the severely mentally ill? *International Journal of Psychiatry in Clinical Practice* 1(2), 95–100.

Wanigaratne, S., Wallace, W., Pullin, J., Keaney, F. & Farmer, R. (1990) *Relapse Prevention for Addictive Behaviours: A Manual for Therapists*. Oxford: Blackwell.

Ward, A. (2002) Good lives. Paper presented at Division of Forensic Psychology annual conference, Manchester.

Warr, P., Allan C. & Birdi K. (1999) Predicting three levels of training outcome. *Journal of Occupational and Organisational Psychology* 72, 351–75.

Watson, T. & Rosborough, J. (2000) Teamworking and the management of flexibility: local and social-structural tensions in high performance work design initiatives. In Procter, S. & Mueller, F. (eds), 2000.

Webster, C.D., Douglas, K.S., Eaves, D. & Hart, S.D. (1997a) Predicting violence in mentally and personality disordered individuals. In Webster, C.D. and Jackson, M.A. (eds), *Impulsivity: Theory, Assessment, and Treatment*. New York: Guilford.

Webster, C.D., Douglas, K.S., Eaves, D. & Hart, S.D. (1997b) *HCR-20 Scheme: Assessing Risk for Violence, Version 2*. Vancouver: Mental Health, Law, and Policy Institute, Simon Fraser University.

Wedge, P. & Prosser, H. (1973) *Born to Fail: The Findings of the National Child Development Study*. London: Arrow Books.

Wells, G.L. (1978) Applied eyewitness testimony research: System variables and estimator variables. *Journal of Personality and Social Psychology* 36(12), 1,546–57.

Wells, G.L. & Lindsay, R.C.L. (1985) Methodological notes on the accuracy-confidence relation in eyewitness identifications. *Journal of Applied Psychology* 70(2), 413–19.

Wells W. & Horney, J. (in press) Weapon effects and individual intent to do harm: influences on the escalation of violence. *Criminology*.

West, A.G. (in press) Current approaches to sex-offender risk assessment: a critical review. *British Journal of Forensic Practice.*

West, D.J. & Farrington, D.P. (1973) *Who Becomes Delinquent?* Second Report of the Cambridge Study in Delinquent Development. London: Heinemann.

Wheelan, S.A. (1999) *Creating Effective Teams: A Guide for Members and Leaders.* Thousand Oaks, CA: Sage.

Whittington, R. & Wykes, T. (1996) Aversive stimulation by staff and violence by psychiatric clients. *British Journal of Clinical Psychology* 35(1), 11–20.

Whybrow, A.C. & Parker, S.K. (2000) Introducing teamworking: managing the process of change. In Procter, S. and Mueller, F. (eds), 2000.

Whyte, B. (1998) Rediscovering juvenile delinquency. In Lockyer, A. & Stone, F. (eds), 1998.

Wilberg, T., Urnes, O., Friis, S., Irion, T., Pederson, G. & Karterud, S. (1999) One year follow up of day treatment for poorly functioning clients with personality disorders. *Psychiatric Services* 50(10), 1,326–30.

Wilkinson, J.D. & Campbell, E.A. (1997) *Psychology in Counselling and Therapeutic Practice.* Chichester: Wiley.

Williams, J.M.G. (1996) Personality disorder and the will: a cognitive neuropsychological approach to schizotypal personality. In Salkovskis, P. (ed.) *Trends in Cognitive and Behavioural Therapies.* Chichester: Wiley.

Willmot, P (2000) What else works? Unpublished report. Psychology Group, HM Prison and National Probation Service.

Wilson, M. (1980a) Parental supervision: A neglected aspect of delinquency. *British Journal of Criminology* 20, 203–35.

Wilson, M. (1980b) Assessment centres: How well do they fulfil their role in the Scottish juvenile justice system? M.App.Sci. thesis, University of Glasgow.

Wilson, M. (1985) Social strategy for the 80's: What relevance to child guidance? *SALGEP Quarterly* 4(1), 18–25.

Wilson, M. (1991) Assessing assessment. *Scottish Child* (June/July), 15.

Wilson, M. (1994a) Community psychology in practice – Prevention and childcare. Paper presented at First National Conference of Community Psychology Network, Newark, UK, May.

Wilson, M. (1994b) Violent lives. *Scottish Child* (June/July), 12–13.

Wilson, M. (1998a) From secure unit to prison. Presentation to ISTD Conference, HM YOI Aylesbury, 4 September.

Wilson, M. (1998b) Prevention of youth crime – What might we learn from the Scottish Children's Hearing system? Paper presented at DCLP Annual Conference, University of Durham, 11 September.

Wilson, M. (1998c) Community psychology and youth crime. *Clinical Psychology Forum* 122, 25–7.

Winchester, R. (2000) Falling through. *Community Care* 1332 (July), 20.

Winkel, F.W., Koppelaar, L. & Vrij, A. (1988) Creating suspects in police–citizen encounters: two studies on personal space and being suspect. *Social Behaviour* 3, 307–19.

Winnicott, D. (1949) Hate in the counter-transference. *International Journal of Psychoanalysis* 30, 674–99.

Winter, N., Holland, A.J. & Collins, S. (1997) Factors predisposing to suspected offending by adults with self-reported learning disabilities. *Psychological Medicine* 27, 595–607.

Wolfe, D.A. (1994) Preventing gender-based violence: the significance of adolescence. *Violence Update* 5(1), 1–10.

Woodcock, J. (1994) *The Escape from Whitemoor Prison on Friday 9th September 1994.* London: HMSO.

Woodruffe, C. (2000) *Development and Assessment Centres* (3rd edn). London: Institute of Personal Development.

World Health Organisation (WHO) (1992) *The ICD-10 Classification of Mental and Behavioural Disorders.* Geneva: WHO.

Wright, R.T. & Decker, S. (1994), *Burglars on the Job: Streetlife and Residential Break-ins.* Boston: Northeastern University Press.

Wright, R.T. & Decker, S. (1997) *Armed Robbers in Action.* Boston: Northeastern University Press.

Xenitidis, K.I., Henry, J., Russell, A.J., Ward, A. & Murphy, D.G. (1999) An in-patient treatment model for adults with mild intellectual disability and challenging behaviour. *Journal of Intellectual Research* 43, 128–34.

Young, J.E. (1994) *Cognitive Therapy for Personality Disorders: A Schema Focussed Approach,* rev. Sarasota, FI: Professional Resource Exchange.

Yuille, J. C. & Cutshall, J. L. (1986) A case study of eyewitness memory for a crime. *Journal of Applied Psychology* 71, 291–301.

Zajonc, R. (1965) Social facilitation. *Science* 149, 269–74.

Zajonc, R. (1980) Compresence. In Paulus, B.P. (ed.), *Psychology of Group Influence.* Hillsdale, NJ: Erlbaum.

Zillmann, D. (1983) Transfer of excitation in emotional behaviour. In Cacioo, J. & Petty, R. (eds), *Social Psychophysiology: A Sourcebook.* New York: Guilford.

Index